The TRUSTWORTHINESS of GOD

Perspectives on the nature of Scripture

Edited by

PAUL HELM & CARL TRUEMAN

APOLLOS

APOLLOS (an imprint of Inter-Varsity Press),
38 De Montfort Street, Leicester LE1 7GP, England
Email: ivp@uccf.org.uk
Website: www.ivpbooks.com

Published in the United States of America by Wm. B. Eerdmans Publishing Co., 255 Jefferson Ave. S.E., Grand Rapids, Michigan 49503.

First published in Great Britain in 2002

British Library Cataloguing in Publication Data
A catalogue record for this book is available from the British Library.

ISBN 0-85111-476-8

Typeset in the United States of America.
Printed and bound in Great Britain by Creative Print and Design Group, Ebbw Vale.

Contents

NEW TESTAMENT

HISTORICAL, SYSTEMATIC, AND PHILOSOPHICAL PERSPECTIVES

RESPONSES

Introduction

Paul Helm & Carl R. Trueman

Why bother to put together a collection of essays on the theme "The Trustworthiness of God"? While, historically speaking, the notion of divinity and trustworthiness have not been inextricably linked — witness the antics of the Greek gods, where their very untrustworthiness and capriciousness supplied much of the drama, not to mention comic touches, of classical literature — is there any Christian theologian worth his or her salt who would argue the contrary, that God is inherently untrustworthy? The answer, of course, is almost certainly "No." Nevertheless, there are degrees of trustworthiness, and there are forms of trustworthiness; and the purpose of this volume is to explore, from biblical, systematic, philosophical, and historical perspectives, the nature and the implications of the trustworthiness of the God portrayed in the Bible and worshipped in the Christian Church for some two thousand years.

The title itself highlights the agenda. First, it is our God about whom we are talking. This is not a collection that is designed to convince those who are not Christian or who do not believe that there is a God who has spoken — as if such a project could ever be successful. It is rather addressed to those people — academic, clergy, and lay — who do believe in the God who has spoken and who believe he is trustworthy, and who are interested in seeing both how this notion of a speaking, trustworthy God is reflected within the Bible and Christian theology, and what implications this understanding of God has for the various disciplines represented here. Each essay has been written with the needs of the outsider in mind — if this were not the case, then the collection would merely reinforce disciplinary boundaries, not stimulate and encourage interdisciplinary dialogue, which is part of the collection's purpose.

Second, it is our God's *trustworthiness* that provides the theme. This choice of theme is very important, raising as it does a variety of significant issues for the Christian theologian — and all Christians are theologians, that is, those who think and speak about God, whether they are aware of it or not. It is of the essence of personal trustworthiness that people are who they claim to be; that, if you like, there is an intimate connection between their words and who they are, between what they say about themselves and the actions they can and do perform. The woman who promises a friend that she will give her £1,000 yet does not have two pennies to rub together may have the best intentions in the world; but her inability to honor the promise indicates that she is, however reluctantly, untrustworthy. Likewise, the husband who tells his wife that he loves her but loses no opportunity to insult her, beat her, and cheat on her is profoundly untrustworthy precisely because his actions reveal his words as empty lies and show that he is not the man he claims to be. His words speak of love and respect, but his deeds demonstrate hatred and contempt; the only conclusion one can draw is that the intention behind the words is insincere, if not downright deceptive, and that the man is therefore utterly untrustworthy. Christ himself makes a not dissimilar point about trustworthiness in the Sermon on the Mount:

> "Which of you, if his son asks for bread, will give him a stone? Or if he asks for a fish, will give him a snake? If you, then, though you are evil, know how to give good gifts to your children, how much more will your Father in heaven give good gifts to those who ask him!" (Matt. 7:9-11)

The point is simple: God has said that he is good; therefore, we can expect God to act in a manner that is consistent with that statement, especially when we consider how even unreliable human beings can be expected to be that trustworthy. God has both the ability and the intention to act in a manner consistent with his goodness; he is, therefore, trustworthy.

The trustworthiness of God, therefore, focuses attention on the relationship between who God is and what he has said about himself, or, to put it in more technical jargon, between the ontological and the epistemological aspects of theology. It is at this point, at this "interface," that Christian theology has traditionally placed the phenomenon of scriptural revelation, which, as the source for our knowledge of God, is the foundation for knowing who God is; and it is the relationship of revelation to God that establishes and defines the nature of his trustworthiness and that is thus of vital importance for all involved in the theological task, whether scholars, teachers, or straightforward believers. To take an imperfect though helpful analogy from the world of geography, the geographer who spent his or her entire life studying a map of Europe without once asking how the various symbolic conventions on the chart related to the realities to which they pointed would be a strange geographer indeed. The key issue that makes the map a reliable, trustworthy guide is that the map is itself, through the set of standard conventions that it uses, an accurate representation of the realities to which it refers; otherwise, it is simply a useless piece of paper, at best fantasy, at worst dangerously misleading. Again, one might receive a letter from someone one has never met. If the contents of the letter reflect his or her actual abilities and intentions, it is a trustworthy production, and the author is also trustworthy; if not, both letter and author must be considered both misleading and deceptive. The key question is simply this: Is the letter a trustworthy statement of the writer's feelings and intentions?

Such a point, one might argue, is little more than common sense, but it is in fact much more than that. As a number of the essays in this volume indicate, it is a central theme of the Bible itself. That God is, in a sense, the words he speaks, or, perhaps better, that God is towards his people the same as the words he speaks to them, is a recurring theme, from the Pentateuch, through the Wisdom Literature and the prophets, and on to the New Testament, the teaching of Christ himself and the letters. In addition, it has also been an important presupposition of the Church's own theology through the years and is the position that makes the most philosophical sense within the framework of historic Christian orthodoxy, whether considered in terms of modern analytic approaches to God, orthodox responses to the Enlightenment, or the challenges posed by recent hermeneutical theory. Each of these points is made with clarity in the essays that follow. Taken individually, each essay makes a specific contribution to the theme when approached from a particular disciplinary perspective; taken as a whole, the collection will hopefully stimulate reflection on what exactly it means when we say that God is trustworthy, on what implications the claim has for the whole spectrum of theological disciplines, and on what conditions must hold if the claim that the Christian God is a trustworthy God is to be at all coherent or comprehensible.

Introduction

The arrival of a book on Scripture will no doubt provoke a mixed reaction: some will certainly sigh, despairing that, at the start of the twenty-first century, individuals should still be preoccupied with issues that they regard as having been put to death by the Enlightenment; some will feel some trepidation, wondering if the unpleasant and damaging debates of the past, in which so many individuals, churches, and organizations were badly wounded, are about to be reopened with similar bloody consequences; still others might suspect much the same but look forward to such conflict as a way of sifting the wheat from the tares (which side is wheat and which tares depends, of course, on the perspective of the specific individual concerned). Such has been the controversial nature of discussions of Scripture, particularly over recent decades, that few will have no strong feelings about such a collection. The editors and contributors to this volume, however, hope that all of those who fall into the above categories will be disappointed. We do not intend this volume to provide a spark to re-ignite the fires of past unpleasantness, still less to be a final and definitive dogmatic statement on the issue with which it deals. Its aim rather is at once both more modest and more constructive than such polemical goals would suggest, and, to be correctly understood, it must be set within both a broader and a narrower context.

There is no doubt that one of the major legacies of the Enlightenment, which postmodernity has served only to exacerbate and extend, has been the fragmentation of knowledge and the disciplines that seek to organize and correlate that knowledge. This is not only a problem caused simply by the abstract philosophical concerns of Enlightenment and postmodern thinking; it is also the result of the technological revolution. By massively expanding the amount of knowledge and information available, this revolution has rendered almost impossible the ideal of the renaissance man or woman, competent in a whole range of spheres, replacing them with specialists who find that even mastering all the information in their own chosen sphere is a full-time commitment. The effect in theology, as in other disciplines, has been quantitatively earth shattering and qualitatively little short of disastrous. Whereas the past gave us theologians who were competent in biblical exegesis, systematic theology, church history, and practical theology, we now have specialists in minute subdisciplines (Pentateuchal studies, Pauline studies, ethics, etc.) who are frequently ignorant of, and certainly incompetent in, the current state of research and scholarship in other areas.

One of the casualties in the fragmentation of recent years has therefore been the dialogue that did, and should still, exist between theological disciplines. The work of biblical scholars, systematicians, historians, and others suffers if there is no correlation or interaction among the disciplines. If all truth is God's truth, then the findings in one sphere of theological endeavor cannot be developed in complete isolation from those in another. There is, rather, an organic link between the fields that requires that such dialogue take place. One can, of course, reject the idea that this is the case, but to do so is to subscribe implicitly to a notion of a plurality of truth, as in the medieval notion of double truth, where something could be true in theology and false in philosophy, or vice versa. Many in the postmodern world would find such a position thoroughly acceptable, no doubt echoing the title of a recent pop music album, "This is my truth; tell me yours." But for the Christian theologian, committed to the idea of one God who has definitively revealed himself in the Bible and supremely revealed himself in the person of the Lord Jesus Christ, such an option would seem to point inexorably towards an idea of God as fundamentally unknown and unknowable.

This, then, is the broader context of the essays gathered here. Seen in this light, the collection is intended as an attempt to bring together scholars from various theological disciplines, Old Testament studies, New Testament studies, Systematic Theology, Historical Theology, and Philosophy of Religion to discuss a particular theme, each from his own disciplinary perspective, in order to draw out the significant relationships that exist between their different subjects and approaches and to hint at what gains might be made if some means of correlating different disciplines could once again be found.

Contributors

CRAIG BARTHOLOMEW, Research Fellow, School of Humanities, University of Gloucestershire

GERALD BRAY, Anglican Professor of Divinity, Beeson Divinity School, Samford University, Birmingham, Alabama

COLIN GUNTON, Professor of Systematic Theology, Department of Theology and Religious Studies, King's College, London

PAUL HELM, J. I. Packer Professor of Theology and Philosophy, Regent College, Vancouver, British Colombia; formerly Professor of History and Philosophy of Religion, King's College, London

DAVID INSTONE-BREWER, Librarian, Tyndale House, Cambridge

DONALD MACLEOD, Professor of Systematic Theology, Free Church of Scotland College, Edinburgh

J. G. McCONVILLE, Senior Lecturer in Old Testament, School of Humanities, University of Gloucestershire

GARY MILLAR, Minister, Presbyterian Church of Ireland, Howth and Malahide, Republic of Ireland

DAVID PETERSON, Principal, Oak Hill Theological College, London

SEBASTIAN REHNMAN, Lecturer in Theology and Philosophy, Johannelund Theological Seminary, Uppsala, Sweden

CARL TRUEMAN, Associate Professor of Church History and Historical Theology, Westminster Theological Seminary, Philadelphia; formerly Senior Lecturer in Church History, University of Aberdeen

TIMOTHY WARD, Curate, Crowborough, East Sussex, England

FRANCIS WATSON, Professor of New Testament Exegesis, University of Aberdeen

H. H. DRAKE WILLIAMS III, Associate Minister, Central Schwenkfelder Church; Adjunct Faculty Member, Biblical Theological Seminary, Pennsylvania

P. J. WILLIAMS, Research Fellow, Tyndale House, Cambridge

STEPHEN WILLIAMS, Professor of Systematic Theology, Union Theological College, Belfast

OLD TESTAMENT

"A Faithful God Who Does No Wrong": History, Theology, and Reliability in Deuteronomy

J. Gary Millar

Introduction

Deuteronomy is not an easy book to characterize. It has been described as patriarchal and prophetic, sapiential and priestly, pro- and anti-monarchical, conservative and reactionary, legalistic and dominated by grace. Powerful claims have been advanced both for a strongly nationalistic agenda and for a missiological, international concern. Proponents of every date from the time of Moses to that of Ezra queue up to stake their claims!

Historical-critical questions, however, no longer dominate the scholarly agenda in the way they once did. Since the publication of Robert Polzin's *Moses and the Deuteronomist* in 1980, there have been few works that have not at least nodded in the direction of a holistic reading of the text. Even though one should not make the mistake of assuming that similarities in approach reflect similar methodologies, it is clear that a sea change has occurred. Rhetorical analysis and ideological readings now take their place alongside more conventional studies. It is fair to say that the past twenty years has seen a revival of interest in the subtleties of the canonical text. This has breathed new life into the study of Deuteronomy and the Old Testament as a whole. The preoccupation with sources of the last fifty years has been augmented by a growing concern with the rhetorical impact of the final form of the book.

In some ways, the new "pluralism" in biblical studies, if one can call it that, has made life easier for conservative evangelicals. It is no longer untenable to study the text of the Bible as it stands. Nor is there the same need to defend the doctrine of the Bible on behalf of the wider Church, for the threat of the old adversarial critical orthodoxy is not what it once was. Most evangelicals now feel free to adopt a more positive approach.

There is no doubt that a strong argument can be made for "making hay while the sun shines," but a note of caution must be sounded. Much recent biblical scholarship, while less overtly antagonistic to a holistic reading of the text, is ultimately no more compatible with an evangelical approach to the text than the liberal orthodoxy of the past. Now we must contend not only with confrontation but with relativization as well.

In the past, a traditional view of the authority of the Bible was seen as academically untenable simply because it refused to bow to the "assured" results of sociohistorical analysis of the text. This line of reasoning is no longer the sole challenge to evangelical orthodoxy, for increasingly there is no need to ridicule conservative interpretations of the text. Such "readings" can simply be relativized, "lost" among the plurality of other "readings," all of which, of course, possess equal validity. Any claim that the biblical text is in some way authoritative today is seen as outrageous, not for historical-critical reasons but simply because it flies in the face of the dogmatic uncertainty of our postmodern age. No text can have *authority* because we cannot be certain of its meaning (in fact, to speak of *the meaning* at all is highly dubious). To claim that any one text has *unique authority* is therefore out of the question. The nature of debate may have changed, but evangelicals seeking to play their part in the world of biblical scholarship still face the same essential conflict. The key issue dividing confessing evangelicals from the rest of the academic world is still that of the *authority* of the text, and of the nature of the God who stands behind it.

Since the advent of new "literary readings," many Old Testament specialists have attempted to build literary approaches on a foundation of historical criticism. This always seems to result in a rather shaky structure — and in real terms amounts to a strange marriage of the old skepticism and the ability to read the text holistically with a clear conscience! Others, more radically, abandon traditional methods completely in favor of poststructuralism and other reading strategies derived from mainstream literary criticism. The end result is basically the same: the text is once more construed as a purely human construct, and to speak of "authority" is irrelevant.

It is clear, then, that despite the changing face of Old Testament criticism, and the study of Deuteronomy in particular, the key issues are unchanged. The gulf between those who regard the biblical text as authoritative and those who do not remains as wide as ever. It is important, however, that we understand the origins of this division. Evangelicals are often accused of imposing nonbiblical categories, such as infallibility or inerrancy, on the Bible, but that is simply not the issue here — for it is the text of Deuteronomy itself that raises the questions.

The book of Deuteronomy presents itself to a large degree as the words of God (mediated by Moses). This is an important claim because it instantly ties the text to the God behind the text. The way in which we think of the text, then, is intimately linked to the way in which we think of the God behind the text. This clearly raises problems both for the traditional critical and for the new literary approaches to Deuteronomy discussed above. How, for example, do we react to a seventh-century fictional document designed to fool people, which talks of a "faithful God who does no wrong"? Similarly, how do we relate to a God who claims to lay down the law and yet is happy for each of us to make of it what we will? Such tensions are only the beginning, for the whole doctrine of God in Deuteronomy is predicated on the reliability of a faithful God acting in history. If one dispenses with the historical claims of the text, surely then one cannot continue to believe in a reliable God? There is an unbreakable connection with our doctrine of God, the words of God as presented in the biblical text, and the actions of God to which the text bears witness.[1] Any attempt to drive a wedge between these elements must have disastrous consequences. Inevitably, we will be left with a God who is less than God.

In the rest of this essay, then, I shall attempt to show how the inner logic of the book of Deuteronomy demands that if we are to believe in a God who can be trusted, then we must of necessity trust what he claims to have said in Scripture concerning his actions in history.

1. Contra Robert Polzin's contention that the voice of the narrator silences the voice of God (*Moses and the Deuteronomist* [New York: Seabury, 1980], pp. 25-72). See also Dennis T. Olson, *Deuteronomy and the Death of Moses* (Minneapolis: Fortress, 1994), pp. 178-82.

The Reliability of God and Israel's Past

Over the years there have been many attempts to characterize the genre of Deuteronomy.[2] Yet however one understands the book, it is clear that the opening chapters are essentially a retrospective on Israel's experience in the wilderness. They are evidently sermonic, as Moses draws lessons from the successes and failures of the past.

Carefully selected historical detail peppers chapters 1–3 — detail that evinces both the activity and the reliability of God. In the opening verses, the emphasis is placed on Yahweh's initiative — it was he who instigated Israel's exodus journey, he who maintained its momentum after the potential disaster of Horeb, and he who smoothed the way through the Transjordan, despite Og and Bashan. In marked contrast to this, the democratization of power in the infant nation (1:9-18) leads only to the catastrophic decision of Kadesh-barnea.

It is interesting that the central issue to be faced at Kadesh was that of the trustworthiness of God. Despite Moses' plaintive appeal in 1:30-31, assuring Israel of the Lord's military protection and fatherly provision, in 1:32 he announces that "you did not *trust* the LORD your God." Even though Yahweh had proven a reliable guide in the past, Israel tragically assumed responsibility for her own future. The exclusion of all but Caleb and Joshua from the land is therefore a simple matter of trust, or, to be more accurate, of refusal to trust.

However, such is the nature of Yahweh's commitment to them that even their experience in the wilderness bears witness to his sheer reliability. They did not merely survive but sailed through this remedial period, thanks only to him (2:7). More striking still is the lesson to be learned by paying attention as they pass through the environs of Canaan. Remarkably, there is evidence of God's trustworthiness on display all around them. In one of the most daring passages in the whole of the Old Testament, Moses asserts that God had already given land to Israel's "cousins": Edom, Moab, and Ammon.[3] God had proven himself utterly trustworthy even to those

2. Dennis Olson, in one of the more recent attempts, tries to use the umbrella term "catechesis," which he argues is flexible enough to include the elements of covenant, sermon, law code, constitution, and so forth. In doing this, he has in fact broadened the reference of genre to make it almost meaningless (Olson, *Deuteronomy and the Death of Moses*, pp. 7-14).

3. The parentheses seem to be editorial here but simply spell out the implications of Moses' words, particularly with reference to the nations who previously occupied these

who were not "his own." Surely his own people could stir themselves sufficiently to take him at his word?

According to Moses, God has shown himself to be reliable in the way he has acted towards his people. The foundation of these chapters is that God has acted faithfully at every twist and turn of Israel's history. If God has not acted faithfully, or if Moses had not recorded events faithfully, then we have no reason whatsoever to give any credence to the doctrine of the reliability of God preached so powerfully here. We simply cannot have our cake and eat it.

This becomes even more evident when we examine Deuteronomy 4, probably the most complex chapter in the entire book. Deuteronomy 4:1-40 comprises a carefully conceived unit, beginning and ending with the assertion that Israel's initial and enduring occupation of the land depend on conformity to the decrees and laws about to be proclaimed (4:1-4, 40). The other theme dominating the chapter forms an "inner inclusion" (4:5-8, 32-39). In 4:5-8, the emphasis is on God's immanence, demonstrated particularly by his accessibility (and proximity) to his praying people, and his laws enunciated by Moses. At the end of the chapter, a restatement of God's immanence is beautifully balanced by an insistence on his transcendence. This paradox is evident in the election of Israel and the events of the Exodus, but, above all, it is to be seen in God speaking to Israel from on high at Horeb (v. 36). Israel's God is a God who talks. To deny that he speaks amounts to denying that he is both transcendent and immanent, for in the view of Deuteronomy, his speech-acts are the ultimate demonstration of both.

These ideas are developed in the body of the chapter, where the inextricable link between the character of God and both the nature and content of the revelation at Horeb is set forth. God's appearance (or rather lack of it) in verses 12 and 15 underscores his transcendence. The divine origin of both the Ten Words and the ensuing preaching of Moses in 4:13-14 illustrates the intimate presence of God among his people. In the light of this awesome paradox, any attempt to deny the absolute reliability of God is utter folly, as Moses himself affirmed (4:21-24), for not only does he speak from the fire, but he is in himself a consuming fire.

It should be said that many have sought to argue that this chapter has

---

lands. The allusion to the "Anakites," the mythical giants the spies had allegedly seen, is probably ironic.

neither integrity nor authenticity (it is usually dated at the time of the Exile or later). Yet as we have seen already, any attempt to prize these words apart from the nature of the events they describe inevitably undermines the Deuteronomic doctrine of God. It is precisely *because* God is both transcendent and immanent that his words spoken in history can carry weight. It is precisely *because* he has spoken at Horeb, and continued to speak at Moab, that his words can continue to have not only abiding significance but abiding authority. Any denial of the validity of his original speech-act or of the commentary of his appointed go-between, must have serious repercussions for the nature of the God who claims to be speaking.

This is further highlighted by the presence of the Decalogue in chapter 5. With a couple of minor exceptions, this version of the commandments is identical to that in Exodus 20.[4] The opening verses of the chapter make the reason for the recapitulation clear. Moses insists that Horeb was not simply an unrepeatable watershed in the nation's past; rather, it was a defining moment for both the present and the future. It was at Horeb that God established his *b^{e}rit* with Israel, a covenant that was forged prospectively with every future generation. I have explored this at some length elsewhere.[5] The important issue for us is that the primary element both of the covenant-making act and of the enduring covenant relationship is the divine word. This is emphasized by the striking phrase with which 5:4 opens in Hebrew: "Face to face I spoke to you. . . ." Clearly at odds with the traditional view that humans cannot look on the face of God and live (represented by the parenthesis of 5:5), this shocking statement aims to convey the nature of God's verbal commitment. He will continue to speak to his people.

It is then that the Ten Commandments are rehearsed, as the definitive illustration that Israel's God is a talking God. This statement is no longer negotiable, for God has spoken "in a loud voice" and literally set the tone of his ongoing relationship with Israel. In the rest of the chapter, a continuity is established between these original words and the Mosaic exposition of torah in much of the rest of the book. Verse 24 is particularly inter-

4. It is almost universally accepted that the Exodus version is the earlier.

5. See "Living at the Place of Decision," in J. G. McConville and J. Gary Millar, *Time and Place in Deuteronomy,* Journal for the Study of the Old Testament, Supplement Series 179 (Sheffield: Sheffield Academic Press, 1994), pp. 15-88; and J. Gary Millar, *Now Choose Life: Theology and Ethics in Deuteronomy,* New Studies in Biblical Theology 6 (Leicester: Apollos, 1998), pp. 67-98.

esting for us: "The Lord our God has shown us his glory and his greatness, and we have heard his voice from the midst of the fire. Today we have seen that even if God speaks to a human being, he may live on!" The divine verbal communication has had a twofold effect: first, it has revealed the nature of the God who is speaking (showing his glory and greatness); second, it has established a new *modus vivendi* for Israel — the nation is, from now on, to be dependent on every word that comes from the mouth of the Lord (8:3). Once again, the trustworthiness of God is inextricably linked to the trustworthiness of what he has said, first at Horeb, and then at Moab. Moses' address then flows smoothly into the long exhortation that eventually introduces the collection of laws in chapters 12–26. Throughout chapters 6–11, the emphasis is still on the connections between God's words, actions, and character. Nowhere is this connection to be seen more clearly than in the "Shema" of Deuteronomy 6. It is rather surprising that the obvious connection of 6:1-5 to the preceding account of God speaking at Horeb has not been recognized more often. For the double call to hear of 6:3-4 is sounded against the background of the voice of God in chapter 5. This is not merely a rhetorical device to gain attention.[6] It is an appeal to Israel to take seriously the way of life begun at Horeb, living out the covenant made there "with all who are alive today" by listening to the ongoing revelation of Yahweh. This revelation will, of course, be both personal and propositional, as these verses make clear. The slightly enigmatic terms of verse 4 cannot disguise the fact that the essential nature of God cannot be separated from his words, whatever their precise nuance. If the Lord is to be "one," whether "one" is taken to be an affirmation of loyalty or an expression of Yahweh's singleness of purpose, it will inevitably involve giving credence to the reliability of his words, his actions, and his essential nature.

This linkage is highlighted in two other ways later in this same chapter. It is positively presented in typically Deuteronomic fashion in the conjunction of the Exodus and future obedience (6:21-25). His past reliability provides the motivation for obedience, a theme that increasingly dominates Moses' discourse, as we shall see. Deuteronomy 6:25 is particularly interesting. Literally translated "And righteousness *(ṣᵉdāqah)* will be to/for us if we are careful to obey this whole body of legislation before God, just as he has commanded us," the emphasis is placed on the fact that "righ-

6. These verses show a similar rhetorical technique to Jesus' "If anyone has ears to hear . . ." sayings.

teousness" will somehow accrue to Israel through obedience. When we take the broader context of chapters 1–6 into account, it seems most likely that the verse is suggesting that if Israel follows God's example and instruction, then the trustworthiness and reliability (the righteousness) exhibited by him will also become a reality within the life of his people.[7]

This theme of God's consistency is pursued throughout the next chapter, as Moses turns for the first time to the problem of the Canaanites in chapter 7. Yahweh's unyielding opposition to the present occupants of the land is entirely consistent with what we have already seen. As he was unerringly benevolent to Israel and her relatives (see ch. 2), so he is equally implacable in his enmity towards her enemies in the land. The election of Israel and rejection of the evil Canaanites (who are presented as "God-haters" [7:10] without further comment) are corollaries. Both sides of the coin bear witness to his absolute trustworthiness (7:9). The God who speaks and acts on behalf of Israel against the occupants of the land is "a great and awesome God" (7:21).

The relentless insistence on God's flawless record of faithfulness to his people continues in chapters 8–11, where Moses returns to a sustained reflection on the past. He draws on the wilderness tradition in chapter 8 (where God's faithfulness is shown in manna, clothing, and lack of blisters) and the Exodus events in 9:1-6 before he gives an extended retelling of the Golden Calf incident. The narrative here is rather more personal than that in Exodus, focusing on the contrast between God, who is reliably gracious, and Israel, who can only be counted on to rebel (summed up in 9:22-23). Moses' appeal for clemency in 9:27-29 amplifies contrast. The only grounds upon which Moses can mount his plea for forgiveness are the nature and reputation of God. There are no mitigating circumstances, nor can he summon witnesses to vouch for Israel's good character. Instead, he boldly points out that excessive punitive action would call God's trustworthiness into question. In the eyes of the nations looking on, the end of Israel would speak of the weakness and capriciousness of God, undermining the message of the Exodus. This then explains the act of grace that follows. God speaks again in the form of replica tablets to be placed in the ark at the very center of the national life of his people.

The extended and persuasive plea that follows in 10:12–11:32 repeatedly returns to the same theme of God's trustworthiness, which has been

7. This thought is also present in 16:18-20. See Millar, *Now Choose Life*, p. 25.

demonstrated in the Exodus. This trustworthiness is held up as a model for Israel's own behavior in 10:17-18: "For the LORD your God is God of gods and Lord of lords, the great God, mighty and awesome, who shows no partiality and accepts no bribes. He defends the cause of the fatherless and the widow, and loves the alien, giving him food and clothing." His action in fulfilling his promises to the patriarchs has established his reputation; his words at Horeb set it in stone. The fate of Pharaoh, the Egyptian army, Dathan, and Abiram, add to the overwhelming evidence attesting to the reliability of God. The choice that the people face on the threshold of the land is then clear: they can either go the way of a God who can be trusted and enjoy blessing, or they can do their own thing and face the frightening prospect of bringing down the curses of the covenant on themselves.

The preaching of Moses in chapters 1–11 draws heavily on the Exodus tradition to demonstrate the trustworthiness of God both in action and in word. He has proven himself to be utterly reliable in bringing Israel to the threshold of the land for the second time. If they needed any further persuasion to take him at his word, their encounters with other nations, both "friendly" and "hostile," should have been more than enough. Moses, however, does not simply appeal to these mighty acts of God — the most significant moment in the history of Israel to date involved not action per se but speech. The Horeb theophany makes concrete the link between God's words and actions. Yahweh can never again simply be a God who acts on behalf of his people; he has become a God who talks. In speaking, he expresses his character just as surely as when he acts. The nature of God in Deuteronomy then rests equally on what God does and what he says. This tripartite alliance cannot be sundered without diminishing the God who stands behind the text.

The Reliability of God and Israel's Future

If the opening chapters of Deuteronomy preach a doctrine of God that rests on his faithful words and actions in the past, then the rest of the book, consisting of the collection of laws and reflections on Israel's prospects in the context of Moses' death, takes these basic convictions and applies them to the future of God's own people.

The laws in Deuteronomy 12–26 address Israel's immediate future, giving the nation a blueprint for successful life within God's land. They do so, however, on a twofold basis: these stipulations come with divine authority, and they rest on the prior action of Yahweh in bringing Israel to, and establishing her in, the land. This is not simply commonsense advice for those intending to live in Canaan! That becomes apparent on the most cursory glance at the laws. In the opening verse, obedience is tied to God's prior action in fulfillment of the promise — divine action stands over the entire collection as the ultimate motive clause.

In addition to this, many of the laws are intricately linked to divine action in the present or the future. Take the so-called "altar law" of chapter 12. The "place" where Israel is to worship is to be chosen exclusively by God. Their whole system of worship is to be shaped by divine action in appointing such a place (or places). The warning of 12:31 that "you must not worship Yahweh your God in their way" is simply a corollary of the fact that Israel as a result of divine action is not a free agent but belongs exclusively to God. This same theme echoes throughout chapters 13–16. Explicitly in the condemnation of fifth columnists who are either prophets or family members, and implicitly in the guidelines for dealing with apostates in a nearby town, appeal is made to the fact of Yahweh's redemption of Israel from slavery in Egypt.

The requirement to abstain from certain quasi-religious practices at the beginning of chapter 14 is justified in terms of Exodus 19:6: Israel is now a holy people (14:2, 21) and must behave in ways that demonstrate this. The same presupposition underlies the rules for tithes at the end of Deuteronomy 14, and those on canceling debts and freeing slaves in chapter 15. Surrendering a tenth of all your produce, canceling all debts, or freeing servants at the end of every seven years can only be justified by the fact that a trustworthy God is watching over the economy of Israel. If Israel were to forget or ignore this fact, then the drive for personal gain would surely have obliterated such practices in an instant. However, the injunctions to remember the Exodus are repeated frequently, lest Israel forget and revert to a more conventional financial system!

It may be stating the obvious to say that the great festivals of Israel called the people to reflect on the character of their God as exemplified in his acts of redemption and providence, but this is particularly evident in the Deuteronomic legislation. Not only Passover but also Weeks is linked directly to the Exodus, and Tabernacles is drawn into this same nexus of ideas through the inclusive formula of verse 14 (see 16:11-12). The ongoing festal life of the people is built on the faithfulness of God, expressed par excellence in the Exodus, but now an enduring reality in the life of the nation. The pithy statement of the transitional 16:18-20 rests on the assumption that the God of Israel is just.[8] This is reiterated in the guidance given to judges, kings, and prophets in particular. Each in his own way is to be dependent on the word of the Lord: the judges are to seek the guidance of the priests and "the judge who is in office" at the place chosen by God; the king must look to his copy of the law; and the prophet is only to speak in the name of Yahweh. Wherever one turns in the laws, it is asserted that Yahweh alone has authority over Israel's future, as he continues to speak and act through his word and his appointed leaders.

Even within the disparate stipulations gathered together in chapters 21–25, there are occasional references to the actions of God in the past. The laws concerning the admission of foreigners to the assembly in 23:1-7 follow a similar line of argument to chapter 2. The citation of Amalekite dishonesty in 25:17-19 and the accompanying statement of the Lord's attitude to such behavior undergird the demand for probity in commerce. In a similar way, a strange incident involving God's punishment of Miriam (24:8-9) adds weight to regulations for treating skin conditions. Alongside these, 21:8-9 and 24:17-18, 22 recall God's Exodus actions in a more conventional way.

It is clear that there is no dichotomy between the perspective of the first eleven chapters and the laws that follow. In both cases, the emphasis is placed firmly on the prior action of God — first in bringing about the Exodus, then in speaking to his people. This nexus of speech and action establishes the trustworthiness of God in Israel's eyes. God is faithful, and now Israel's role is to respond obediently to his ongoing requirements in the light of what she has seen and heard.

Chapter 26 is the hinge on which the rest of the book turns. In one sense, it is the climax of the collection of laws, drawing on a further ritual act to emphasize the nature of the response that God is seeking from Israel. In another, it introduces the whole question of the long-term future of Israel in the light of the reliability of God and the unreliability of his people.

Chapter 27 develops the idea introduced in 11:26-27 that a basic choice confronts Israel. On entering the land, the people are to proceed to

8. Verse 20 begins with a unique collocation: the word *ṣedeq* is repeated. The best explanation of this is that it is drawing attention to the righteousness/justice of God as the foundation of the Jewish legal system.

Shechem, where they are to set up stones bearing the divine words on Mt. Ebal. There are several very interesting dimensions to this suggested dramatic enactment of Israel's covenantal obligations, but perhaps the most significant is that there is no mention of the blessings to be pronounced, only curses.[9] Israel seems bound to fail.

It is as if Moses thinks that there will be no need to pronounce the blessings, for such blessings will never actually accrue to Israel, who will be cursed. The fact that these stones are to be set up on Mt. Ebal, the mountain of curse, confirms this rather depressing observation, as does the nature of the final curse in 27:26. The shape of chapter 28 simply adds further weight to this view. However one understands the list of blessings, their relative brevity compared to the almost overwhelming barrage of curses is all too obvious. Moses at the very least *fears* that the future holds curse rather than blessing for Israel. The "return to Egypt" described in chapter 28 seems inevitable (28:45-48).[10] Ultimately, it seems that Israel's only hope rests on God himself.

The "covenant at Moab," introduced at the beginning of chapter 29, seems to come at the perfect time, and one does not have to read far to see that it is, in fact, more of the same. It sits comfortably alongside Horeb, granted, but now we become aware of a negative side to that equation. Deuteronomy 29:4 (MT 29:3) is one of the most important verses in the whole book, for, although God has done much for Israel (e.g., vv. 5-8 [MT 4-7]), it seems that he has not as yet done that which they needed most (see also 29:25-28 [MT 24-27]). It is as if Moses is again describing events that have already been decreed, rather than events that are one possibility among many. This casts a long shadow back over what has gone before. When 29:29 (MT 29:28) is read in the light of the rest of chapter 29, this enigmatic verse takes on a new importance. The "revealed things" are best taken as referring to the content of Moses' preaching at Moab and, in particular, to the insight that this covenant is doomed to failure. The "secret things," however, anticipate the radical, hopeful initiative of chapter 30, to which we now turn.

9. See Paul Barker's excellent discussion, "The Theology of Deuteronomy 27," *The Tyndale Bulletin* 49 (1998): 277-304.

10. Yet it would not be true to say that the picture is entirely gloomy. Paul Barker has shown that the presence of the "offering of well-being" in 27:4-7, the affirmation of Israel's election in 27:9-10, and the role of Shechem as a place of promise in other Pentateuchal narratives all keep more than a glimmer of hope alive.

We have seen how the reliability of God, as shown through his action in Israel's history, is the foundation of Moses' preaching in Deuteronomy. However, by the end of chapter 29, we have reached a point where there are fresh questions to be asked. It seems that the failure of Israel is inevitable. God's people will invoke the curses of the covenant through their foolish disobedience. Therefore, we ask, Is that the end? Is the ultimate implication of God's trustworthiness that he can be counted on to reject his people as they deserve? Not according to chapter 30, where a new facet of God's faithfulness to Israel comes into view.[11] It is not simply that God can be trusted to keep on speaking, or even to honor his covenant pledges. God's trustworthiness ultimately finds its fullest expression in the greatest demonstration of grace yet seen. His reliability stretches even to solving one problem that the Israelites cannot solve themselves: the problem of their sinful nature. At the beginning of chapter 30, we encounter another "new covenant," although it would not be called such until the time of Jeremiah and Ezekiel. God promises to do for Israel exactly what they cannot do for themselves. In 10:16, Moses had pleaded with the people, "Circumcise your hearts." Now he announces that the necessary surgery would be performed by God himself.

This is the ultimate evidence of the reliability and trustworthiness of God in the book. In his grace, he can be counted upon to reverse the effects even of the covenant curses themselves. The prospect of the Lord once more deriving delight from his relationship with his own people (31:9) is the greatest hope in the entire book. Then, the choice faced by Israel will have been transformed by the change that God has wrought in their lives.

In the meantime, Moses lays before them the immediate choice to be faced at Moab, and then in the land of Canaan (30:15-20). Here is the message of Deuteronomy in a nutshell, culminating in the statement "For Yahweh is your life, and he will extend your days in the land he swore to give to your forefathers, Abraham, Isaac and Jacob" (my translation). The life or death choice of Deuteronomy is, in essence, a choice between trusting Yahweh or rejecting him. To choose life means accepting the Mosaic account of God's actions in the past, recognizing the wisdom of his prescriptions for life in the present, and, above all, putting faith in the solution promised in the distant future. The text as we now have it insists that noth-

11. This was, of course, hinted at in chapter 4, which acts as a kind of overture to the book.

ing less than this wholehearted commitment will do, for the God who demands is the Lord of heaven and earth.

The remainder of the book, while in some ways providing a postscript to the moving appeal of Moses, contributes in and of itself to the argument I have been trying to construct. Chapter 31 underlines that in the future it is not Joshua in whom the people need to trust, but the one who goes ahead of him (31:3-5). The formula "he will never leave you nor forsake you" (vv. 6, 8; see also v. 23) is a succinct expression of the reliability of Yahweh expounded throughout the book. The faithfulness of God yet again is brought into sharp relief by the faithlessness of Israel. In 31:14-22, the most strongly deterministic passage in the book, God himself asserts that Israel will fail to keep the law and will face the curses of the covenant. Moses echoes what he has heard (31:27, 29) and then "performs" the song that God has given him (31:21). The song is essentially a meditation on the faithfulness of God (see, e.g., vv. 3-4) and the perversity of Israel (e.g., v. 15). All the important Deuteronomic elements are present: the central role of God's words (vv. 1-2), his actions in history (vv. 10-14), the inevitability of those who rebel to experience the "curse" (vv. 36-38), and even the willingness of God to come to meet the deepest need of his people (v. 39). Whereas Moses himself cannot finally be trusted (32:48-52), Moses' God is utterly reliable. This is precisely the message that emerges from the gritty realism of Moses' blessing of the infant nation. The summary in verses 26-29, which is in fact Moses' final recorded utterance, dwells on this theme. Israel may be a mixed bunch, but their hope rests on the reliability of God, for the trustworthiness of the almighty God, the God who talks and acts, overshadows even the death of a great leader like Moses.

Conclusion

In 1985, Gordon Wenham wrote an important article in *Themelios* entitled "The Date of Deuteronomy: Linch-pin of Old Testament Criticism." He presented a powerful case for reexamining conclusions that had long since become critical orthodoxy concerning the date and provenance of the book. However, I believe that we can go further than simply arguing about the most likely time of writing of this magisterial document. It is not simply the date of Deuteronomy that is a linchpin of Old Testament criticism; it is the Deuteronomic doctrines of God and of Scripture.

The two cannot easily be separated because in Moses' discourse, the God who speaks is the God who acts — the God who acted in the Exodus and who will act in Canaan, finally and decisively by establishing the new covenant. God's words and God's actions can both be relied upon, and the preaching contained in this book demands a no-holds-barred commitment from the people of God.

This is where some interpretations of the book can lead to all sorts of problems. Say, for example, that we held that this book was a propaganda pamphlet attempting to bolster the claims of a reformist regime. How could we reconcile the fact that people were using deception to advance the claims of a God who is faithful and does no wrong? How could people, for whatever motives, manipulate God to achieve their own ends? How does this fit with the innate spirituality of the text? Ultimately such an approach is inconsistent. One cannot believe in the God of Deuteronomy and at the same time silence him. The choice boils down to that expounded by Moses: a choice between life and death, although this time the life or death in view is not ours, but God's.

In a different vein, the sustained exposition of the authority of the God of Moses, whose words and acts demand a response, must surely cause all sorts of problems for those who want to avoid any claim of truth in the text. One cannot read this book without coming face-to-face with the outrageous claims of God on the lives of his people. Once more, the choice is between taking the text seriously (and therefore the God who stands behind the text seriously) or dismissing it. It is hard to see where there might be any middle ground.

Deuteronomy unequivocally states that God is a faithful God who can do no wrong. In other words, God can be relied upon. The question is, Are we willing to rely on him? If he is the God of Deuteronomy — the God of salvation, past, present, and future, and the God of revelation — then can we do anything else? But if he is not, then he is quite simply not God and not worthy of our interest, never mind our wholehearted worship.

Divine Speech and the Book of Jeremiah

Gordon McConville

Preamble

Jeremiah is one of the best books in the Old Testament by which to test the idea of the word of God coming through a written text. This is because of its length and diversity, and its resistance to the imposition of a structure or a single point of view, complicated by the fact that it is actually extant in two major ancient versions (MT and LXX). To put it differently, the relationship between the spoken word of Jeremiah and the form(s) of the book is complex. The problem of Jeremiah as word of God is by no means new, and the story of how it has been understood as such is in itself revealing. In what follows I will attempt to show how interpretations of the book have tried to deal with the problem of its authority, to offer some evaluation of these interpretations, and then to articulate an understanding of the authority of the book that does justice both to the idea of the specific divine speech to and through Jeremiah and to the nature of the book as such.

Jeremiah and Modern Criticism

The early criticism of Jeremiah in the modern period looked for the "authentic" words of the prophet. The quest for this authenticity was spearheaded by B. Duhm, who reduced the "original" Jeremiah to the prophet's poetic oracles.[1] Duhm's purpose was strictly a historical-critical one; he was not overtly presenting a theory of authority. Even so, a notion of authority was implicit, namely, what may be called a "prophetic" concept of inspiration. The poetic oracles were regarded more highly than the prosaic parts of the book. This sort of value judgment has persisted in studies of Jeremiah, with many scholars taking the view that the prosaic, or Deuteronomistic, parts were inferior in thought and expression.[2] As in much literary criticism of the Old Testament, the notion of "secondariness" became a cipher for "less true," or negligible. The correlation of poetic oracle and quality of religious thought reached a high point in Jeremiah studies with J. Skinner, for whom the prophet was an outstanding example of the religious life, marking an advance in internalized, individual religion, exemplified above all in the prophet's prayers.[3] All such studies were pursued broadly under the aegis of the historical-critical mode of Old Testament interpretation.

In the tussle over authenticity one attempt to put the authority of the book on a firmer basis was John Bright's influential proposal, on the basis of a comparative lexical analysis, that a large proportion of the prosaic material along with the poetry could be attributed to the prophet.[4] Here too the issue of authority was not overtly at stake, yet the implication was that, if the book consisted to a large extent of the authentic words of the prophet, it would be the more authoritative. In the correlation of prophetic words and authentic message Bright was like Duhm; they simply differed on the extent of those words. Bright's thesis required an attempt to locate the various words of the prophet as far as possible in his life and ministry; hence, he reordered the sections of Jeremiah in his Anchor Bible commentary.[5] W. L. Holladay has more recently proposed his own realign-

1. B. Duhm, *Jeremia,* Kurzer Hand-commentar zum Alten Testament (Tübingen: Mohr, 1901), pp. XI-XIII.

2. L. Stulman cites the scholarly use of terms such as "legalistic, monotonous, impoverished" to characterize these parts of the book (*The Prose Sermons of the Book of Jeremiah,* Society for Biblical Literature Dissertation Series 833 [Atlanta: Scholars Press, 1986], pp. 12-13).

3. J. Skinner, *Prophecy and Religion* (Cambridge: Cambridge University Press, 1922), p. 201. J. Wellhausen had thought that the prayers actually had no part in the prophet's public ministry (*Israelitische und Jüdische Geschichte,* 5th ed. [Berlin: G. Reimer, 1904], p. 149).

4. J. Bright, "The Date of the Prose Sermons of Jeremiah," *Journal of Biblical Literature* 70 (1951): 15-35.

5. J. Bright, *Jeremiah,* Anchor Bible (New York: Doubleday, 1965).

ment of the prophet's words and his life,[6] and H. Weippert, who also attributed much of the prose to Jeremiah, tried to put Bright's linguistic analysis on a better footing by analyzing the book's discourse at sentence level rather than lexical level.[7] These attempts have kept open the lively minority line of interpretation that maximizes the actual prophetic deposit and resists the Deuteronomistic type of interpretation. However, by focusing on the words of the prophet, they have left the implicit questions of the authority of the *book* unanswered. The prevailing hermeneutic remained historical-critical.

The alternative direction in Jeremiah studies after Duhm took the book as the locus of the message more seriously. J. P. Hyatt, writing in the same year as Bright, examined the theology of the Deuteronomistic author of the book, an impetus later developed by W. Thiel;[8] and E. W. Nicholson charted a movement from the words of the prophet to reinterpretation and reapplication within the Exilic community.[9] Some of this type of work continues to show a concern for a real connection between the words of the prophet and the later developments.[10] In general, however, this sort of move in the book's interpretation may be thought consonant with the fashion for the "canonical criticism" of B. S. Childs. The history of composition was observed but made subordinate to the "final form," which was a function of the canonizing community. There is thus a significant shift away from the authentic voice of the prophet to the way in which the prophet continued to be heard in the community that remembered his words as mediated by a tradition.

The most recent developments, however, are in line with the modern

6. W. L. Holladay, *Jeremiah* I, II (Philadelphia: Fortress, 1986; Minneapolis: Augsburg/Fortress, 1989).

7. H. Weippert, *Die Prosareden des Jeremiabuches,* Beihefte zur Zeitschrift für die alttestamentliche Wissenschaft 132 (Berlin: de Gruyter, 1973).

8. J. P. Hyatt, "The Deuteronomic Edition of Jeremiah," *Vanderbilt Studies in the Humanities* 1 (1951): 71-95. W. Thiel, *Die Deuteronomistische Redaktion von Jeremiah 1–25,* Wissenschaftliche Monographien zum Alten und Neuen Testament 41 (Neukirchen-Vluyn: Neukirchener Verlag, 1973); idem, *Die Deuteronomistische Redaktion von Jeremiah 26–45,* Wissenschaftliche Monographien zum Alten und Neuen Testament 52 (Neukirchen-Vluyn: Neukirchener Verlag, 1981).

9. E. W. Nicholson, *Preaching to the Exiles: A Study of the Prose Tradition in the Book of Jeremiah* (Oxford: Blackwell, 1970).

10. J. A. Thompson's commentary may be cited in this connection (*Jeremiah,* New International Commentary on the Old Testament [Grand Rapids: Eerdmans, 1980]).

interest in the polyphonic character of texts. The commentaries of W. McKane and R. P. Carroll mark an important stage in this move, each in its own way emphasizing the diversity and ultimate shapelessness of the material in the book.[11] McKane's concept of a "rolling corpus" remains more in touch with the older interest in the prophet and a dependent tradition of interpretation; Carroll is the more radical, pursuing a thesis of mere disparateness, a vast number of possible settings in diverse communities, and the impossibility of finding system or meaning in the book as a whole. The voice of the prophet can hardly be heard at all in this many-sided conversation.

Polyphony is taken in a slightly different direction by Mark E. Biddle. Taking issue with all interpretations that seek a final authoritative voice (whether that of the prophet or of the canonical or literary form), he finds an interplay of voices in what he calls "a variety of redaction criticism informed by literary and canonical concerns."[12] These voices air problems that the dialogue gradually resolves. A consequence of his approach is that the text stands a long way from the message originally given by the prophet. For example, there is no record of preaching true repentance in the book, nor are the "confessions" (the prayers of Jeremiah) actual intercessions for the people; they are simply a part of the book's demonstration that the punishment of the Exile was justified. Texts purporting to record incidents in the prophet's life have in reality no interest in original settings, but rather the "narrator's interests lie with the universal workings of Yahweh's mind," with an accent on theodicy. The prophet himself "is irrelevant except as he functions as a cipher for the exploration of theodicy."[13] The implications of this are extensive, not least in relation to the "confessions," which (as I will argue) make a strong statement for the presence of God in and through the experience of the prophet. Biddle's work is cogent in its insistence on the rights of the lineaments of the text, but a question exists over the detachment from the voice of the prophet since the book's self-commendation depends so heavily on the concept that God spoke through Jeremiah.

11. W. McKane, *Jeremiah I–XXV; Jeremiah XXVI–LII,* International Critical Commentary (Edinburgh: T. & T. Clark, 1986, 1996); R. P. Carroll, *Jeremiah,* Old Testament Library (London: SCM, 1986).

12. Mark E. Biddle, *Polyphony and Symphony in Prophetic Literature: Rereading Jeremiah 7–20,* Studies in Old Testament Interpretation 2 (Macon, Ga.: Mercer University Press, 1996), p. 7.

13. Biddle, *Polyphony,* p. 85.

Criteria for Authority

In this selective charting of atolls in the sea of Jeremiah interpretation we have described some outer limits: at one horizon stands the prophet, mediated by a more or less pure text (including even Duhm's reduced canon); at the other stands the book, a vessel of meaning in itself, removed from the life of the prophet who has retreated into misty detachment. The proven viability of both these directions in Jeremiah studies suggests that there is force in each and that, whatever other criteria we can establish for authority and interpretation, each pole should figure in a conceptualization of the authority of the book.

Our questions are whether there is a way to such a conceptualization, and what criteria should be established in doing so. It should be said at this stage that the resolution of the tension between the two extremes is not necessarily found by appeal to "canonical" or "final form" alone. As I have mentioned, this concept, in the case of Jeremiah, highlights a problem as much as it offers a solution (because of the large variation between the main texts). Certainly, once a decision is made in principle for the MT, some scholars have found it possible to describe the "final form" as a coherent structure with a specific theological trajectory.[14] However, even on these terms, "final form" is not universally equated with "single authoritative voice." Carroll's understanding of the "final form" of the MT as a medley, lacking an organizing principle, poses the question of authority starkly. Certain nonhistorical "final form" treatments promise more synthesis. This is true of T. Polk's treatment of the "persona" of Jeremiah as presented in the book. In his interpretation, the "persona" of the title is a construct, and the book a sophisticated staging of theological issues.[15] Biddle's gradual resolution of the variant voices tends towards synthesis in a different way. The menu of "book" interpretations, therefore, is varied, and they pose different problems. Carroll makes a bid for the incoherence of the book and indeterminateness in interpretation. Others have seen cohesion in the book but cut the link with the prophet. Both of these moves can end

14. The monographs of T. M. Raitt, J. Unterman, and the present writer are such attempts: T. M. Raitt, *A Theology of Exile: Judgment/Deliverance in Jeremiah and Ezekiel* (Philadelphia: Fortress, 1977); J. Unterman, *From Repentance to Redemption: Jeremiah's Thought in Transition* (Sheffield: JSOT Press, 1987); J. G. McConville, *Judgment and Promise: An Interpretation of the Book of Jeremiah* (Leicester: Apollos; Winona Lake: Eisenbrauns, 1993).

15. T. Polk, *The Prophetic Persona* (Sheffield: JSOT Press, 1984).

in pessimism about meaning.[16] Against Carroll, it may be urged, provisionally, that his approach is in principle "anti-book," and therefore the existence of the book stands against it. The nonhistorical interpretations, however, beg the question why the concept of the word of God coming to the figure of Jeremiah occupies so central a place in the book. Both these points need further elaboration.

Communication, Text, and Audience

We take up first the challenge of Carroll, namely, that the book does not speak with a coherent voice. In his concept it is the product of a vast number of interventions and additions, with no governing principle, each deriving from its own particular place and interest. How does such a view square with the nature of the material? Childs indicated that the way to an answer to this question is by highlighting the significance of the text *as Scripture.* As such it was received as authoritative by a community, or communities. The question is thus put back to interpreters who insist on anarchy in the generation of the text: By what means it can be shown that no governing principle existed? The theory of bandwagoning incoherence assumes a minimal attachment on the community's part to the concept that God spoke authoritatively through the prophet. Yet the evidence that derives from the preservation of the text, as well as the concept of canon, points in the opposite direction.

To Childs's stimulus other, somewhat different voices may now be added. These are those that try to establish a connection between the initial communication and the written text. The tendency may loosely be defined as rhetorical criticism. This development has gone well beyond the work of James Muilenburg, who first appealed against the dominance of historical criticism in interpretation and pointed to the potential for meaning in the text in its stylistic features. The term may now be defined, in the words of D. Patrick and A. Scult, as "the means by which a text establishes and manages its relationship to its audience in order to achieve a

16. Mark Brett warns against a self-defeating pessimism and pleads for an overt ethics of interpretation in which negotiations are made between the iconoclastic and the traditional ("Biblical Studies and Theology: Negotiating the Intersections," *Biblical Interpretation* 6 [1998]: 140-41).

particular effect."[17] The crucial point is the relationship between text and audience, and the assumption that the form of the text is a function of the need to communicate and to hear a message. An audience may not hear the text in any way they please. Rather, "the speaker or author attempts to constrain that freedom and direct interpretation by giving the audience clues and indicators as to how he or she means the discourse to function for them." He does so via "[his] management of the conventional forms of discourse prevalent in the community to which speaker and audience belong." The assumption of Patrick and Scult is that the text had a theological purpose and aimed to speak authoritatively. The text, indeed, can only be understood as an attempt to elicit faith. They also claim a unity or correspondence between the concept of the text (in the mind of speaker or writer) and the understanding of the intended audience(s) by appeal to conventional forms of discourse.

The direction given by Patrick and Scult does not negate the role of the modern interpreter. On the contrary, her role is defined in relation to the nature of the text as bearing authority for a community: "[she] needs to find those conventions of engagement through which the text might have originally exercised its authority over an audience."[18] The scholar's task is further defined as the reconstruction of the "significant interpretive moments" in a text's life; "the interpreter, therefore, must synthesize the meanings a text has had into the meaning it has" and "judge which moments in a text's history constitute the effective movement of meaning from the text to the interpreter."[19] This will be done with chosen interpretive companions, and this "judging with" is an inescapable part of interpretation.[20]

It will be clear too that the approach taken here does not try to avoid or reduce the specific issues of interpretation posed by Jeremiah. Their understanding is of a text that grows within a community. There is no problem in principle with the fact that the book exists in more than one form. Judgments as to best text are part of the interpretative process. This means, for example, that the decision as between MT and LXX of Jeremiah need not wholly uphold the one while discrediting the other. The issue is how

17. Dale Patrick and Allen Scult, *Rhetorical Criticism and Biblical Exegesis,* Journal for the Study of the Old Testament Supplement Series 82 (Sheffield: Almond, 1990), p. 12.

18. Patrick and Scult, *Rhetorical Criticism,* p. 15.

19. Patrick and Scult, *Rhetorical Criticism,* p. 20.

20. Patrick and Scult, *Rhetorical Criticism,* p. 21.

well each form of the text brings out its essential rhetorical force, as far as the interpreter can judge from all the evidence. His interpretation, furthermore, is done within an interpretive community, to whom he has to make an effective case for his interpretation.[21] The text, in fact, has an "ideal reader" in view, and the interpreter, acting in community herself, fulfills the role of such a reader. Where diverse statements stand together in a text, it is the reader's role to piece them together so that sense is made of them.[22]

In this way a brake is put on on the reading of a complex text from two different sides: the act of interpretation implied in the formation of the text is constrained by its location within a believing, canonizing community; and its continuing interpretation is governed by the concept of an ideal reader, who judges and sifts possible interpretations for their validity in the light of the original communicative intention, while he himself is located within an interpreting community.[23]

The book of Jeremiah well illustrates the sort of interpretative issues raised by rhetorical criticism. Jeremiah 36 has always been a key text in critical theories about its composition. Interpretation of it has tended to focus on questions of authenticity: Could the text be trusted as a reliable indicator of Jeremiah's own involvement in the book's production? Answers have ranged from those in which the role of Baruch as Jeremiah's scribe has been emphasized, thus maximizing the link between prophet and book, to those that see the narrative as a Deuteronomistic invention, a foil to King Josiah's discovery of the Book of the Law (2 Kings 22). Against the background of modern interpretation (and leaving aside whatever the narrative may imply about kingship), the text takes on a new kind of significance, namely, addressing the specifically hermeneutical question of the authority of the prophet in the community and subsequent communities. The issue is the relationship between original words of the prophet and their authority in his absence. The absence of the prophet in the incident itself accentuates the point, Baruch standing in a mediatorial role. The book of Jeremiah is like Deuteronomy in this respect (more interest-

21. Patrick and Scult, *Rhetorical Criticism,* p. 22.

22. Patrick and Scult, *Rhetorical Criticism,* pp. 131-36.

23. Other interpreters who draw on the idea of a communicative event in relation to a text are G. A. Kennedy, *New Testament Interpretation through Rhetorical Criticism* (Chapel Hill: University of North Carolina Press, 1984); C. G. Bartholomew, *Reading Ecclesiastes: Old Testament Exegesis and Hermeneutical Theory,* Analecta Biblica 139 (Rome: Pontifical Biblical Institute, 1998).

ingly than simply in terms of vocabulary and phraseology), that is, in establishing how the word of God might continue to be living reality in times and places beyond the word given in one place to one community. In Deuteronomy, Moses' teaching of the word given at Horeb represents the ongoing presence of the word in all foreseeable communities of God's people. There Moses embraces the roles of prophet and teacher. Here Jeremiah has the prophetic role, while Baruch has the humbler scribal part. Even so, there is no "magic" in the scroll itself as read by Baruch (a magic sometimes held to be countered symbolically by Jehoiakim's destruction of the scroll in the fire). The point is simply that the word given once to the prophet is living and effective beyond the moment and first circumstances of its giving and hearing. The production of a second scroll shows that this fundamental fact cannot be undone, rather the reverse. The word lives on, mediated by and within the faithful in the community. The "many similar words [that were] added to [the first scroll]" (Jer. 36:32c) even let in the idea of the word taking different forms. It is not far from this to seeing in Baruch a figure of the interpreter, or of the community as interpreter, hearing the word afresh in new situations, even weighing together words that stand in some tension with each other.

A slightly different angle on the same question comes from what is known as speech-act theory, a province first charted by J. L. Austin and explored further by authors such as John Searle. They considered language events as performing certain communicative actions and thus effecting changes in relationships by their utterance. The approach is more strictly linguistic than rhetorical criticism in the sense that it analyzes and classifies types of speech-acts, showing how and what they communicate. It is clear that there is an immediate application to the prophets. The idea of a prophet's audience is more or less built into the concept of prophet itself. The shape of the audience has varied in the mind of scholars over the decades, from the schools and disciples of older criticism to the support groups of more recent sociologically orientated study.[24] Furthermore, the prophetic books themselves often depict the prophet as addressing the community of Israel or Judah generally, as when Jeremiah stands at the gate of the temple and declaims the "temple sermon" (Jer. 7:1-15). The word proclaimed is sometimes seen to produce repentance, the classic case being

24. Cf. R. R. Wilson, *Prophecy and Society in Ancient Israel* (Philadelphia: Fortress, 1980); D. L. Petersen, *The Roles of Israel's Prophets* (Sheffield: JSOT Press, 1981).

the repentance of Nineveh at the preaching of Jonah (Jonah 3). Elijah's demonstration on Mt. Carmel elicits a confession of faith from the panic-stricken onlookers, though there is no sign of lasting effects (1 Kings 18:39). In the prophetic books themselves there are no clear records of penitence and turning to Yahweh in response to the prophetic word. The effectiveness of the prophetic word is apparent only in the fear on the part of the prophets' opponents that their word might be disruptive: hence, the burning of the scroll by Jehoiakim (Jeremiah 36), the same king's murder of the prophet Uriah (Jeremiah 26), and Zedekiah's imprisonment of Jeremiah despite his hesitant clandestine consultations (Jer. 32:1-5; 34:1-7, 37-38).[25]

The failure of the people to respond to the prophetic word is one of the central issues of the prophetic books. In that sense the books are precisely exercises in prophetic hermeneutics. The original speech event of the prophet is now carried in the book, in full cognizance of the fact that the outcome of the first event was a failure to respond. This is the paradox involved in these books: they are prophetic calls for response, while being themselves records of nonresponse. This is not to say that the words spoken have been ineffective. In a sense they have been fully effective, in that they have compelled a response of one sort or another — even a refusal to repent is a response — and the "performance" of the prophets (to borrow a key term from speech-act theory) is therefore to have pronounced judgment that is then shown to fall, duly and justifiably.[26] The existence of the book, furthermore, is a testimony to the fact that the word has been recognized, by someone, as effective, and to their expectation that the record of the word spoken can be so still.

Yet can a speech-act be mediated by a book? Austin originally applied speech-act theory to the spoken word, and it has been held by some to be inapplicable to written texts. This view, however, is now changing. Francis

25. On the texts concerning Jeremiah and Zedekiah, see J. Applegate, "The Date of Zedekiah: Redactional Debate in the Book of Jeremiah," *Vetus Testamentum* 48 (1998): 137-60, 301-8.

26. On this Walter Houston rightly dissents from Carroll's view that a successful performative speech was one that persuaded the hearers to the view of the speaker (Walter Houston, "What Did the Prophets Think They Were Doing? Speech Acts and Prophetic Discourse in the Old Testament," *Biblical Interpretation* 1 [1993]: 176-77). Carroll's discussion of speech-act theory, referred to by Houston, is in *When Prophecy Failed* (London: SCM Press, 1979), pp. 72-74. Houston argues that the force of the prophetic utterance is that it declares, or brings into being, a state of judgment ("What Did the Prophets Think?" p. 180).

Watson, agreeing that speech is "the paradigmatic instance of the category of communicative action,"[27] argues that writing is also communicative action. The basic criteria that govern a successful speech-act apply first of all to spoken communication, and therefore written communication is entirely dependent upon the spoken. These criteria are: (1) a shared medium of communication, (2) some form of proximity between speaker and hearer, (3) a common concern between speaker and hearer, (4) an intention to produce both understanding and response from the hearer, and (5) the possibility of further communication. In applying such criteria to writing, certain adjustments have to be made. The most important of these is that the audience is not necessarily close in space or time to the writing of the text. This has further important consequences. It means, for example, that the identification of the "shared concern" that characterizes spoken acts of communication lies with the reader rather than the speaker. It also increases the risk of misunderstanding that is involved in all speech-acts.[28]

None of these problems is fatal to the notion of writing as speech-act, however. Two of Watson's adjustments of the speech-act to writing are important for our purpose. First, the audience must clearly be redefined. Once a piece of discourse is "published" in written form it has in theory any number of possible audiences.[29] Yet audiences will not in practice be random; they are defined by certain factors. The concept of "proximity" of speaker and hearer may be met in the case of writing by "institutional" continuity (e.g., educational or ecclesial) or "tradition"; "author and intended readers are conscious of participating in a tradition that mediates the historical and/or geographical distance that separates them and brings them into a certain proximity to one another."[30] Second, the interaction between speaker and hearer may be substituted by the activity of interpre-

27. Francis Watson, *Text and Truth: Redefining Biblical Theology* (Edinburgh: T. & T. Clark, 1997), p. 98.

28. Watson, *Text and Truth*, pp. 98-103.

29. The idea of "utterance become text" is crucial in Walter Brueggemann's work on Old Testament theology and in his central concept of the Old Testament as Israel's "testimony" to Yahweh (*Theology of the Old Testament* [Minneapolis: Augsburg/Fortress, 1997], pp. 117-44, 721-25). He has a distinctive line on the question of the text's audiences; its primary audiences are the twin households of faith, Church and Synagogue, while the "secondary listening community" is "the larger public, that is willing to listen to many alternative construals of reality" (Brueggemann, *Theology*, p. 87 and n.).

30. Watson, *Text and Truth*, p. 100.

tation. An interpreter who is close in space and time to the reader may even be able to clarify the speaker's meaning in ways that the speaker might not have been able to, or where he had not foreseen unclarities.[31]

The Book of Jeremiah as Speech of God

Our consideration of the book as speech-act has focused up to now on the relationship between the prophet's utterance and the written text. The root question, however, is whether and how the book may be regarded as speech of God, and indeed how God may be thought to be a speaker. This question has been addressed directly by N. Wolterstorff. Wolterstorff's work is a philosophical inquiry into the claim that God speaks. As such it focuses directly on the idea of divine speech, distinguishing this from the category of revelation. The argument is a reflection on speech as predicated specially of God.[32] In the course of it he considers ways in which human speech might "count as" speech of God, having the prophets primarily in view. Recognizing that there are "many modes of discourse," he uses the examples of a secretary and an ambassador as cases in which a person is deemed to speak through the agency of another, what he calls "double agency" discourse. The nature of the agent's representation of the person may be seen as superintending, authorizing, or deputizing, or more than one of these. A secretary may write a letter, using his own words, on behalf of an executive, with the latter's full authority, on the grounds that the secretary knows the executive's mind on the matter in hand (both superintending and authorizing are involved here). An ambassador may convey a message from the president, perhaps using some of the president's own words and some of his own. In this case the ambassador "deputizes," and the words he speaks have all the force of words spoken by the president. It is the latter analogy that Wolterstorff applies especially to prophecy. In Hosea 9:11-17 certain words appear to be the words of God himself, conveyed directly by the prophet (9:11-12); others are words of the prophet ad-

31. Others are less sanguine about the amenability of text to dialogue; see P. Ricoeur, *Interpretation Theory: Discourse and the Surplus of Meaning* (Fort Worth, Tex.: Texas Christian University Press, 1976), pp. 25-37; cited in Bartholomew, *Rereading Ecclesiastes,* p. 214 and n.

32. Nicholas Wolterstorff, *Divine Discourse: Philosophical Reflections on the Claim That God Speaks* (Cambridge: Cambridge University Press, 1995).

dressed back to God in the dialogue between God and Hosea (9:14); and still others might be regarded as either God's words or those of the prophet (9:16). The first and last of these cases correspond to the example of the ambassador, who sometimes uses the president's own words and sometimes his own. The biblical books themselves reflect on the idea of deputized discourse in passages such as Deuteronomy 18:15-22 (note v. 18) and Jeremiah 1:4-10.[33]

There are limitations to this model, as Wolterstorff himself recognizes. In order to accommodate biblical books that are not prophetic, such as Psalms and Wisdom books, he uses the additional category of "appropriated discourse," that is, when one allows the words of another to stand as one's position or view.[34] More important, however, is the question of what happens to the divine speech when it becomes embodied in a written text.

We have already argued that the idea of a speech-act can be extended in principle to written texts. Can the same thing hold true for speech of God? Wolterstorff deals with this by making the valid points that the words of the apostle (his example in this case is Paul) may come to mean different things to different audiences once they have become a "letter." Watson's points, noted above, concerning continuity within an interpreting tradition strengthen this contention. Can the same solution be applied to the book of Jeremiah?

The problem is complicated in Jeremiah (and most prophetic books) because, as we have noticed, scholarship has placed greater or lesser distance between the ministry of Jeremiah and the book that bears his name. We are compelled, therefore, to go beyond the question we have already addressed about the relation between prophet and book in principle to consider the extensions of the authority of the prophet's speech that the book tolerates. These extensions may be stated minimally, as when the prophet himself stands close to the process by which his words are preserved in writing, or maximally, as when the prestige of the prophet's name is simply borrowed in furtherance of some program distant from his own.

In this case some extension of Wolterstorff's notion of double agency is needed to cover not merely the conveying of the words of the speaker

33. Wolterstorff, *Divine Discourse*, pp. 38-51. He is careful to avoid the imputation of a "mechanical" theory of inspiration on the grounds that nothing is said in the biblical books about the way in which the words of God are "put in the prophet's mouth" (p. 48).

34. Wolterstorff, *Divine Discourse*, pp. 51-54.

into new situations but also their adaptation and reinterpretation. This can be done, I think, with two qualifications. The first is the centrality in the book of the actual speech of Jeremiah. That is not to say that all the words come directly from him, but rather that they both form the core of the book and give it its concept of what constitutes word of God. This seems to me to be required not only by the book's centering of the prophet's word and experience but also by the larger prophetic tradition within which this is situated. The community that preserved Jeremiah's message was heir to a tradition that went back to Hosea and beyond him to Elijah and Moses. The ancientness of the concept of prophet as mediator may be illustrated by Numbers 12:6-8, where the generality of prophetic experience is made incidental to the special standing of Moses. Jeremiah's hearers and readers knew that prophets mediated the word of God. For them the issue was not how God speaks but rather how to know the true prophet from the false. This issue is writ large in Jeremiah (Jer. 23:9-40; 28). The true prophet is the one who has "stood in the council of the LORD" (23:18, 22); the false is merely a pretender. The problem is itself a widespread theme in the Old Testament's thinking about validity. The same contention that erupts in this book between Jeremiah and Hananiah (Jeremiah 28) may be found in 1 Kings 22, in which Micaiah reports his receiving God's message for Jehoshaphat and Ahab in the divine council (1 Kings 22:19), and in which another prophet, Zedekiah ben Chenaanah, confronts Micaiah because the word has passed from him (Zedekiah) to the other (v. 24). It is implicit in the confrontation between Elijah and the prophets of Baal (1 Kings 18; cf. Num. 11:26-30), and it is theologized in Deuteronomy 18:15-20. In view of the strength of this topic in various strands of the Old Testament, the importance of the voice of the prophet in the book cannot be minimized. In charting the relationship between prophet and book the biblical witness suggests that the speech of Jeremiah *as* speech of God is fundamental to the authority of the book, whatever forms the book should actually take.

Having said that the prophet's experience is essential to the Old Testament's thinking about prophecy, the book of Jeremiah remains the chief example of the point. Here the experience of Jeremiah goes well beyond the simple reception of a verbal message to his whole life experience. His rejection by the people to the extent of threats to his life (Jer. 11:18-23; 18:18), his banishment from normal society, including marriage (15:17; 16:1-4), his psychological anguish (15:18; 20:7-18), and his imprisonment and banishment (32:1-5; 37–38; 43:1-7) all in some sense mark the involvement of God in Israel's history, in a way that may be called "incarnational."[35] As in Hosea it was sometimes impossible to tell the voice of the prophet apart from that of God; so it is with Jeremiah (Jer. 8:22–9:6 [MT 9:5]). The force of the identification in this case, however, is to suggest that Yahweh himself weeps over his people. The suffering of God because of the waywardness of Israel is mirrored in the life of Jeremiah.

The validity of the message of the book of Jeremiah therefore depends on what is asserted about the prophet's experience. It can be argued, of course, that the persona of Jeremiah is a mere figment, detached from the prophet's life.[36] Yet this runs counter to what we have observed about the strength of the notion of the prophetic experience in Israel. The suffering prophet can scarcely be invented if the idea has no rooting in what is known and expected of prophets.

The second condition for the validity of the book of Jeremiah as speech-act is implied in the first. It is that the activity of preserving and reflecting on the prophet's own words is done in the context of a tradition of knowing God and his word that imposes constraints on interpretation. This contention cannot readily be demonstrated since the process involved is not accessible to scrutiny. It is a reasonable inference, however, from the simple existence of the canon, a cumulation of words of God understood and presented as a single entity, and therefore bearing witness to a frame of mind that sought to understand God's words in the totality of their relationships to each other. In my view this should predispose us to read the traditioning that brought the book of Jeremiah to its present form(s) as responsibly concerned to convey the true import of the words of the prophet.

Particularity and Universality in Jeremiah

The two conditions described correspond to the inescapable poles of any reading of Jeremiah: the prophet and the book. These poles symbolize the whole process of interpretation, the movement from particular to univer-

35. The classic treatment of this "incarnational" aspect of Jeremiah's ministry is U. Mauser, *Gottesbild und Menschwerdung* (Tübingen: Mohr, 1971); in addition to Jeremiah it deals with Hosea and Jesus. The present author has a fuller discussion of the topic in *Judgment and Promise,* pp. 61-78.

36. As Polk does in *The Prophetic Persona.*

sal that is involved in all reading of the Bible. This idea is contained within that of Scripture itself, namely, words that were given in certain times and places and that are preserved and conveyed because they are believed to have validity in an indefinite number of other times and places.

The particularity of God's word to and through Jeremiah should not be underestimated. It extends to the way in which the prophet speaks about God. An example is the theme of Yahweh's incomparability (10:1-16).[37] In this sequence, the claims made for Yahweh are part of an argument that contains claims made for other gods and powers. When Yahweh is called "King of the nations" (10:7), this is a metaphor drawn from contemporary religio-politics; Yahweh is king, not an imperialistic Babylonian monarch, who is thought to reflect hierarchical authority in heaven itself. When he is said to stretch out the heavens, utter his voice, or make lightning for the rain (10:12-13), this is all by assimilation of powers attributed to other deities, in a prophetic habit learned from Hosea. We do not necessarily find, then, a fully formed theoretical monotheism but the application of a belief in Yahweh's power to maintain his covenant with Israel and Judah in spite of all other powers. Hosea's image of Yahweh as husband of Israel is adopted by Jeremiah (Jer. 2:32-33; 3:1-5, 6-10) in a metaphor that says that true divine love does not consist in the love of a male god for his female fertility consort but in a fully engaged love for a people.[38] Indeed, the very use of metaphorical imagery in the poetry of Jeremiah (as of Hosea) may be a deliberate counter to the physical images used in all other ancient religion, and therefore a way of enabling world-rooted thinking about God in face of the danger of losing him into unimagined remoteness as a consequence of the anti-iconic prophetic program.[39]

The process of universalizing the message is already visible in the book. For example, it no longer contains a direct record of Jeremiah's first

37. This passage is highlighted by Brueggemann as expressing the importance of the uniqueness of Yahweh to the testimony of Israel about him (*Theology,* pp. 137-39, 142).

38. For this as the force of the husband-bride metaphor see Brigitte Seifert, *Metaphorisches Reden von Gott im Hoseabuch,* Forschungen zur Religion und Literatur des Alten und Neuen Testaments 166 (Göttingen: Vandenhoeck & Ruprecht, 1996), p. 257. She cites in turn D. Kinet, *Baal und Jahweh: Ein Beitrag zur Theologie des Hoseabuches,* Europäische Hochschulschriften, Reihe XXIII — Theologie 87 (Frankfurt: Peter Lang; Berne: Herbert Lang, 1977), p. 227.

39. Seifert, *Metaphorisches Reden,* p. 250. The point might be extended for Jeremiah to such metaphors as warrior, healer, and redeemer.

calls to the people of Judah to repent. While it must be supposed, from the presence of repentance as a theme, that Jeremiah did preach for it at a time when the historical issues played out in the book were not yet settled, the perspective of the book is from a time when it is known that the message went unheeded, that Judah did in fact go into exile, and therefore the issues have now changed utterly. This change in the issues is reflected in the composition of Jeremiah 3, which looks beyond the failures of both Israel and Judah and forward to a new day when not only these will be restored to their historic land but "all nations" will gather to Zion (3:15-18).[40] Furthermore, the process of universalizing continues more broadly within the biblical canon, and in relation to other themes. New covenant theology, perhaps the chief glory of the book of Jeremiah, is by its nature suitable for extension into new spheres of thought and experience. It appears (in effect, if not in name) in other prophetic books, not least Ezekiel 11:19-20, as a way of expressing the need for a covenant loyalty that transcends the immediate physical and political forms. It is found in principle in Deuteronomy, with its demand for "circumcision of the heart" (Deut. 10:16; cf. Jer. 4:4), placed in the province of Yahweh's own responsibility (Deut. 30:6). It becomes one of the central ideas of the New Testament's affirmation that the covenant promises find their "yes" in Jesus Christ. The formation of the canon, therefore, is a testimony to the power of the thought of the book (as of all the canonical books) to enter new worlds and receive new potencies of meaning and communication. The diverse textual forms of the book may be understood in this connection, as witnesses to the effectiveness of the speech of God by Jeremiah, the major texts possibly corresponding to quite different communities.

These early "hearings" of the book of Jeremiah form the backcloth to any modern reading of it. So too, we may add, do influential later readings, such as the casting of Jeremiah as a religious genius, the founder of individualism in religion. This view, characteristic of the early twentieth century and the piety of religious liberalism, has suffered in the course of further study of the book (though it still has adherents), but it focuses rightly on an aspect of the book (the profound personal experience of the prophet) and illustrates its power to speak to a situation far removed from the ancient settings in which the book was formed.

40. For a fuller explanation of the redaction of Jeremiah see the present author's *Judgment and Promise*, pp. 27-41.

The Book of Jeremiah as Communication Event

In the light of the discussion so far, we can claim that the book of Jeremiah constitutes a speech-act, or communication event, capable of speaking to generations well beyond that of the prophet. As such it fulfills the criteria we observed for a successful speech-act. The text, while it should be a matter for continuing research as to "best text," is in its diversity a testimony to the activity of interpretation and the life of the communication in different communities (yet joined by a common tradition). The language has a function beyond the grammar of its sentences. The poetry, with its rich metaphors, belongs to the message about the character of Yahweh as opposed to other gods. The "Deuteronomic" parts put the reader in touch with the covenantal language and thought of large sections of the Old Testament. The "institutional context" is broadly defined as all those who have understood the book and passed it on to further generations of readers, always in the context of believing communities. Finally the "shared concern" of text and reader must be broadly conceived as a concern for the possibility of God continuing with people, laying out the twin possibilities of judgment and salvation, and as a call to faithfulness and obedience. With this in mind, the focus falls on the final organizing voice of the book, the voice that knows that the word of Yahweh came to Jeremiah and that he was set apart before he was born to be "a prophet to the nations" (Jer. 1:4-5); the voice that arranged for his words to enter new literary contexts and thus take on new theological possibilities; and the voice that finds in the interaction of prophetic word and historical event in the period from Josiah's reform to the release of Jehoiachin in Babylon a progression from judgment to salvation, the turning again of Yahweh to his sinful people and retribution upon the foe that was once the instrument of his wrath. Whether or not we call this organizing voice "Deuteronomistic," the concept is a long way from the older critical view that tried to look past the book to the words of the prophet in their purest form. The instinct to find in the prophet's words something of lasting value was right. It was impossible, however, to bypass the book, and indeed the attempt underestimated the extent to which the ability of the prophet's words to be made universal required not just that particular mediation but the possibility of mediation in principle.

Conclusion

The argument presented may be summed up under seven points.

1. A model was adopted for the possibility of divine speech by means of human agency. It was found in Wolterstorff's extension of speech-act theory, in which an agent may convey meaning through proxies, acting under his supervision or deputizing for him.
2. The primary speech-act in the book of Jeremiah is God's speech to the prophet, commissioning him to speak in turn to the people of Judah, or certain members of it. The deputizing model works well for the book, most evidently when the prophet conveys God's words directly. It follows that Jeremiah's speech *as* speech of God is central to the concept of the book. This is consistent too with the biblical tradition concerning prophecy, which places Jeremiah in a line of such speakers, Hosea having the most in common with him.
3. The centrality of the prophet's speech as God's speech remains even when that speech is cast in the form of a book. Both rhetorical criticism and speech-act theory allow for the extension of the spoken word into writing as communicative event. We saw how the book of Jeremiah contains its own reflection on the process from utterance to text in Jeremiah 36. This means that the book itself favors a model that reckons with the poles of actual speech of the prophet and the book itself as communicative event. The force of the word is neither identified with the pure voice of the prophet nor with the book as dehistoricized text. The book rides on the speech of the prophet; conversely, the speech of the prophet is accessible only through the book, with all the mediation and interpretation that is implied in this.[41] The guarantee that the relaying of the prophet's words is true and faithful lies in the nature of the community. New meanings do not arise in a vacuum but are understood within a tradition of knowing

41. Bartholomew, following Ricoeur and Wolterstorff, calls this "the space between Romanticism and structuralism" (*Rereading Ecclesiastes,* pp. 214-15). Wolterstorff is cited in "The Importance of Hermeneutics for a Christian Worldview," in *Disciplining Hermeneutics: Interpretation in Christian Perspective,* ed. R. Lundin (Leicester: Apollos, 1997), p. 44. Houston also dealt with the relationship between the original spoken word and its written realization, especially in relation to Oracles of Judgment ("What Did the Prophets Think?"); see also n. 26.

and believing. The idea of the prophetic word as speech of God, further constrained by anxieties about false prophecy, guards the traditioning of the word.

4. The book of Jeremiah, dependent on underlying speech-acts (of God through the prophet), becomes in itself a speech-act to the community that hears and preserves it. In turn, it plays its part within the greater communicative event that is Scripture. Its specific contributions to this larger discourse include the concept of the new covenant; its supreme instance of "incarnation" in the OT; its answer to the Old Testament's communal laments generally (in the Psalms and Lamentations) and to other writings that express future hope less definitely (notably Kings).
5. The original speech-acts (spoken and written) belong to their times and settings. Therefore they require the reader to enter their world(s) in order to hear and understand the full force of the communication. It is the world of a Jewish community facing its own world with its startling message of the one unimaged God, who creates, calls, commands, judges, and saves. The force of the communication to new times and settings depends on its meaning within that original Hebraic frame.[42]
6. The specific location of the original speech-act need not imply its inability to be universalized, still less its inherent oppressiveness (*pace* Jeanrond).[43] André Lacocque and Paul Ricoeur insist in reply that the text has in fact been able to live in many diverse communities. This move can result in pluralism. Yet Lacocque agrees that meaning is found at the intersection between constraints imposed by the text's *Sitz im Leben* and subsequent reading events.[44]

42. See Heinzpeter Hempelmann on the Hebraic nature of the Scriptures and its function in their interpretation; "Gottes Wort — unsere Antwort: Sprachtheologische und sprachphilosophische Aspekte der Verkündigung des Evangeliums," *EJT* 3 (1994): 43-59.

43. See Brett's reckoning with an interpretation of Isaiah 49 in which positive meaning can be derived only by challenging the ideology promoted by the text, in this case by resisting the text's preference for the returning exiles at the expense of those who remained in the land ("Biblical Studies," p. 133); he refers to essays by W. Jeanrond and Roland Boer in the same volume.

44. André Lacocque and Paul Ricoeur, *Thinking Biblically: Exegetical and Hermeneutical Studies*, trans. David Pellauer (Chicago: University of Chicago Press, 1998), pp. xi, xii-xiv.

7. When we accept these rather loose-fitting parameters, it follows that the message of Jeremiah for today cannot be defined narrowly. However, the starting point is the book as book; that is, the theologizing that has produced the form(s) of the book known to us is irrevocably part of the communication event bequeathed to history. That being so, modern reappropriations are bound to reckon with its reassertion of the rule of God in history, his incomparable power despite the appearance of the opposite, his irreducible insistence on right, and his will to save, reaching beyond whatever might befall, yet without compromising his readiness to deal with evil. This much should be heard loud and clear within believing communities. "Second audiences" (Walter Brueggemann, Ricoeur) may eavesdrop on this divine discourse and even be asked by believers to exercise an imaginative sympathy with them in hearing the text.[45]

45. Lacocque and Ricoeur, *Thinking Biblically,* p. xvii; and see n. 29.

A God for Life, and Not Just for Christmas! The Revelation of God in the Old Testament Wisdom Literature

Craig G. Bartholomew

Introduction

It is well known that the Wisdom Literature of the Old Testament has had a checkered reception in the nineteenth and twentieth centuries.[1] The dominant historical interests of historical criticism and the seeming lack of theology in the Wisdom books conspired to foster their neglect. A welcome characteristic of the last third of the twentieth century has been a renewal of interest in the Old Testament Wisdom Literature, and at the turn of the millennium a spate of commentaries on Job, Proverbs, and Ecclesiastes have appeared. Without doubt wisdom is back on biblical studies' agenda!

And so it ought to be! OT wisdom is an indispensable part of the older testament and a vital part of the background to the Jesus tradition of the NT.[2] Neglect of the Wisdom books may say rather more about the defi-

1. See H. G. Reventlow, *Problems of Old Testament Theology in the Twentieth Century* (London: SCM, 1985), pp. 168ff.

2. B. Witherington (*Jesus the Sage: The Pilgrimage of Wisdom* [Edinburgh: T. & T. Clarke, 1994], p. 156), for example, suggests that some 70 percent of the Jesus tradition has its background in OT wisdom. Not all NT scholars would agree with Witherington's portrayal of Jesus as a sage, but this gives us some idea of the importance of the OT Wisdom Literature for the NT.

ciencies of our own theologies than about the deficiencies of these books.[3] The Wisdom books are a vital part of *tota Scriptura* and fundamental to a full-orbed view of God and humankind. In this chapter my aim is to reflect positively on how the Wisdom books help us to know and follow God.

A God for *All* of Life: Wisdom and Creation

An important element in wisdom's renaissance was W. Zimmerli's 1964 essay on the place and limit of wisdom in OT theology, in which he argued that OT wisdom is theological through and through in its presupposition of the doctrine of creation: "If we now try to characterize the theological attitude of Wisdom, we must say: Wisdom thinks resolutely within the framework of a theology of creation."[4] According to Zimmerli wisdom has no connection with Israel's salvation history, but its articulation of order and active exploration of the world is rooted in Genesis 1. This insight has come to be widely recognized and, as J. Day, R. E. Gordon, and H. G. Williamson acknowledge: "Whatever its special emphases, wisdom as the foremost expression of Israelite intellectual endeavour is, in its more usual manifestations, predicated on a belief in the orderly governance of the world by God. Its character is thus misstated if it is presented merely as a secular alternative to the religious outlook of the rest of the Hebrew scriptures."[5] The relationship of wisdom to the history of Israel will be discussed below. Suffice it here to note that the rediscovery of wisdom as deeply religious and of creation as fundamental to wisdom represents major progress towards understanding the Wisdom Literature of the OT.

3. J. L. Crenshaw (*Urgent Advice and Probing Questions: Collected Writings on Old Testament Wisdom* [Atlanta, Ga.: Mercer University Press, 1995], p. 79) says of the earlier neglect of wisdom that "one could hardly find a better example of interpretive bias, the point made so often today by practitioners of literary interpretation. The imperialism of a particular view of theology excluded wisdom literature from consideration. Dissatisfaction with salvation history coincided with revived interest in Israel's wisdom, which had earlier captured the imagination after its intimate connection with Egyptian wisdom literature was recognized."

4. W. Zimmerli, "The Place and Limit of the Wisdom in the Framework of the Old Testament Theology," *Scottish Journal of Theology* 17 (1964): 148.

5. J. Day, R. E. Gordon, and H. G. Williamson, *Wisdom in Ancient Israel* (Cambridge: Cambridge University Press, 1995), p. 1.

In Proverbs there are two major types of wisdom — the wisdom of God and the wisdom of humans — and the bridge between these is the doctrine of creation. In Proverbs 1–9, the hermeneutical key to the book as a whole, there are two key passages in this respect (Prov. 3:19, 20 and 8:22-31).

Proverbs 3:19, 20

Proverbs 3:13-20 is a wisdom poem positioned between an instruction about right behavior towards God (3:1-12) and an instruction about right behavior towards other people (3:21-35). Proverbs 3:13-18 extols wisdom as leading to prosperity and peace. The reference to the tree of life in verse 18 is intriguing. In the OT it occurs elsewhere only in Genesis 2–3. Proverbs 3:19, 20 contain the theological rationale for wisdom being so valuable and so worthy a goal.

According to this rationale, wisdom is so desirable because it is by *wisdom* that Yahweh founded the earth and by *understanding* that he established the heavens. The very things that are the goal of the quest for wisdom in Proverbs (cf. 3:13 — the same two words are used as in 3:19) are the means by which Yahweh created the world in which humans live. The reference to "the earth," "the heavens," and "the deeps" in 3:19, 20 speaks of the entire creation.[6] The entire, complex fabric of the world, as it were, has been woven by Yahweh, so that to attain wisdom is truly to find the tree of life because it positions one to live according to the warp and woof of the world. This understanding of wisdom as shaping the whole of creation should not somehow be spiritualized away from the real world in all its dimensions. Proverbs 3:20 maintains that the entire shape of the world down to the way in which rain falls from the clouds embodies God's wisdom. This wisdom embodied in the fabric of the world has immense practical significance, as R. J. Clifford recognizes: "Whoever lives in accord with wisdom will not go against but with the grain of the world. Such a person will receive all the goods a wisely constructed world can offer."[7]

6. R. van Leeuwen, "Proverbs," in *The New Interpreter's Bible*, vol. 5 (Nashville: Abingdon, 1997), p. 53.

7. R. J. Clifford, *Proverbs*, The Old Testament Library (Louisville, Ky.: Westminster/John Knox, 1999), p. 54.

Proverbs 8

In a much expanded version we find the same emphases in Proverbs 8:22-31. Proverbs 8 is Lady Wisdom's longest speech in Proverbs, and one in which she makes a passionate appeal to God's people to embrace wisdom by elaborating on its many advantages. The precise identity of Lady Wisdom and her relationship to Yahweh, particularly as expressed in verse 22, remain controversial. Is wisdom an attribute of Yahweh? If *qānah* in verse 22 is taken to mean "acquire" or "possess," then this understanding of wisdom is likely. However, if in verse 22 we have the language of (pre)creation, then the identity of wisdom becomes more complex.[8] In my opinion we have a literary personification of wisdom rather than a literal creation of a separate being. This is a highly poetic and metaphoric section, and it would, I think, be wrong to extrapolate details about the Godhead from this section.[9]

However we resolve the identity of wisdom, the important point in this section is that nothing was created without God's wisdom being involved. This, rather than the precreation of the being of wisdom, is, I suggest, the implication of the negatives in 8:24-26.[10] To use the language of Proverbs 3, it is by wisdom that Yahweh creates. How to understand *āmon* in 8:30 also remains controversial. *Amon* has been understood in three principal ways: as "artisan," as "trustworthy friend," and as "ward," nursling.[11] Clifford has recently argued that *āmon* is a loanword from Akkadian *ummanu,* meaning "scribe, sage." An *ummanu* in Mesopotamian mythology is a divine or semidivine bringer of culture and skill to the human race.[12]

8. For a useful discussion of Lady Wisdom's identity see R. E. Murphy, *The Tree of Life: An Exploration of Biblical Wisdom Literature,* 2nd ed. (Grand Rapids: Eerdmans, 1990), pp. 133ff.

9. I agree with R. van Leeuwen ("Liminality and Worldview in Proverbs 1–9," *Semeia* 50 [1990]: 116) that "in Woman Wisdom we have the 'self-revelation' of an archetypal normativity built into the cosmos, a *tertium quid* that mediates between God and the world, a something embedded in the fabric of creation, but which is not simply to be identified with created things. This cosmic Wisdom serves to ground and legitimate wisdom teaching." See also van Leeuwen, "Proverbs," pp. 96, 97 for a stronger emphasis on the intermediary nature of wisdom.

10. Cf. Clifford, *Proverbs,* p. 96.

11. See Clifford, *Proverbs,* p. 99.

12. Clifford, *Proverbs,* pp. 99-101.

However we resolve the meaning of *amon*, the point of the passage is clear. It is by and with wisdom that Yahweh creates the world, and this is a process of delight and great joy. The very fabric of the world embodies Yahweh's wisdom, and hence there is great advantage in embracing wisdom in one's life, and great folly in rejecting it. Clifford's understanding of the background of *amon* in the bringers of culture in Mesopotamian mythology is attractive in its focus on the potential for cultural development that is built into Yahweh's creation. This would strongly affirm cultural development (cf. Gen. 4:17-22) while also alerting one to the need for *wise* cultural development.

This understanding in the OT Wisdom books of the whole of creation as having come into existence by Yahweh's wise activity is similar to the positive depiction of the creation as shaped by God's "Let there be's" in Genesis 1. True wisdom consequently involves discovering and living according to the shape Yahweh has given to the world. This is a delight and not a burden — it is sharing in the dance of wisdom in God's world! It should be noted here that just as Genesis 1 insists that the creation is good and in accordance with God's will, so too wisdom knows nothing of a Gnostic anti-creation tendency. All of creation comes from God and embodies his wisdom.

R. van Leeuwen shows how this idea of a creation ordered by God underlies the main metaphors of Proverbs 1–9, the hermeneutical key to the book of Proverbs as a whole. There are several key metaphors in 1–9: the two ways, the two women, the two houses, and so on. However, at a deeper level the root metaphor is that of a creation ordered by God:

> . . . underlying the bipolar metaphorical system of positive and negative youths, invitations/calls, 'ways', 'women', and 'houses' in Proverbs 1–9, is a yet more fundamental reality which these images together portray. These chapters depict the world as the arena of human existence. This world possesses two fundamental characteristics. First is its structure of boundaries or limits. Second is the bi-polar human *eros* for the beauty of Wisdom, who prescribes life within limits, or for the seeming beauty of Folly, who offers bogus delights in defiance of created limits. Love of Wisdom means staying within her prescribed cosmic-social boundaries. . . . Thus, recognition of cosmic structure or limits is inseparable from proper eros or direction. . . . The socio-ethical order of Proverbs

1-9 is grounded in the creation order revealed by Wisdom who accompanied God as he set the cosmic boundaries.[13]

An implication of this theology of creation is that Proverbs assumes that all of life is the terrain for service of God. Proverbs knows nothing of the sacred/secular dichotomy that has dogged the footsteps of theology and Church life in the twentieth century. The debate continues about the *Sitz im Leben* of wisdom.[14] Does it originate in school or court circles? In their quest for the *Sitz im Leben* scholars have noted the diverse parts of Israelite society that are referred to in Proverbs. While the *Sitz im Leben* is not irrelevant, the whole point of wisdom is that it is discernible in every aspect of life as God has made it, and certainly not just in the cultic, royal, educational, or family sphere.

In line with Proverbs's theology of creation, wisdom is pictured as crucial to all aspects of life. Proverbs 1 begins by asserting the great value of wisdom for education. In 1:20 wisdom cries out in the busiest parts of the city, presumably the marketplace and the city gates, home *inter alia* of the law courts. Indeed, there are no areas of life that wisdom does not reflect upon: leadership and royalty, wealth and poverty, economics and law, and justice, marriage, and developing sexuality — they are all here, reminding us that *all* of life is a response to God.

This is not to say that the Wisdom books assume that wisdom provides quick and easy answers to the challenges of life. Job and Ecclesiastes, in particular, witness to the complexity of finding wise ways in our broken lives. However, even in Proverbs wisdom has the nature of a quest. The call of Lady Wisdom has to be responded to, her house has to be entered, and her hospitality has to be taken; the path of wisdom has to be followed; wisdom has to be sought in an ongoing way. Indeed, the fear of Yahweh can be understood as the beginning of wisdom in two ways. On the one hand it is the foundation upon which a wise life is built. On the other hand, the fear of Yahweh is the beginning of wisdom in the sense that it is the starting point of a lifelong journey towards wisdom. Proverbs is well aware of the role of tradition and the handing on of wisdom in the community and the family. Its epistemology, as M. Fox rightly points out, is not that of empiricism, although observation of the world through the glasses of Israelite

13. Van Leeuwen, "Liminality," pp. 116, 117.

14. For a useful summary of the debate see Crenshaw, *Urgent Advice*, pp. 79-85.

tradition does play an important role.[15] As Proverbs 26:1-12 makes clear, the wise person has to relate his or her wisdom to the actual situations in life, and that calls for interpretation (see especially 26:7, 9). This is an implication of the antithetical proverbs in Proverbs 26:4, 5. It is no easy matter to know whether to speak up in the context of folly or to remain silent. Each situation has to be assessed on its own merits. In this way wisdom is very much akin to what Lesslie Newbigin said repeatedly of Christ, that he is the clue to creation — the implication being that he is the answer but not in any simplistic way. The clue has to be followed and pursued in all areas of life with all the available human resources.

The fundamental notion of the fear of the Lord as the beginning of wisdom also helps, I think, to resolve a tension that some see between the availability and hiddenness of wisdom. Proverbs seems to see wisdom as calling out in the streets and everywhere else and to be readily available. In the marvelous poem in Job 28, however, wisdom is nowhere to be found. The repetition in 28:12, 20 focuses on the question, Where shall wisdom be found, where is the place of understanding? Even Abaddon and death only hear a rumor of wisdom (8:22)! The answer to this paradox is that God alone is the source of wisdom; he, if you like, is wisdom. This is why real wisdom starts with existential reverence for Yahweh, rather than just reading off his order from the creation. The order is only known out of such existential relationship.[16] This is what G. von Rad infers in his earlier description of Lady Wisdom:

> None the less it is correct to say that wisdom is the form in which Jahweh's will and his accompanying of man (i.e. his salvation) approach man. Wisdom is the essence of what man needs for a proper life, and of what God grants him. Still, the most important thing is that wisdom does not turn towards man in the shape of an "It," teaching, guidance, salvation or the like, but of a person, a summoning "I." So wisdom is truly the form in which Jahweh makes himself present and in which he wishes to be sought by man.[17]

15. See M. Fox, *A Time to Tear Down and a Time to Build Up: A Rereading of Ecclesiastes* (Grand Rapids: Eerdmans, 1999), pp. 80, 81.

16. Cf. in this respect Murphy's discussion of von Rad's positions on creation order in *The Tree of Life,* pp. 138, 139.

17. G. von Rad, *Old Testament Theology,* vol. 1 (Edinburgh: Oliver and Boyd, 1962), p. 444.

It is this insight that underlies O. O'Donovan's Christian ethics in his *Resurrection and Moral Order.*[18] O'Donovan rightly sees that it is a false dichotomy to set kingdom ethics against creation ethics. Indeed, Christ's resurrection reaffirms creation and its order. There is a dynamic, objective order that graciously presses down on all of creation, but it is only rightly known and discerned out of an existential relationship with God through and in Christ.

This hiddenness *and* availability of wisdom is connected with wisdom's doctrine of the two ways. The surface metaphors of Proverbs 1–9 — two women, two houses, two roads, wisdom versus folly, life and death — make it quite clear that although creation is carved along a certain grain, humans can direct themselves in two different ways in relation to the grain of creation. All of life is inevitably a response to God, but there is a wise response and a foolish response, a response of obedience that leads to life and a path of disobedience that leads to death. The wisdom books do not refer explicitly to Genesis 3 and the fall of humankind, but the very real possibility of disobedience and folly is assumed at every point in the Wisdom Literature, so that, although wisdom is rooted in God's good creation, the Wisdom books deal with the practical reality of finding wise paths in a world in which folly is a constant threat. Just as it is possible to follow God in all areas of life, so too disobedience is a threat in all areas of life. Theologically we might say that creation and fall are comprehensive realities. Yet so too is redemption. Commenting on the tree of life in Proverbs 3:18 Clifford says, "The Genesis story ends with the tree of life guarded by angelic figures (Gen. 3:24). Proverbs reverses Genesis and ends the sequestering of the tree of life. One who finds wisdom finds life."[19] Amid the threat of folly the Wisdom books hold out the hope of truly finding life in God's good creation. In this respect it is no accident that God is regularly described as Yahweh in Proverbs. Historical critics continue to discuss the extent to which these Yahweh sayings cast their shadow over the wider context of Proverbs. However we construe the origin and development of Proverbs, and it is clearly complex, in its canonical shape it is Yahweh as Israel's redeemer God who is the source of wisdom.

18. O. O'Donovan, *Resurrection and Moral Order: An Outline for Evangelical Ethics* (Leicester: Inter-Varsity; Grand Rapids: Eerdmans, 1986).

19. Clifford, *Proverbs,* p. 55. Yet cf. R. E. Murphy (*Proverbs,* Word Biblical Commentary 22 [Nashville: Nelson, 1998], p. 22), who argues that in Proverbs the tree no longer enjoys the original mythological background that it has in Genesis and is here simply a metaphor for the good life resulting from wisdom teaching.

It is no mistake that Proverbs ends with the description of the virtuous woman, for this extraordinary woman embodies the wisdom that begins with the fear of Yahweh. A. M. Wolters argues that the form of this pericope is that of a heroic hymn,[20] a form generally reserved for God! This woman is presented to us as a great hero of the faith embodying the fear of the Lord. What has perplexed interpreters down through the ages is that read literally this woman does not appear to be very spiritual! There is no mention of prayer and cultic activity. Indeed, her activities are very secular. Yes, she is a good homemaker, but she is also an estate agent and a wine merchant (31:16). She manufactures and trades in fabrics of the highest international quality (31:22, 24). Because of all these secular activities interpreters down through the ages have been tempted to allegorize this woman. It was particularly, as Wolters tracks, with the Reformation that it became clear that this woman's fear of Yahweh manifests itself precisely in her daily, "secular" activities.[21] She models for us that wise understanding of all of life as religion.

A God for *Life*

Wisdom and Retribution

Most scholars now agree that OT wisdom is rooted in a theology of creation and that in this sense it is religious and not secular. However, whether or not the OT Wisdom books *are* in touch with the realities of life remains highly controversial. A view has become commonplace that Proverbs articulates a fairly naive view of the relationship between deeds and their consequences (referred to hereafter as the "act-consequence structure") in which wisdom automatically leads to prosperity and well being. Inevitably this theology of retribution resulted with time in a crisis in Israel's view of wisdom, a crisis that is reflected in Job and Ecclesiastes, albeit in different ways. Now, of course, the whole point of wisdom is that it helps one to negotiate the challenges of life in a happy and successful way.

20. A. M. Wolters, "Proverbs XXXI 10-31 as Heroic Hymn: A Form-Critical Analysis," *Vetus Testamentum* 38 (1988): 446-57.

21. A. M. Wolters, "The Song of the Valiant Woman (Prov. 31:10-31): A Pattern in the History of Interpretation (To 1600)," M.A. thesis, McMaster University, Ontario, Canada, 1987.

And Proverbs is all about encouraging people to embrace that wisdom that is written into the fabric of the world. Thus, there is much at stake if this view of the world and of wisdom is fatally flawed by a naive optimism.

R. E. Murphy refers to H. D. Preuss as a representative example of the presuppositions that many scholars hold about wisdom.[22] In this view:

1. Wisdom is marginal to Israel's faith.
2. The God of wisdom is not Yahweh.
3. Wisdom concentrates on the orders in reality.
4. Retribution is one of these orders. The sages sought to discover this mechanical correspondence between action and consequence, as reflected in Proverbs.
5. A deed-consequence viewpoint is the basic dogma of early wisdom.

Clearly, if one understands early wisdom in this way, then Job and Ecclesiastes will be seen as reacting against this mechanical understanding of retribution, thus embodying a crisis of wisdom. Literary and canonical readings of the Wisdom books are casting new light on the doctrine of retribution in them and on their relationships to each other. The reconstruction of the original naive doctrine of retribution followed by a crisis as reflected in Job and Ecclesiastes depends on reconstructing earlier layers of the Wisdom books and then reading these and determining their relationships with each other. This is clear, for example, in Preuss's reconstruction. However, Brevard Childs's canonical hermeneutic and, since the 1970s, the literary turn in biblical studies have helped us to reappropriate the Wisdom books as whole literary units. This is not to deny complex histories of development — clearly a book like Proverbs has a long and complex history — but it is to insist that the juxtaposition of proverbs and of collections and their editing into a book creates a literary unit that is more than the sum of its individual parts and that is intended to speak in its totality.

Work in this direction is still in its early stages. However, already there is considerable fruit to be shown. Fox has opened up highly creative directions in the study of Ecclesiastes, scholars such as R. Polzin have shown how Job can be read as crafted literature, and in Proverbs's study a spate of highly creative works have appeared. Scholars remain divided over the ex-

22. R. E. Murphy, *Ecclesiastes,* Word Biblical Commentary 23A (Waco, Tex.: Word, 1992), p. lxi.

tent to which Proverbs can or should be read as a literary whole,[23] and two of the most recent commentaries on Proverbs fail to really explore the shape of the book. Clifford notes that Proverbs does not primarily provide information but rather gives its readers a perspective, a vision for life.[24] However, his superb commentary still focuses primarily on historical and ancient Near Eastern contextual issues in the introduction. There is virtually no analysis of the insights that exploration of Proverbs as a literary unit is unearthing. Sadly, Murphy, for all his excellent work on OT wisdom, has even less to say on these issues than Clifford in his 1998 commentary!

An OT scholar who is alert to the literary shape of Proverbs as a whole is van Leeuwen. In particular van Leeuwen has argued that reading Proverbs casts light on the act-consequence structure. Van Leeuwen points out that there are large groups of sayings in Proverbs that assert a simple cause-and-effect relationship, whereby righteousness leads to wealth and wickedness to poverty. These are examples of the "character-consequence-nexus." However, these sayings do not concern concrete, individual acts and their consequences: "It is the long-term character and direction of a person or group (as 'righteous' or 'wicked') which determines life consequences and 'destiny.'"[25] It is a failure to recognize this long-term character that leads scholars to the mechanical view of retribution in Ecclesiastes.

> These proverbs, *when taken by themselves,* are the basis for the view of some scholars that the tidy dogmatism of Proverbs does not correspond to reality and is doomed to collapse under the weight of reality, as happened in Job and Qoheleth. Since the foregoing sayings are not always exemplified in human experience, their falsification presumably led to a crisis of faith in Yahweh's maintenance of a just world order.[26]

However, proverbs are *partial utterances,* and the mechanical approach does not do justice to the many sayings in Proverbs that manifest a more complex understanding of the way God works in creation. Particularly relevant in this respect are the "better-than" sayings in Proverbs (cf. 15:16-17;

23. Crenshaw (*Urgent Advice,* pp. 82, 83, 89) urges caution in this respect.

24. Clifford, *Proverbs,* p. vii.

25. R. van Leeuwen, "Wealth and Poverty: System and Contradiction in Proverbs," *Hebrew Studies* 33 (1992): 27.

26. Van Leeuwen, "Wealth and Poverty," pp. 28-29.

16:16, 19, etc.). The overall picture is a complex one that van Leeuwen sums up as follows:

> *In general,* the sages clearly believed that wise and righteous behaviour did make life better and richer, though virtue did not *guarantee* those consequences. Conversely, injustice, sloth, and the like generally have bad consequences. The editor-sages who structured Proverbs sought first to teach these basic "rules of life," thus the heavy emphasis on character-consequence patterns in both Proverbs 1-9 and 10-15. We must first learn the basic rules; the exceptions can come later. Though very aware of exceptions to the character-consequence rule, the sages insisted that righteousness is better than wickedness. The most fundamental and profound reason for this is that they believed that God loves the one and hates the other. For Israel's sages that sometimes seems the only answer. . . . the sages knew that there are limits to human wisdom. General patterns may be discerned, but many particular events may be unjust, irrational, and ultimately inscrutable.[27]

Van Leeuwen also discerns a future-oriented retribution perspective in Proverbs. Proverbs lacks a doctrine of resurrection and yet insists on the triumph of God's justice. For van Leeuwen this is a hallmark of Yahwistic faith:

> The sages' stance is to maintain faith in God's justice, even when they personally cannot see it or touch it, even when the recorded past does not verify it. Here religion provides no escape from the pain or absurdities of existence. The book of Job was inevitable, not because Proverbs was too simplistic, but because life's inequities, as reflected in Proverbs, drive faith to argue with the Deity.[28]

Once one recognizes that Proverbs's understanding of retribution is more complex than a mechanical deed-consequence notion, then Ecclesiastes' and Job's relationship to Proverbs and traditional wisdom has to be reevaluated.[29]

27. Van Leeuwen, "Wealth and Poverty," pp. 32, 33.

28. Van Leeuwen, "Wealth and Poverty," p. 34.

29. Admittedly, van Leeuwen's understanding of this greater complexity is only one

Job and Ecclesiastes — Living Wisely amid Theodicy and Incomplete Knowledge

Job and Ecclesiastes are, I suggest, best understood as complementary to Proverbs. They explore wise living *in the midst of* particular exceptions to the act-consequence structure. For example, although the book of Job does overall affirm this structure, the book focuses in detail on a particular exception to that structure. Even though Job ends up "seeing" God and his prosperity is restored (Job 42), between the introduction and conclusion Job is a story of harrowing pain and bad counsel heaped upon a truly wise and godly person.

Job is deliberately portrayed as a great example of a wise, God-fearing man (1:1, 5). Yet, it is precisely to *this* man that this series of terrible events happen. From the introductory scenes in heaven, we, but not Job, are given some understanding that there is a cosmic dimension to Job's suffering. However, after the Satan's introductory appearances, we never hear from him again, and thus, in the context of Job, we should probably not make too much of the "test" aspect of Job's suffering. Indeed, the logic of Job's suffering remains enigmatic throughout the book. Job's counselors try to close the circle of this logic, but they are not portrayed as examples to be followed (cf. 42:7).

The resolution of Job's enigmatic suffering comes through personal encounter with God himself, and particularly with God as transcendent creator. Indeed, in 38–41 the doctrine of creation functions as the key to theodicy. Somehow, this personal encounter resolves at an existential level Job's desperate struggle with the radical exceptions to the act-consequence structure that he has experienced, and he finds his relationship with God immeasurably deepened and his prosperity restored.

Ecclesiastes struggles with the question of the meaning of life amid many exceptions to the act-consequence structure. "What does man gain from all his labor at which he labors under the sun?" (1:3) is the rhetorical question that casts its shadow over the whole of Ecclesiastes. *Qoheleth* —

---

possibility among a number. J. A. Gladson (*Retributive Paradoxes in Proverbs 10–29* [Ann Arbor, Mich.: University Microfilms International, 1979]), for example, makes retributive paradox a function of pluralism and dissent already present in early wisdom traditions. For van Leeuwen ("Wealth and Poverty," pp. 32-33), by comparison, "whatever their historical origin, within Proverbs they have come to express *one* broad worldview which acknowledges the conflict of dogma and experience, yet maintains both."

portrayed initially as the great, wise Solomon,[30] embarks on a quest for an answer to this poignant question. Adopting a methodology that he calls "wisdom" (1:13, 2:3), Qoheleth embarks on his quest by examining different aspects of life to see if meaning can be discerned there. With his wisdom methodology he keeps coming to a *hebel* conclusion.[31] In my view *hebel* is best translated in these conclusions as "enigmatic."[32] In the light of his methodology, the horrible exceptions to the act-consequence structure that Qoheleth keeps discovering lead him to conclude repeatedly that all of life is utterly enigmatic!

Intriguingly, these *hebel* conclusions are juxtaposed throughout Ecclesiastes with what I like to call the *carpe diem* passages, affirming joy and the shalom of life.[33] There is much discussion among scholars about how the *hebel* conclusions relate to the *carpe diem* passages, with scholars continually trying to smooth out Qoheleth's message in accordance with one or the other of these poles. Either he has a negative message or he affirms joy! I have argued that the positioning of the *hebel* conclusions next to the joy passages, a pattern that is repeated throughout Ecclesiastes, is an example of *contradictory juxtaposition*.[34] This pattern, in which opposing perspectives sit in tension with each other, is common in literature and raises the question for the reader of how the two perspectives relate to each other and how they are to be negotiated in an integrating way.

Qoheleth's method and analysis lead him continually, no matter what aspect of life he analyzes, to the *hebel* conclusion that life is utterly enigmatic. If there is meaning, it cannot be discerned. At the same time he knows from his believing Israelite background that God's world is good, and that it is humankind's lot to live life fully in the creation and to enjoy life and labor under the sun! These perspectives sit in strong tension with each other throughout the main body of the text and epitomize what the book is about. Qoheleth knows that his religious tradition is right — there

30. Most scholars agree that Ecclesiastes was not written by Solomon. However, in the early part of Ecclesiastes, Qoheleth is portrayed *as* Solomon, and this is significant. We are to think of Qoheleth as gifted with great wisdom.

31. Variously translated as "meaningless," "vanity," "useless," etc.

32. This is G. Ogden's view (*Qoheleth,* Readings: A New Biblical Commentary [Sheffield: JSOT Press, 1987]).

33. The joy passages are 2:24-26; 3:12-13; 3:22; 5:18-20; 8:15; 9:7-10; 11:8-10.

34. See C. G. Bartholomew, *Reading Ecclesiastes: Old Testament Exegesis and Hermeneutical Theory,* Analecta Biblica 139 (Rome: Pontifical Biblical Institute, 1998), pp. 237-54.

is a wonderful *shalom* to life under the sun! Yet, in whatever area of life he examines, examples can be found in which the act-consequence structure is broken. These examples lead him to conclude that all is *hebel!*

Does Ecclesiastes give us any clues as to how this very real and existential tension is resolved? I think it does. There are two main clues.[35] First, there is the clue of Qoheleth's *methodology.* He goes out of his way to describe this as "wisdom," but careful analysis of it shows it to be very different from the methodology of Proverbs. Fox rightly picks up the difference between Qoheleth's methodology and that of Proverbs.[36] Qoheleth is empirical in a way that Proverbs is not. Qoheleth's methodology revolves around experience and logic *alone,* whereas Proverbs's approach is rooted in the tradition of the fear of the Lord. Qoheleth's "empiricism" means that any exception undermines the very possibility of meaning and leads to the *hebel* conclusion. For Proverbs, there are, as we have seen, exceptions, but these do not undermine the overall shape of the act-consequence structure. Thus, epistemologically, Proverbs uses observation but to illustrate and support its views, not to prove or establish them in any decisive way.

This difference is crucial, especially in the practical business of affirming meaning amid apparent meaninglessness. It becomes apparent as one reads on in Ecclesiastes that, ironically, what Qoheleth describes as a method of "wisdom" is folly, especially in the canonical light of Proverbs's fear of the Lord, which is the beginning of wisdom. The latter is precisely *not* Qoheleth's starting point, and the result is that he keeps running down to the *hebel* conclusion. In other words, what Qoheleth embodies for us is what happens when we try to find meaning in an ambiguous world without starting from the fear of the Lord — we inevitably conclude that life is utterly enigmatic!

The second clue comes at the end of Ecclesiastes. Normally in Ecclesiastes Qoheleth reaches a *hebel* conclusion, and then this is juxtaposed with a *carpe diem* passage. Right at the end of Ecclesiastes this order is reversed (11:7–12:7/8) — the *carpe diem* passage comes first, and this is followed by one of the strongest passages about death and the struggle with meaning. This change in order is important, as is the exhortation to "Remember your creator . . . before . . . before . . . before . . . !" (12:1-7).

The exhortation to "Remember your creator" must be understood

35. For a detailed discussion of this see my *Reading Ecclesiastes.*

36. See Fox, *A Time to Tear Down,* pp. 71ff.

"thickly." It is not just a thin exhortation not to forget, but rather Ecclesiastes' equivalent of Job's encounter with the Creator, or Proverbs's equivalent of that fear of the Lord that is the *starting* point of wisdom. It is as though Ecclesiastes is telling us that if we are to discern meaning amid the ambiguities of life and thus to find joy in life, then we must early on let our entire perspective be shaped by an understanding of the fabric of the universe as our Father's. This will not remove us from the challenges of life — note what follows after the threefold "before"! — but it will enable us to wake each day with a sense of the sweetness of life under the sun (cf. 11:7)!

This second clue, like the first, is confirmed by the epilogue (12:9-14). At the end of it all the answer is to fear God and live in obedient trust before him.

Wisdom and the Rest of the Old Testament

Read as above, it is apparent how richly the OT Wisdom Literature contributes to our understanding of God. Yet how does it relate to God as revealed in the other types of literature in the OT? In OT theology the relationship between salvation history, law, prophecy, *and* wisdom remains a difficult issue. Law is embedded in narrative in the Old Testament, and prophecy appears to presuppose the historical covenant with Israel. So it is not too difficult to see the connection between salvation history, law, and prophecy, at least on the surface level of the Old Testament. However, the relationship of these three to wisdom is controversial.

Murphy has helpfully suggested that "[t]he problem of the relationship between wisdom literature and other portions of the Old Testament needs to be reformulated in terms of a shared approach to reality."[37] We certainly need to guard against anachronistically imposing modern notions of a sacred-secular dualism upon ancient Israel.[38] Personally I think it is in the area of a shared approach to reality, or what one might call a worldview, that the solution is to be found.

The wisdom and legal traditions in the OT are clearly distinct, and yet

37. R. E. Murphy, "Wisdom — Theses and Hypotheses," in *Israelite Wisdom: Theological and Literary Essays in Honor of Samuel Terrein,* ed. J. G. Gammie et al. (Missoula, Mont.: Scholars Press, 1978), p. 38.

38. See, for example, J. Goldingay, *Theological Diversity and the Authority of the Old Testament* (Grand Rapids: Eerdmans, 1987), p. 219.

they manifest some awareness of each other.[39] Both have in common the ordering of the life of God's people. Van Leeuwen argues persuasively, as we have seen, that a notion of creation order underlies the surface metaphors of Proverbs 1–9. He says that the worldview that Proverbs exhibits is a "carved" one in that "cultural and personal exhortation is grounded in the reality of the created word with its inbuilt normativity."[40]

This link of wisdom with creation has long been recognized. What is often not noted, though, is that the order that Proverbs finds in the "carved" creation cannot be simply read out of the creation. This is the point that Fox makes about Israelite wisdom: it is not empirical in the way that Ecclesiastes is; it assumes ethical principles that it supports through observation. This is the sort of position in Genesis 1–2. The ordering of creation is not opposed to instruction from Elohim/Yahweh Elohim. Order and instruction or torah go hand-in-hand, and obedience requires both a good creation *and* instruction. Similarly Wisdom Literature assumes certain ethical principles that are not just read off creation but are often very similar to the principles found in the law. Van Leeuwen, for example, says that Proverbs 1–9 indicates that it is in "the liquid abandonment of married love" that healthy *communitas* takes place. As van Leeuwen notes, "This reality has its parallel at Sinai."[41]

Thus it can be argued that while wisdom is most closely related to creation, it presupposes instruction. Similarly, when the narrative frame, within which law always occurs, in the final form of the OT is foregrounded, it becomes apparent that the law of Yahweh the redeemer God is also the law of the creator God.

I suggest, therefore, that law and wisdom share an underlying and often tacit presupposition of a "carved" creation order. This is their shared reality or worldview. Instruction from Yahweh would not be seen to conflict with the way he ordered his creation but would provide the ethical principles for discovery of that liminality.

If salvation history and law and wisdom reflect a shared vision of reality, is there an OT concept that embodies this vision? I think there is: *covenant.* In my opinion by far the best biblical theological work done on cove-

39. See van Leeuwen, "Liminality," p. 122, for some of the links between Proverbs and Job and the Pentateuch. Van Leeuwen argues that certain texts in Proverbs and Job presuppose the historical tradition of the gift of the land.

40. Van Leeuwen, "Liminality," p. 118.

41. Van Leeuwen, "Liminality," p. 132.

nant to date is that by W. J. Dumbrell.[42] With meticulous exegesis Dumbrell has shown that there is one major covenant in the OT and that it is rooted in creation and is all about God achieving his purposes for his good creation. Beneath this umbrella the dynamic order of creation, the historical unfolding of creation, instruction about how to live in the creation, and reflection on the creation order are thoroughly complementary and not in the least antithetical. It is modern historicism and not biblical religion that sets creation order against history. Yahweh is, as the second creation narrative reminds us, Yahweh Elohim[43] (as Genesis 1 and 2 so clearly show)!

Conclusion

In this chapter we have looked at the revelation of God in the OT Wisdom books. The emerging picture is rich and challenging, for the Wisdom Literature confronts us with a God who wishes to be with us and to rule over us in all areas of our individual and communal lives. Truly, *this* God is for life, and not just for Christmas!

Much could be said about the importance of OT Wisdom Literature for contemporary Christian thought. Suffice it here to make two points. First, wisdom stands adamantly against the privatization of religion that characterizes modernity and much evangelicalism. Modernity allows freedom of religion as long as it is kept private and out of the major cultural areas of education, politics, economics, art, etc. Much contemporary Christianity goes along with this and concentrates on building the institutional Church and evangelism while seeing "secular" activities as second rate and distinctly less spiritual. OT wisdom, by comparison, sees all of life as an arena for serving God by being wise in that area of life. Wisdom calls us to follow its paths in education, politics, the marketplace, and so forth.

My second point follows from this. Such a comprehensive understanding of what service of God involves alerts us to the Christian journey as far bigger, more exciting, and daunting than we may have imagined be-

42. See especially W. J. Dumbrell, *Covenant and Creation: An Old Testament Covenantal Theology* (Exeter: Paternoster, 1984).

43. See Gen. 2:4-9. Gen. 1:1–2:3 refers to God as Elohim; 2:4-9 refers to God as Yahweh Elohim. The implication is that Yahweh (the redeemer God of Israel, see Exodus 3 and 6) is the creator.

fore. Truly, from this perspective, the fear of Yahweh *is* the beginning of wisdom! The whole of the creation and history opens up before us as the terrain of our journey *coram deo.* Such a journey in this fallen and yet fundamentally good world will require real skill, and the Bible — and in our context the OT Wisdom books — is there as a travel guide to keep us going in the right direction.

Lying Spirits Sent by God? The Case of Micaiah's Prophecy

P. J. Williams

A passage that might seem to strike a discord with other biblical passages dealing with God's truthfulness is 1 Kings 22 (= 2 Chronicles 18). For a start the passage records how the good prophet Micaiah, initially at least, predicted the king of Israel's success in a battle he subsequently lost. Then it talks of a "lying spirit" sent with God's express approval in order to deceive the king of Israel. It is necessary therefore to examine whether this passage can be fitted without distortion into a theology of God's truthfulness.

The Context

The books of Kings are generally viewed as part of a whole work that stretches from Joshua to 2 Kings, is introduced by the historical prologue to Deuteronomy, and usually is called the Deuteronomistic History (DH). 1 Kings 22 finds itself within a section of Kings, or the DH, that gives special prominence to prophecy and, in particular, to the strained relationships between prophets and monarchs. The passage itself is set within chapters that highlight the dynamic figures of Elijah and Elisha (most inclusively 1 Kings 17–2 Kings 13). Within these chapters there is little doubt that the monarchs should listen to the words of God's prophets and that they are reprehensible when they do not do so. Prophets come to the fore continually from the time of the encounter of Ahijah the Shilonite with Jeroboam (1 Kings 11:26-40), and the exact fulfillment of their words is recorded (1 Kings 20:22, cf. 20:26; 1 Kings 21:23, cf. 2 Kings 9:36-37; 2 Kings 7:1-2, cf. 7:16-20).[1]

A peculiarly graphic example of the emphasis on certain fulfillment is found in 1 Kings 13. There, in response to Jeroboam's worship of the golden calves, an unnamed prophet is sent to Bethel, one of the centers of Jeroboam's new cult, to predict that someone called Josiah would be born and would destroy the altar there. Jeroboam's initial hostility to the prophet only earns him a temporarily withered hand, no doubt to convince him of the power behind the prophet's words. The prophet, though having delivered his unpopular message faithfully, is tricked into disobeying God's original command not to eat or drink in Bethel by an old prophet who utters a false oracle saying that the other prophet should stay with him. For listening to this oracle the prophet who had prophesied against Bethel is killed by a lion on the way home. The punishment of death for eating a single meal seems disproportionate. However, it is precisely the scale of the punishment that highlights what the prophet had done wrong: he had allowed himself to think that God might annul previous revelation (his initial instructions not to eat or drink in Bethel) by subsequent revelation (the old prophet's words). By doing so he had undermined his own message to Jeroboam that the altar at Bethel would be destroyed. By allowing for the possibility of a subsequent change of God's word he had also allowed for the possibility that Jeroboam's altar might not be destroyed. The scale of the punishment seems carefully designed to illustrate that God's word does not change.[2] That this is a major focus of the account is further shown as the old prophet, whose deceit had led the other astray, buries him, saying to his sons:

1. Even long-range predictions by people not specifically designated as prophets may be fulfilled (e.g., Josh. 6:26; cf. 1 Kings 16:34).

2. Perhaps more strictly, some of God's word does not change. 1 Kings 21:20-29 shows that some of God's words may contain conditional elements that are not initially marked as conditional. However, even in this case the most conditional element seems to be the timing, and fulfillment of the oracle is still recorded (2 Kings 9:36-37). 1 Kings 21:19 may not be part of the conditional oracle as a whole, and its fulfillment is recorded in 1 Kings 22:38 (this much is clear despite the different descriptions of the location). Thus, even the context dealing with unmarked conditional oracles affirms the necessary fulfillment of God's word generally.

> When I die, bury me in the grave in which the man of God is buried; lay my bones beside his bones. For the saying that he proclaimed by the word of the LORD against the altar in Bethel, and against all the houses of the high places that are in the cities of Samaria, shall surely come to pass. (1 Kings 13:31-32, NRSV)

The fulfillment of the oracle of destruction is carefully recorded in 2 Kings 23:16-18. Everything serves to highlight the certain fulfillment of what God predicts.

1 Kings 22:15 and Micaiah's Initial Prediction of Success

This contextual focus on the fulfillment of God's words makes it, at least initially, unlikely that 1 Kings 22 is somehow illustrating the opposite, namely, that God speaks words that are not fulfilled. This chapter also deals with true and false prophecy. The king of Israel and Jehoshaphat, king of Judah, are deciding whether to go up and fight against Syria in order to gain possession of Ramoth-gilead. The king of Israel has gathered four hundred prophets round him to endorse his action in the conflict and to predict the success he wants to hear. Jehoshaphat, more anxious to hear what God has to say, asks for a prophet of Yahweh to be brought, and thus Micaiah son of Imlah is summoned.

The narrator, rather than introducing Micaiah straightaway, describes in more detail the setting for the ensuing dialogue (vv. 10-12). His description of how the kings were seated (v. 10), of a particular prophet's horns of iron as a visual aid for his prophecy (v. 11), and of the repetition of the general consensus of prophets (v. 12, cf. v. 6) serves to increase the suspense in the narrative before the introduction of Micaiah himself.

A further element of suspense is inserted before Micaiah's audience with the kings. This is produced by the dialogue of verses 13 and 14, in which the messenger sent to summon Micaiah primes him to give a favorable message, and Micaiah, on oath, swears that he will only say what Yahweh actually says to him, as if it is a case of repeating the *ipsissima verba* of God.

In verse 15 the awaited moment arrives, and Micaiah is asked by the king of Israel the same question that was posed to the other prophets: "Shall we go to Ramoth-gilead to battle, or shall we refrain?" His answer is no little surprise: "Go up and be successful, and the LORD will give [it] into the hand of the king." The scene is well characterized by J. Fichtner: "And again the reader is amazed: the well known prophet of doom announces salvation, and that with the same words as the other prophets (v. 15)!"[3] It is only in response to being put on oath by the king of Israel in verse 16 that in verse 17 Micaiah finally gives the expected oracle of doom.

The question immediately arises concerning the relationship between what Micaiah has said in verse 15 and divine revelation. Given the strong dichotomy between true and false prophecy in this chapter it would seem incongruous to admit that a "true" prophet had uttered something false. Further, given the emphasis in the surrounding chapters on the certain fulfillment of God's word, it is difficult to say that somehow God's revelation failed at this point. Several unsatisfactory solutions have been proposed to this problem.

(1) A solution proposed by some older commentators is that Micaiah indicated that his statement was ironical by some sign not mentioned in the text. This is put rather quaintly by Matthew Henry: ". . . he bade him go, but with such an air of pronunciation, as plainly showed he spake it by way of derision. . . ."[4] A more recent exponent of this view is Gene Rice: "It is clear, however, whether by the tone of Micaiah's voice or his nonverbal behavior, that his word is not genuine."[5]

3. J. Fichtner, *Das erste Buch von den Königen, nach dem Tode des Verfassers herausgegeben von Klaus Dietrich Fricke* (Stuttgart: Calwer Verlag, 1964), p. 331: "Und wieder erstaunt der Leser: der bekannte Unheilsprophet verkündet Heil, mit denselben Worten wie die andern Propheten (V.15)!"

4. M. Henry, *A Commentary on the Holy Bible,* vol. 2 (London/Edinburgh: Marshall Brothers, 1890), p. 923. See also, e.g., Adam Clarke, *Commentary on the Bible,* vol. 2 (London, 1860), p. 1365, who says that the words "were spoken by Micaiah in such a tone and manner as at once showed to Ahab that he did not believe them." Cf. further J. R. Lumby, *The First Book of the Kings,* The Cambridge Bible for Schools and Colleges (Cambridge: Cambridge University Press, 1896), pp. 231-32.

5. G. Rice, *1 Kings: Nations under God,* International Theological Commentary (Grand Rapids: Eerdmans, 1990), p. 184. Another recent author who assumes the same is Robert Goldenberg, in "The Problem of False Prophecy: Talmudic Interpretations of Jeremiah 28 and 1 Kings 22," in *The Biblical Mosaic: Changing Perspectives,* ed. R. Polzin and E. Rothman (Philadelphia: Fortress; Chico, Calif.: Scholars Press, 1982), p. 88: "His tone, however, must have been heavily ironic. . . ." I am deeply grateful to Dr. Magnar Kartveit for bringing this article to my attention.

One of the reasons that this solution is unsatisfactory is precisely its appeal to extratextual information. It is now widely recognized that in most forms of communication people compensate for the deficiencies of the medium through which they communicate. Steps are usually made to avoid ambiguity, and humor or irony in written form, when it would be infelicitous to understand them as other than humor or irony, are clearly marked.

(2) It has been suggested that at verse 15 it is not yet clear to Micaiah what Yahweh would have him say; this becomes clear only after verse 16. A version of this view is held by S. J. DeVries:

> Though many interpreters suggest that Micaiah was deliberately lying, it is better to interpret his words as a preliminary message expressive of a patriotic strain in his ideology. But the king's adjuration makes him see clearly what Yahweh truly intends.[6]

If this is the case, however, it must be asked why the narrator would want to present Micaiah as initially making up an oracle of his own and why, in particular, he would create narrative suspense for such an anticlimax. Furthermore, though the imperfect tense *wayōmer,* "he will say," in verse 14 stresses the futurity of God speaking to Micaiah, thus perhaps indicating that he had not yet received the words from God to say, when Micaiah responds to the king's oath with a negative oracle, he does not indicate any regret for what he has just said. Nor does he even hesitate before declaring what he had previously seen (cf. *rāʾiti,* v. 17).[7]

(3) The view that Micaiah is deliberately lying, alluded to above by DeVries, demands the question *why?* Support for this view might be sought in the absence of any "thus says the LORD" in verse 15. This might be in contrast with verse 19, where the ensuing vision is introduced as the "word of the LORD." Though this may partially solve the problem, the absence of any indication that the oracle of doom in verse 17 is also a word of Yahweh should give us pause about seeing this as the main component of a solution. Furthermore, with the prefatory "As the LORD lives, whatever Yahweh says to me, that I will speak" (v. 14) as the immediate context for verse 15, it seems that Yahweh, though distanced from Micaiah's words in

6. S. J. DeVries, *1 Kings,* Word Biblical Commentary (Waco, Tex.: Word, 1985), p. 268.

7. The perfect *rāʾiti* could have present significance; cf. 1 Sam. 28:13.

verse 15 by the absence of an introductory formula, is not completely dissociated from the statement.[8]

Yet if God is not completely dissociated from the statement, and he is also true, do we have a paradox? Before answering this we must first try to understand the purpose of the initially favorable oracle.

Taking the simplest hypothesis that no nonverbal indication was given to the king that the oracle of verse 15 was not true, we may ask how it was that the king recognized it not to be true. If he did not decide this on the basis of the mode of delivery, he must have realized this on the basis of the message's *content.* If the king was capable of recognizing that the oracle was not true merely on the basis of content, he must have been equally capable of recognizing it as untrue when almost the same words as Micaiah pronounces in verse 15 were used by his own prophets (vv. 6, 12). The king, by his response in verse 16, has in fact given away that at some level in his consciousness he was aware all along that what his prophets were telling him was not true. Micaiah's words in verse 15 have elicited that admission from him in a way that a simple statement of doom could not have done.

Yet we still have to explain how God can be associated with a statement that seems so false as verse 15 does. Part of a solution to this may be found in Tim Ward's article later in this volume (pp. 192-218), where he illustrates the wrongness of isolating utterances in understanding a work. When Micaiah's initial statement in verse 15 is separated from its context and set up as an individual proposition, the truth or falseness of which is to be evaluated, the statement is clearly false. However, in its context it neither deceived anyone nor had the intention of deceiving anyone, but was acting as a preface to a full explanation of the truth. The dialogue as a whole is entirely truth-illustrating, somewhat akin to Solomon's "wise" initial ruling that the baby whose parentage was being debated should be cut in half (1 Kings 3:25). It seems clear that, however God is associated with Micaiah's statement in verse 15, he cannot be charged with deceit.

Yet the passage itself has been understood to mean that God deceives.

8. To these three solutions one might also add Clarke's view (*Commentary on the Bible,* p. 1365) that the statements of both the false prophets and Micaiah initially are ambiguous (almost Delphic), the "hand of the king" being equally applicable to the king of Syria. The object of "give" in vv. 6, 12, and 15, supplied by most translations as "it," could equally well be "you."

1 Kings 22:19-25 and the Lying Spirit from God

When Micaiah does finally get around to prefacing something unambiguously as "the word of the LORD," the revelation he describes is quite striking. Micaiah describes his vision of a heavenly court scene quite similar to that in Job 1 (and even Isaiah 6). God asks, "Who will entice Ahab, so that he may go up and fall at Ramoth-gilead?" (1 Kings 22:20, NRSV). The verb translated "entice" is *pth* (piel). However, the verbs used here by early versions have the general sense of "deceive" or "beguile": ἀπατάω (LXX), *šdl* pael (Peshitta; also "seduce"), *ṭ*ʿʿ aphel (*Targum Jonathan;* also "lead astray"), *decipio* (Vulgate). English Bible translations have usually refrained from using such a strong verb and prefer "persuade" (AV) or more commonly "entice" (JPSA, NASB, NEB, NIV, NRSV, REB, RV), leaving "deceive" to the margins of the AV and RV, and their unusual ally the GNB. The piel of *pth* may mean "seduce (sexually)," as in Exodus 22:15, and it is used for deceit by sexual charms in Judges 14:15 and 16:5. The action involves deceit in 2 Samuel 3:25. However, in Hosea 2:14 the word is used of a more tender and loving "wooing." The pual in Proverbs 25:15 seems also to be more positive in meaning: "By patience a ruler may be persuaded." The verb is cognate with the Hebrew noun *pty*, "simple." Like its antonym *ʿrwm* (Prov. 14:15), it can have, but need not have, negative connotations, and occasionally it may have positive connotations (Ps. 116:6; cf. *ʿrwm* in Prov. 12:23).

If a close relationship is traced between *pty* and *pth* piel, the latter is most likely to mean "to make (someone) *pty*'" since the piel is best understood as a factitive.[9] The verb could therefore mean, in the case of 1 Kings 22:20, "make simple," that is, "make without intelligence." The meaning would then be somewhat akin to the Homeric εὔθ' αὖτε Γλαύκῳ Κρονίδης φρένας ἐξέλετο Ζεύς, "Zeus the son of Cronos then took away Glaucus' good senses" (*Iliad* 6.234; cf. 18.311). The divinity took away the senses of a human, who then suffered the consequences of their subsequent foolish action.

A question related to how we should translate *pth* piel here is the question concerning how we should translate it in Jeremiah 20:7, where the

9. E. Jenni (*Das hebräische piʿel* [Zürich: EVZ-Verlag, 1968], pp. 20-21) describes the verb as factitive. The above-stated relationship of the verb with *petî* goes beyond what Jenni says.

prophet complains: "Lord, you deceived me, and I was deceived." Here more translations than in 1 Kings are prepared to use the verb "deceive" (AV, NASB, NIV, RV), though there is no unanimity: "dupe" (NEB), "entice" (JPSA, NRSV, RV margin), "persuade" (NIV footnote), and "seduce" (JB). Perhaps it is felt here that Jeremiah's complaint is more likely to accuse God of deceit than Micaiah's vision is to associate a deceiving spirit with divine permission.

D. J. A. Clines and D. M. Gunn seek to show that the verb in Jeremiah 20:7 means "tried to persuade."[10] In this context they argue that *pth* piel in 1 Kings 22:20 cannot mean something like "deceive" (a verb that presumes its own success). To put it briefly, "If *pittâ* meant 'persuade,' that is, 'be successful in persuading,' *w^{e}gam-tûkāl* would be unnecessary."[11] Yet their argument would work even if in this context the verb meant "try to deceive" rather than "deceive."

However, no uncertainty concerning the meaning of the verb *pth* piel can make more palatable the fact that in 1 Kings God gives positive encouragement to a *rwḥ šqr,* "lying spirit." The relationship between the force of evil and God is somewhat akin to that presented in the first chapter of Job.

Is God then condoning lies? The text clearly presents a God who is truthful. At the end, Micaiah is quite prepared to stake his validity as a prophet upon the sure outcome of his prediction, saying to the king of Israel: "If you really do return in peace, the Lord has not spoken by me" (1 Kings 22:28). This affirmation, together with the record in the passage that the king of Israel did not return safely, indicates that what God says through his prophets is true. This concurs with the contextual emphasis noted earlier that God's prophetic word is certainly fulfilled. This could, arguably, be understood as the central assertion of the whole narrative. After all, God's prediction of the king of Israel's doom is fulfilled against all the odds, despite the king's disguise, and through the strike of an arrow in a most unlikely part of the king's person. With all this emphasis on truth, where does the lying spirit fit in?

These two themes of the truth of God's word and his sovereignty over the lying spirit are such prominent themes in the narrative that it is hard to avoid concluding that they are being set in deliberate tension and that the

10. D. J. A. Clines and D. M. Gunn, "'You tried to persuade me' and 'Violence! Outrage!' in Jeremiah xx 7-8," *Vetus Testamentum* 28 (1978): 20-27.

11. Clines and Gunn, "'You tried to persuade me,'" p. 23.

narrator believes that both must be held to firmly. The narrative, though using an active verb for God's action in relation to the lying spirit — he "put" *(ntn)* a lying spirit in the mouths of the prophets — makes it clear that this spirit is not God's. This is even presupposed by the false prophet Zedekiah as he responds to Micaiah (v. 24): "Which way did the spirit of the LORD cross over from me to speak to you?" Zedekiah clearly thought that if a spirit was a lying spirit, it was not God's spirit. The assertion then of the narrative of God's sovereignty over lying spirits is precisely that, an assertion of sovereignty. According to the narrative it does not in any way compromise the utter truthfulness of God's word, nor is a lie to be associated with God's spirit. Zedekiah's words are certainly not to be classed as "inspired."[12]

Conclusion

The narrative of 1 Kings 22 certainly has some strong tensions concerning truth and falsehood. It seems that it is the narrator's special desire to bring these tensions to the fore. The narrative asserts that God is utterly sovereign and still utterly truthful in what he says. This may be a difficult conclusion to accept, but these two assertions are made so strongly that it seems hard to deny that either is the narrator's intention. The overarching contextual theme of the truthfulness of God's word is not felt to be compromised in any way by his sovereign control over spirits of deceit. The sentiment is remarkably similar to that of Ezekiel 14:9:[13]

> If a prophet is deceived [*pth* pual] and speaks a word, I, the LORD, have deceived [*pth* piel] that prophet, and I will stretch out my hand against him, and will destroy him from the midst of my people Israel.

While God's sovereignty over the prophet is asserted, the prophet's action is also the object of deep displeasure on the part of God.

12. Contra P. Buis, *Le Livre des Rois* (Paris: J. Gabalda, 1997), p. 171.

13. This understanding of Ezek. 14:9 is in contrast to that of R. Mosis, *Theologisches Wörterbuch zum alten Testament,* vol. 6, ed. G. J. Botterweck and H. Ringgren (Stuttgart: W. Kohlhammer, 1989-90), p. 830. Mosis says that *pittêṯî* in v. 9ab "is thus to be translated as a future or as a present with future significance" ("ist also futurisch oder präsentisch mit futurischer Bedeutung zu übersetzen").

NEW TESTAMENT

Jesus and Scripture

Donald Macleod

Jesus laid out his position on the Old Testament at the very beginning of his ministry: "Think not that I have come to abolish the law and the prophets; I have come not to abolish them but to fulfill them" (Matt. 5:17, RSV). As Donald A. Hagner points out, the placing of the passage at this early point in the Gospel is no accident: "It is necessary at the outset to indicate Jesus' full and unswerving loyalty to the law."[1] The form of Jesus' statement suggests that he had been accused of doing exactly what he denies: advocating a heretical attitude towards the Torah. His response to the criticism is unambiguous: "I have not come to abolish the law and the prophets." The phrase "the law and the prophets" indicates Jesus' concern to endorse not only the Torah in the strict sense of "the Law of Moses," but the entire Old Testament. He does not subscribe to the view that the Pentateuch had a unique glory. For him, the prophets were on the same level. That endorsement carried with it an endorsement of the prophets' priorities ("I desire steadfast love and not sacrifice," Hos. 6:6) and of their criticism of legalistic ritualism ("'What to me is the multitude of your sacrifices?' says the LORD," Isa. 1:11).

Jesus clearly disclaims all intention of setting aside the Old Testament. There is a hint in the language he uses that if anyone had the authority to do so, *he* had: "I have *come to*. . . ." Such sayings are rare in Matthew. There are

1. D. A. Hagner, *Matthew 1–13*, Word Biblical Commentary 33A (Dallas: Word, 1993), p. 103.

only three others: Matthew 9:13; 10:34; and 10:35. They convey the clear idea that Jesus is a man with a mission: a divine mission. Yet that mission is not to abolish the Old Testament. On the contrary, his mission is to fulfill it.

Fulfilling the Law and the Prophets

It is difficult (and probably unwise) to try to pin down *plērōsai* in this context to a single meaning. Apart from all else, the Law may have to be fulfilled in one sense and the Prophets in another. Jesus will bring both to their messianic fulfillment. But how?

First, Jesus' mission is to make sure that everything foretold by the Law and the Prophets is accomplished. This is confirmed at many later points in his life. Often, for example, his explanation of particular events is that they occurred so that Scripture might be fulfilled. There is a clear instance of this in Matthew 26:53-54: "Do you think that I cannot appeal to my Father, and he will at once send me more than twelve legions of angels? But how then should the scriptures be fulfilled, that it must be so?" B. B. Warfield comments: "Although holding at His command ample means of escape, He bows before on-coming calamities, for, He asks, how otherwise 'should the scriptures be fulfilled, that thus it must be?'"[2] The program for the Messiah is already set out in the Law and the Prophets, and he has come to bring that program not only to some temporary, provisional implementation but to its final, definitive fulfillment. This is why he rebukes so bluntly the two disciples on the road to Emmaus: "'O foolish men, and slow of heart to believe all that the prophets have spoken! Was it not necessary that the Christ should suffer these things and enter into his glory?' And beginning with Moses and all the prophets, he interpreted to them in all the scriptures the things concerning himself" (Luke 24:25-27). Had they reflected properly on the Old Testament, he clearly insinuates, they would have known that suffering, death, and resurrection were a clear part of God's program for the Messiah; and had they known that, the crucifixion would not have shaken their faith as it clearly had.

Conversely, this would have been Jesus' own consolation as he moved through the various phases of the messianic calling. None of them was un-

2. B. B. Warfield, *The Inspiration and Authority of the Bible* (Philadelphia: Presbyterian and Reformed Publishing Company, 1948), p. 141.

expected. Instead, each was an act of compliance with God's will as made known through the Law and the Prophets.

Second, Jesus' mission is to bring out the radical ethical force of the Law and the Prophets. One clear implication of this is that there is, strictly speaking, no new kingdom ethic. The King has come, his coming has apocalyptic significance, and the old order (even the old Israel) is gone forever. However, the Law and the Prophets are not gone. They are part of the new order, in which the two greatest commandments remain, as in the old: "You shall love the Lord your God with all your heart" and "You shall love your neighbor as yourself" (Matt. 22:36-40). W. D. Davies is fully justified, therefore, in commenting, "Not antithesis but completion expresses the relationship between the Law of Moses and the teaching of Jesus."[3]

Jesus' radicalism consists not in his coming with a new canon but in his rigorous application of the old. Just how rigorous appears in Matthew 5:19-20. The kingdom has not been inaugurated on the basis of relaxing the commandments. On the contrary, "unless your righteousness exceeds that of the scribes and Pharisees, you will never enter the kingdom of heaven" (Matt. 5:20). This means, in terms of overall biblical theology, that our covenant keeping (our *ḥesed*) has to be far more thorough and consistent than what passed for such under the old order. In the immediate context, it means that our compliance with even the least of the commandments set forth in the Law and the Prophets has to be far more thorough than that of the scribes and Pharisees.

What this means is illustrated in Matthew 5:21-48, where Jesus contrasts traditional, evasive interpretations of the Law with the searching inwardness of the divine intent. We shall return to this later. Yet we should note in the meantime that, far from discarding the Old Testament, Jesus concludes his treatment of this particular theme by declaring, "You, therefore, must be perfect, as your heavenly Father is perfect." Within the bounds of the Sermon on the Mount, "perfection" consists in compliance with the Old Testament. It is in the Law laid down in these ancient Scriptures that God disclosed the categorical imperative of love: a love that insists, "Love your enemies and pray for those who persecute you" (Matt. 5:44). To achieve that standard is to be perfect as our Father in heaven is perfect (Matt. 5:48).

3. W. D. Davies, *The Setting of the Sermon on the Mount* (Cambridge: Cambridge University Press, 1964), p. 107.

One clear conclusion to be drawn from Jesus' mission statement as recorded in Matthew 5:17-20 is that Christians should not be embarrassed by claims that there is little originality in the ethical teaching of Jesus. He specifically disclaimed such originality. His uniqueness lay in more challenging areas: in his identity as the eternal Son, in the redemptive object of his mission (to give his life a ransom for many, Mark 10:45), and in his projection of himself as not merely a devout worshipper but as the worshipped one. He is not a rival Moses, but Moses' Lord (Heb. 3:5, 6).

In his ethical teaching, however, he is content to be a mere expositor, transcending Mosaic categories but not abolishing them.[4] If, then, there is clear continuity between his teaching and that of the Old Testament, this is hardly surprising; and if respected rabbis occasionally made radical statements remarkably similar to those of Jesus, that, again, is no more than we would expect. Even where the Christian ethic comes closest to originality (in the principle of *kenosis*), the self-abasement that lies at its heart is no more than the final, heroic application of the principle of love. When the Law and the Prophets demanded love, they were demanding conduct in accordance with the nature of God himself. He is love (1 John 4:8). When God in Christ made himself nothing, he was exercising love. When we make ourselves nothing, we are reciprocating love.

From this point of view, there is no possibility of supererogation. We can never go beyond what the law requires or do better than the law expects. It requires love as limitless as the love of the lawgiver himself. It was an act of supererogation for the Eternal Son to put himself under the law (Gal. 4:4), but once under it, he could not do more than fulfill it. He could not earn the merit of supererogation. He could only fulfill all righteousness (Matt. 3:15).

Not content with making clear that it is no part of his mission to abrogate the Law and the Prophets, Jesus also makes plain his belief that the law is of enduring authority: "till heaven and earth pass away, not an iota, not a jot, will pass from the law until all is accomplished" (Matt. 5:18). The clause "till all is accomplished" cannot be taken in any relative sense, such as, for example, that the law will not pass away till Christ has accomplished his death and resurrection. The dominant chronological phrase is "till heaven and earth pass away," and this rules out any transitional fulfillment. To adopt, for the moment, a Pauline perspective, the Law (and the

4. See Davies, *The Setting of the Sermon on the Mount,* pp. 93-108.

Prophets) will remain canonical until "the perfect" comes (1 Cor. 13:10) and Christ delivers the kingdom to God the Father (1 Cor. 15:24). The emergence of the New Testament canon does not alter this. On the contrary, the process of New Testament canon formation represents only the addition of the apostolic literature to the already existing canon of "the Law and the Prophets." This is why the author of 2 Peter places the Pauline epistles on a level with "the other scriptures" (2 Pet. 3:15). The New Testament church has an augmented canon. It does not have a new one.

It is significant, too, that Jesus deliberately underlines the fact that it is precisely the Law as written that he has in mind. Only in such a form does it have *iotas* and *dots.* It is not the mere spirit of the Law that is permanent. Nor is it some law within the Law. It is the Law *written.* Its text demands absolute respect. It merits, for example, the meticulous diligence of textual scholars, seeking accuracy to the last iota. Equally, it merits the labors of the exegete, toiling to ascertain the exact meaning and precise significance of every sentence.

This is no plea for pedantry. Nor is it a plea for atomistic exegesis, overinterpreting individual words and drawing huge inferences from what may be no more than incidentals and elegant variations. Even less is it an endorsement of wooden, legalistic exegesis: the kind, for example, that looks at the command, "Love your neighbor," and says, "It is limited to our 'neighbor' and says nothing about our 'enemy'. Therefore we may hate our enemy."

For Jesus, jot-and-tittle loyalty to Scripture is neither legalistic nor evasive. He spells out its true meaning in the remainder of the Sermon on the Mount. Jot-and-tittle fulfillment of the law means avoiding anger as well as homicide; lust as well as fornication; swearing as well as perjury. It means turning the other cheek, going the extra mile, and blowing no trumpets when we make donations to charity. It means, too, the kind of rigorous obedience illustrated by the Good Samaritan. What he did was neither more nor less than jot-and-tittle fulfillment of the Law and the Prophets. The same is true of the Parable of the Sheep and the Goats. Here, too, we have jot-and-tittle compliance with the Law: feeding the hungry, welcoming the stranger, clothing the naked, relieving the sick, and visiting the imprisoned (Matt. 25:35-36). These are clear implications of the Mosaic covenant, "Love your neighbor as yourself." Without such levels of covenant compliance we shall never enter the kingdom of heaven.

Challenges

Inevitably, however, the position laid down in Matthew 5:17-20 has been challenged. *Prima facie,* there have been two challenges. Some have argued that the passage cannot be authentic; others have argued that whatever Jesus said on this particular occasion, in practice he was critical of the torah and even, sometimes, dismissive of it.

In reality, these two challenges merge: Jesus cannot have said what Matthew attributes to him here because in the general tenor of his teaching Jesus' attitude to the law differed radically from that of his Jewish contemporaries.

One of those who questioned the authenticity of the passage was A. M. Hunter. "These verses as they stand," he wrote, "can hardly be words of Christ; for (a) the doctrine of the Law's permanence is pure rabbinism; and (b) Jesus himself 'relaxed' the Sabbath law, annulled the law about purity, and rejected Moses' commandment about divorce. They read, rather, like some early Jewish Christian misapplication of some words of Jesus. . . . What we have in Matthew is Christian legalism such as may have arisen in ultra-conservative circles which were shocked by the attitude of Paul and his friends to the Law."[5]

This echoes the position of Rudolf Bultmann, who categorically dismissed Matthew 5:17-20 as "words which Jesus surely cannot have said" and referred them instead to a time after Jesus' death "when Paul and other Hellenistic missionaries preached to the Gentiles a gospel apart from the Law."[6] Curiously, this is linked in Bultmann to the conviction that Jesus never attacked the law or combated its authority, any more than he opposed worship in the temple or such standard Jewish practices as almsgiving, prayer, and fasting. Yet when we move, he argues, from Jesus' formal pronouncements on the authority of the law to his actual practice, the difference between him and Jewish legalistic piety becomes clear: "For the essential fact about a teacher is not his acceptance of an authoritative mass of tradition, but the way in which he interprets it."[7]

The first point to be made in response to this is a matter of detail. Jesus

5. A. M. Hunter, *Design for Life: An Exposition of the Sermon on the Mount* (London: SCM, 1953), p. 43.

6. R. Bultmann, *Jesus and the Word* (London: Collins/Fontana, 1958), p. 52.

7. Bultmann, *Jesus and the Word,* p. 53.

is affirming the permanent validity not only of the Law but of "the law *and the prophets*." No one seriously suggests that Jesus came to abolish the latter, yet his statement must be taken as a whole. Those who are anxious to jettison the Law normally cite the Prophets in their own support. Jesus' statement in Matthew 5:17-20 does not allow this. It leaves no place for appealing to the Prophets against the Law. Even less does it endorse the rabbinic preference for the Law over against the Prophets. Instead, the Law and the Prophets together constitute the Old Testament and as such provide a canon that is to serve the kingdom till its consummation.

Second, the endorsement of the law given in Matthew 5:17-20 is no isolated phenomenon in Jesus' teaching. It represents his consistent, emphatic, and frequently asserted view of the status of the torah. The evidence for this is conveniently summarized in John Wenham:[8] Jesus repeatedly treated the early chapters of Genesis as straightforward records of fact; constantly used the Old Testament as the final court of appeal on matters of controversy; encouraged his hearers to go beyond the mere externals of Scripture and think out its underlying principles; unquestioningly assumed its authority in matters of ethics; and even when not consciously quoting it used its words and phrases as vehicles for his own thoughts.

This is enough, surely, to show that Jesus shared fully the contemporary Jewish belief in the inspiration of Scripture, even to the extent of equating "Scripture says" with "God says." This appears in, for example, the words recorded in Matthew 19:4-5: "he who made them from the beginning made them male and female, and said, 'For this reason shall a man leave his father and mother and be joined to his wife, and the two shall become one.'" In the original Old Testament text (Gen. 2:24) the words quoted by Jesus are not attributed to God. They represent only the comment of the human author. For Jesus, however, the fact that they are part of the Old Testament text is sufficient proof that they are God's words. If Scripture says it, God says it.

Amid the welter of detail, one saying stands out: the declaration of Jesus that "scripture cannot be broken" (John 10:35). The occasion was remarkable enough. The Jews were on the point of stoning Jesus. He challenged them as to why: "I have shown you many good works from my Father; for which of these do you stone me?" They reply that they are ston-

8. J. W. Wenham, *Christ and the Bible*, 2nd ed. (Grand Rapids: Baker, 1984), pp. 11-42.

ing him not for his works but for his blasphemy, "because you, being a man, make yourself God." Jesus' riposte is an ad hominem one: "It cannot be blasphemy simply to call a man 'god' because 'your law' does that. In Psalm 82:6 it says, 'You are gods, sons of the Most High, all of you.' And scripture cannot be broken."

The passage has four remarkable features. First, the argument is thoroughly Jewish. Psalm 86, as Raymond E. Brown points out, was "understood as a castigation of unjust judges, who had been given the designation 'gods' because of their quasi-divine functions."[9] Jesus uses this fact in his own defense: "In your Scriptures, judges are addressed as *elohim* by the Divine voice . . . where, then, is the blasphemy in my description of myself as *huios tou theou,* being (as I am) the Ambassador of God and sent by him into the world?"[10] The nature of the interchange is itself strong proof of its authenticity. As J. H. Bernard points out, "The argument is one which would never have occurred to a Greek Christian, and its presence here reveals behind the narrative a genuine reminiscence of one who remembered how Jesus argued with the Pharisees on their own principles."[11]

Second, Jesus equates "your law" and "scripture": "Is it not written in *your law* . . . and *scripture* cannot be broken." It is particularly interesting that the passage quoted by Jesus comes from the Psalter, not the Pentateuch. This indicates that even without the additional phrase, "and the prophets," "the law" denoted the whole of the Scriptures. To propose, therefore, that Jesus was a critic of the Law is to propose that he was a critic of Scripture; and to suggest that it is "pure rabbinism" to speak of the permanence of the Law is to suggest, surely, that it is pure rabbinism to speak of the permanence of the Old Testament canon.

Third, Jesus' argument, by its very nature, shows that he had the highest possible view of the entire Old Testament. He is not setting the seal of his approval on Psalm 82:6 alone. Instead, he is presenting an implicit syllogism: "Scripture cannot be broken; Psalm 82:6 is Scripture; therefore Psalm 82:6 cannot be broken." Here the remark of a forgotten nineteenth-century scholar is strikingly apt: in Jesus' view "it was sufficient proof of

9. Raymond E. Brown, *The Gospel according to John I–XII,* Anchor Bible (New York: Doubleday, 1966), p. 409.

10. J. H. Bernard, *A Critical and Exegetical Commentary on the Gospel according to St. John,* vol. 2 (Edinburgh: T. & T. Clark, 1928), p. 367.

11. Bernard, *Commentary on the Gospel according to St. John,* 2:367.

the infallibility of any sentence or phrase of a clause, to show that it constituted a portion of what the Jews called 'the Scripture.'"[12]

Fourth, there is the verb used by Jesus: "scripture cannot be *broken*" *(lythēnai)*. The literal meaning is, "scripture cannot be loosed": the same verb as is used in Matthew 5:19, "Whosoever then *relaxes* one of the least of these commandments . . . shall be called least in the kingdom of heaven." The rendering "relax" on the part of the RSV is unfortunate, if only because the antithesis reads, "but he who *does* them . . . shall be called great in the kingdom of heaven." To *loose* the commandment is not merely to relax it but to break it: to not do it. The verb must have similar force in John 10:35. Scripture cannot be annulled, set aside, or deprived of its force. This is precisely what Jesus elsewhere accused the Pharisees of doing. They were nullifying the word of God by their traditions (Mark 7:13).

We must bear in mind, however, that Scripture is not homogeneous. It contains a great variety of material, and the precise force of *lyein* varies accordingly. No Scripture command can be *breached.* No Scripture record can be *falsified.* No Scripture threat or promise can *fail of fulfillment.* This last shade of meaning is particularly interesting in view of the evidence gathered by Jungkuntz[13] that *lyein* is the opposite of *plēroun.* Therefore, to say negatively that Scripture cannot be broken is to say positively that Scripture must be fulfilled: in which case the sentiments recorded in John 10:35 are exactly the same as those recorded in Matthew 5:17: "I have not come to destroy the law and the prophets but to *fulfill* them." As canon, Scripture must be obeyed. As prophecy, it must be fulfilled. In neither case can it be set aside.

But why? In the context of John 10:35 the answer lies in Jesus' reference to "the word of God." What "came to" the judges of Israel was "the word of God" (John 10:35). That is why it cannot be broken. Scripture is the word of God, and it is the word of God in its entirety. That is the whole evangelical doctrine of Scripture — the least and the most that we can say, without entangling ourselves in labyrinthine debates about inerrancy and about the nature and the degrees of inspiration. It was God himself who committed his revelation to writing (*Westminster Confession of Faith,* ch.

12. Robert Watts, quoted in Warfield, *The Inspiration and Authority of the Bible,* p. 184 n.

13. See Brown, *The Gospel according to St. John I–XII,* p. 404, and D. Carson, *The Gospel according to John* (Leicester: Inter-Varsity; Grand Rapids: Eerdmans, 1991), p. 397.

I:1), but he did it through men, and virtually all that we know about inspiration is that it is the link between the divine authorship of the Bible and its human authorship. It is the process by which God secured that what men wrote was *his* word. The concept occurs only once in the New Testament, in 2 Timothy 3:16, and there St. Paul attributes it not to the authors of Scripture but to their product. The men, says St. Peter, were "carried" (2 Pet. 1:21). What they wrote is *theopneustos* ("God-breathed"). The result, in the language of Matt. 5:18, is that not one stroke or iota of Scripture falls short of being the word of God.

Did Jesus Criticize the Law?

Did Jesus not criticize the law, even in the context of the Sermon on the Mount itself? The so-called Great Antitheses (Matt. 5:21-48), in the opinion of many scholars, set aside not only rabbinical interpretations of the law but the very letter of the Old Testament itself. According to Günther Bornkamm, for example, some of the antitheses "are in point of fact a rather violent onslaught against jot and tittle, in so far as they not only give the established law a radical interpretation, but abolish it."[14] James D. G. Dunn takes a similar position. Commenting on Jesus' attitude to *lex talionis* (Matt. 5:38-42) he writes, "Jesus sets this law aside as relativised by a higher principle — that of love of neighbour."[15] Eduard Schweizer speaks of Jesus' ambivalence towards the law and claims that "there are even places where Jesus annuls not only the Jewish interpretation but the Old Testament law itself." Like Dunn, he cites as an example Jesus' remarks on the *lex talionis:* "when he goes on to say not to resist evil, the requirement of 'an eye for an eye, a tooth for a tooth' found in the Old Testament is in fact abrogated." The same holds true, he continues, "for the Old Testament commandment that a divorced woman be given a note of dismissal, which Jesus finds totally inapplicable because divorce itself is contrary to God's will."[16]

As these quotations show, only two of the antitheses raise any serious

14. G. Bornkamm, *Jesus of Nazareth,* rev. ed. (London: Hodder and Stoughton, 1963), p. 107.

15. J. D. G. Dunn, *The Living Word* (London: SCM, 1987), p. 49.

16. E. Schweizer, *Jesus* (London: SCM, 1971), p. 32.

difficulty about Jesus' attitude to the Old Testament: his comment on divorce and his comment on *lex talionis.* The former is found in Matthew 5:31. In this instance the saying that Jesus is countering was no mere rabbinical gloss on the law. It was the law itself as laid down in Deuteronomy 24:1-4, stipulating that if a man found "some indecency" in his wife and wished to divorce her, he must follow clear formal procedures.

This was not, however, a law instituting divorce. Divorce was already a fact, even in ancient Israel. A previous chapter of Deuteronomy contains two clear references to it, each carefully circumscribing it. In the first, a man who falsely accuses his wife of not being a virgin when they married thereby forfeits his right ever to divorce her: "he may not put her away all his days" (Deut. 22:19). In the second instance, a man who violates an unbetrothed woman incurs the same penalty (Deut. 22:28-29).[17] The fact that such a forfeiture could be seen as a penalty strongly suggests that the right itself was seen as a valuable privilege. It also suggests that the privilege was widely abused. Jesus was not the first to deplore it. The prophet Malachi, for example, was certainly stirred by the frequency and frivolousness of divorce in his day: "For I hate divorce, says the Lord the God of Israel" (Mal. 2:16).

Against such a background the purpose of Deuteronomy 24:1-4 was clearly regulative, not prescriptive. Its intention was not to encourage or even to condone divorce but to control its abuse. Any man who put away his wife had to prove "some indecency" in her; he had to prepare a bill of divorce; he had to serve it on her; and he had to go through the formal ceremony of putting her out of his home. The law introduced a further dissuasive: the man who took this step was made to know that once his wife had gone he could never again have her back. That, in fact, was the main point of this item of Deuteronomic legislation. There could be no experimental divorces: "her former husband, who sent her away, may not take her again to be his wife, after she has been defiled; for that is an abomination before the Lord" (Deut. 24:4).

These regulations must have gone some way towards limiting the abuse of divorce. Yet Jesus takes higher ground: Deuteronomy 24:1-4 does not give any man the right to divorce. The bare statement of this principle is given in Matthew 5:31-32, but for its rationale we have to go to Matthew 19:3-9. This latter passage gives no support to the view that Jesus rejected

17. The custom of divorce is also taken for granted in Lev. 21:7-14 and Num. 30:10.

the law. His appeal is to the law itself: the creation ordinance of marriage as laid down in the Pentateuch: "Therefore a man leaves his father and his mother and cleaves to his wife, and they become one flesh" (Gen. 2:24). Jesus seizes on the idea of the two becoming one flesh and adds his own comment: "What therefore God has joined together, let no man put asunder" (Matt. 19:6).

The passage as a whole brings out two important principles. First, that there is a hierarchy of rules and principles within the law itself. Deuteronomy 24:1-4 is part of the Pentateuch, but it is not as foundational as Genesis 2:24. The reason is simple. The concept of divorce was not there at the beginning. At the beginning God clearly stated the rule of lifelong monogamy.

This idea that temporal priority implies some kind of moral and theological superiority occurs in other New Testament contexts as well. Paul, for example, more than once argues from the late arrival of the Mosaic law that it could not annul the prior dispensation of grace. Circumcision, for example, came in *after* Abraham was justified (Rom. 4:10); the law came in *(pareisēlthen)* long after God instituted his moral government; and, most telling of all, the Sinaitic covenant came in 430 years after the Abrahamic. It could not, therefore, modify the principle of grace laid down so clearly in God's promises to the patriarch.

By the same argument, the regulations laid down in Deuteronomy 24:1-4 cannot nullify the ordinance of lifelong monogamy promulgated at the very beginning of creation.

Why were divorce regulations laid down at all? The answer lies in the second principle given by Jesus: the principle of accommodation. God had to accommodate his revelation and his precepts to the hardness of the human heart (Matt. 19:8). Originally, in the very nature of the case, there was no need for such an adjustment. Man was in Paradise, unfallen. The fall created an entirely new situation as people began to practice polygamy, sodomy, and divorce. As far as this last was concerned, the choice was between the unregulated breakup of marriages, with all the tragedy and misery that that entailed, and the provision of some legislative framework that would both provide a disincentive to divorce and limit its adverse effects when it became unavoidable. This is a dilemma that faces every legislature. Churches, as Lord Hailsham once pointed out, may wish to make divorce "more difficult" or "less easy," but the problem facing legislators is how "to make the unavoidable consequences of a broken marriage more tolerable to the parties and their children without unnecessarily undermining the public interest which lies in the permanence of the marriage bond."[18]

The clear lesson from Jesus' handling of this topic is that no matter how high our doctrine of Scripture we cannot simply take a biblical text and convert it slavishly into an item of civil or criminal law or even into a personal moral code. As Jesus makes clear, the provisions of Deuteronomy 24:1-4 do not represent the divine ideal (and never did), even though they are unmistakably part of the Old Testament canon. However, it would be equally premature to give legislative sanction to Genesis 2:24 and thus abolish divorce altogether. On a wide range of issues (divorce, liquor, gambling, homosexuality), both Church and society have to seek an *accommodation* between the divine ideal and social reality. Such an accommodation is itself divinely sanctioned.[19] What is not sanctioned is the use of such a text as Deuteronomy 24:1-4 to warrant deliberate violation of the divine ideal. God does not command divorce, but he does command legislators to regulate it.

Lex talionis

When we turn to Jesus' comments on *lex talionis* (Matt. 5:38-42), we have to accept, again, that his target is not rabbinical exegesis but a fundamental element of the law itself: "Your eye shall not pity; it shall be life for life, eye for eye, tooth for tooth, hand for hand, foot for foot" (Deut. 19:21; cf. Exod. 21:24; Lev. 24:20). Is Jesus totally abolishing this principle (and implicitly setting aside the intrinsic authority of the Torah)?

The key to the problem lies in the context addressed by Jesus. It differed entirely from that addressed in Deuteronomy. In Deuteronomy, the

18. Q. H. Hailsham, *A Sparrow's Flight: The Memoirs of Lord Hailsham of Marylebone* (London: Collins, 1990), p. 416.

19. See, for example, Calvin's comment on the institution of Urim and Thummim: "it was a concession made by God to the rudeness of His ancient people" (J. Calvin, *Commentaries on the Last Four Books of Moses*, vol. 2 [Edinburgh: The Calvin Translation Society, 1853], p. 198). See further the excellent study by David Wright, "Calvin's Pentateuchal Criticism: Equity, Hardness of Heart, and Divine Accommodation in the Mosaic Harmony Commentary," *Calvin Theological Journal* (April 1986): 33-50. Cf. F. Watson, *Text and Truth: Redefining Biblical Theology* (Edinburgh: T. & T. Clark, 1997), pp. 313-17 ("Torah as Divine Accommodation").

lawgiver is addressing magistrates ("the priests and the judges who are in office in those days"). They hold office precisely to obviate the need for private revenge and to dispense justice with impartiality and equity. On one level this means that the administration of justice must not be based on sentiment: "Your eye shall not pity." On another level it means that punishment and compensation must not be excessive. A life cannot be taken for an eye, nor a hand for a tooth. This is in marked contrast to the kind of justice demanded by, for example, Lamech: "If Cain is avenged sevenfold, truly Lamech seventy-sevenfold" (Gen. 4:2). It also contrasts with the "exemplary" sentences beloved of modern magistrates, obsessed with deterrence. In this particular context, the judges are charged with safeguarding the rights of others: "*you* shall do to him as he had meant to do to his *brother*" (Deut. 19:19). From this point of view, *lex talionis* has never been abrogated. The state exists to intimidate evil (Rom. 13:3) and to protect the weak against the strong. It can even be argued that Jesus himself clearly resisted evil. He drove the money changers out of the temple (Matt. 21:12). He turned the full force of his rhetoric on those who devoured widows' houses (Matt. 23:14). Above all, the specific mission on which he came was to destroy the works of the devil (1 John 3:8). Sometimes, in our concern to do justice to the fact that "when he was reviled, he did not revile in return" (1 Pet. 2:23), we forget that Jesus' ministry had a negative, destructive edge. He chained the powers of darkness to his triumphal chariot (Col. 2:15). To erase these perspectives from the teaching of Jesus is to repeat the very blunders of the scribes and Pharisees: homing in on one text of Scripture, submitting it to a literalistic exegesis, and using it to undermine fundamental principles of the law. We cannot in the name of loving our neighbor outlaw coercive government. In a society that didn't resist evil our neighbors would go to the gas chambers.

Lex talionis clearly admitted of abuses, and it is these that Jesus is confronting.[20] He addresses his disciples not as judges or magistrates but as private individuals. In that capacity, they are categorically forbidden to pursue the agenda of "an eye for an eye, a tooth for a tooth." Instead, if someone hits them on one side of the face, they are to offer him the other (Matt. 5:39). Jealous for the rights of others, they are indifferent to their own.

20. Cf. the story of the boy in a tough inner-city school who was delighted to receive a Gideon's Bible because the index contained an entry "Revenge": "Now I'll know how to get revenge!"

From the standpoint of postresurrection Christianity, one of the best commentaries on this passage is 1 Corinthians 6:1-8. Rather than go to law with each other to reclaim money or property, Christians should let themselves be wronged and defrauded. This would not, however, preclude their going to law on behalf of others. Any Christian who happened to be a magistrate would be absolutely bound to implement the principle of equity, which lies at the heart of *lex talionis*. However, while the state exists to deter evil, it is not in all respects exempt from the principle of nonretaliation. A Christian democracy wronged by a neighbor state might well feel bound not to press its rights. It might even decide to practice *kenosis*. It would come under an entirely different set of obligations, however, if the wrong were perpetrated against one of its smaller, weaker neighbors. Foreign policy is not exempt from the rigors of the Christian ethic.

The Sabbath

There remain two further passages in which, allegedly, Jesus repudiated the authority of the Old Testament. Both involve crucial elements in Jewish identity: the Sabbath and ritual purity.

Jesus' comments on the Sabbath occur in Matthew 12:1-8 (= Luke 6:1-5; Mark 2:23-28). His disciples, walking through a cornfield one Sabbath, plucked ears of corn and ate them. This specific action was not forbidden in the Old Testament, but it was forbidden in the oral tradition. The rabbis had declared it equivalent to reaping.

Jesus immediately defends his disciples' action. He does not, however, repudiate the Sabbath. He argues instead that their action was no breach of it. The precise form of his argument is worth noting. He does not plead that their action was a work of necessity. His disciples were in no danger of starving to death. Instead he argues from clear Old Testament precedents. Mark and Luke mention only one of these: "what David did when he was hungry." He and his followers had gone to Ahimelech the priest and begged for bread. He had given them the only bread available: the holy bread, reserved for the priests. This action was a clear breach of cultic law, but "the fact that scripture does not condemn David for his action shows that the rigidity with which the Pharisees interpreted the ritual law was not in accordance with scripture, and so was not a proper understanding of the Law itself."[21] Ahimelech's action was justified, says Jesus, on the principle "I desire mercy, and not sacrifice" (Matt. 12:7). Canon law and liturgical rubric cannot be used as pretexts for lack of compassion.

The other precedent is cited only by Matthew and relates specifically to the Sabbath: priests work on the Sabbath and are guiltless (Matt. 12:5). This is not merely a plea that the Old Testament itself sanctions departures from the strict letter of the law on humanitarian grounds. It is also a claim that the disciples, like the priests, are on sacred duty. Indeed, their vocation is higher than that of the priests: "I tell you, something greater than the temple is here" (Matt. 12:6). Their hunger has been incurred in that service, and they are therefore guiltless if they satisfy it.

The account closes with the pronouncement "The sabbath was made for man, not man for the sabbath; so the Son of Man is lord even of the sabbath" (Mark 2:27-28). It is impossible to construe this as a repeal of the Sabbath. On the contrary, it is a clear indication that whatever institutions are swept away by the advent of the Son of Man and the inauguration of the kingdom, the Sabbath is not one of them. In the last analysis, these words of Jesus represent a huge Christological claim. In the Old Testament, God had called the Sabbath "my sabbath" (Isa. 56:14). Here, Jesus calls himself Lord of Yahweh's Sabbath. It is for him, not for the Pharisees, to legislate what is appropriate for it. In saying this he goes right to the heart of its purpose: "the sabbath was made for man, not man for the sabbath." This harmonizes perfectly with the Decalogue itself, where the Fourth Commandment is specifically oriented to the needs of "manservant and maidservant." From this point of view, the Sabbath was the first piece of employee-protection legislation. Such a law, said Jesus, may not be invoked to justify inhumanity. A man should not go hungry (or remain unhealed or unassisted) merely because it is the Sabbath. This point had been grasped even by some of the rabbis: witness, for example, the oft-quoted comment of R. Simeon ben Menasya: "The Sabbath is delivered unto you, and you are not delivered unto the Sabbath." "The cult is perverted," writes Hans Conzelmann, "if one uses it to evade the commandment; the sabbath is abused if one denies love for its sake."[22] It is precisely because Jesus is Lord of all that belongs to man that he is Lord of the Sabbath.

21. C. E. B. Cranfield, *The Gospel according to St. Mark: An Introduction and Commentary* (Cambridge: Cambridge University Press, 1959), p. 115.

22. H. Conzelmann, *Jesus* (Philadelphia: Fortress, 1973), p. 53.

The Food Laws

Jesus' comments on the laws of purity, and particularly on the distinction between clean and unclean foods, are to be found in Mark 7:1-23 (= Matt. 15:1-20). The initial conflict with the Pharisees on this matter revolved around the oral tradition. The written Torah said nothing of the need to wash hands before eating. It was a rabbinical addition based, probably, on the idea that unwashed hands defiled food and rendered the eater unclean. Jesus, however, broadened the discussion. "No food," he said, "defiles a man. We eat and we excrete, but our moral character remains unchanged. It is what comes out of us, not what goes into us, that defiles. What taints us is our speech and our evil desires, not our food."

Mark sums up Jesus' observations with the emphatic comment, "Thus he declared all foods clean" (Mark 7:19). Assuming for the moment that Mark correctly summarizes Jesus' position, this is clearly more than an attack on the oral tradition. It is a rescendment of an extensive and important part of the Torah itself: a rescendment that is clearly reflected in the thought of the early Church, which deemed the food laws no longer binding. Luke relates the change to a vision granted to Peter just prior to his visit to Cornelius. His protest that he has never eaten anything common or unclean is silenced by the Voice, "What God has cleansed, you must not call common" (Acts 10:15). Paul states the principle categorically in Romans 14:14: "I know and am persuaded in the Lord that nothing is unclean in itself." Whether we eat or do not eat is no longer a matter of rules but a matter of deciding what most glorifies God in any given situation (1 Cor. 10:31).

Yet the food laws were only one element in a much wider rescendment. Circumcision was abrogated, and the Passover, and the temple, and the priesthood, and the sacrificial system, and the seventh-day Sabbath, and the special status of Jerusalem as the place of worship.

Is it possible to find a rationale for such a wholesale rescendment, one consistent with Jesus' claim that he had not come to destroy the Law and the Prophets?

The answer lies, surely, in the fact that Jesus came to inaugurate a new age. The kingdom was the reality: the Mosaic ordinances were the shadow (Heb. 8:5; 10:1). When the reality came, the shadows were rendered obsolete. This is further linked to the establishment of the new covenant (Heb. 8:8-13; Jer. 31:31-34). This new covenant is specifically declared by the writer to the Hebrews to be discontinuous with the old. It is "not like" the covenant made with the fathers (Heb. 8:9). It has been rendered "obsolete" by the advent of Christ and therefore "vanishes away." This inevitably involved a paradigm shift in the life setting of the Church.

To some extent, Paul plays a different word game from that of the writer to the Hebrews. He does not use the concept of the new covenant; he emphasizes the continuity of the New Testament church with the old (Rom. 11:17-21); and he stresses the unchanging nature of the dispensations of grace. Against this background, he speaks of the Abrahamic covenant as still in force (Gal. 3:15-18). He does not speak in similar terms of the Mosaic covenant, however. In Romans 5:20, for example, he makes an interesting word choice in describing the coming of the Law: *nomos de pareisēlthen.* C. E. B. Cranfield[23] questions whether the verb necessarily has a depreciatory sense, but its only other occurrence in the New Testament is in Galatians 2:4, where the RSV certainly imparts a tone of disparagement: "false brethren secretly brought in, who *slipped in* to spy out our freedom." There can be no doubt either that the Sinaitic law came in late or that it came in as a parenthesis. It did not exist in the time of Abraham; and it was transcended with the advent of Messiah.

Paul's rationale for this is that the Sinaitic law belonged to the Church's minority: "when we were children, we were slaves to the elemental spirits of the universe. But when the time had fully come, God sent forth his Son . . . to redeem those who were under the law" (Gal. 4:3, 4). Earlier, in Galatians 3:23, he had written, "Now before faith came, we were confined under the law, kept under restraint until faith should be revealed. So that the law was our custodian until Christ came."

This accords perfectly with the perspective of Jesus, who stresses more than once the burdensomeness of the Mosaic regulations (Matt. 11:28; 23:4; Luke 11:46). Deliverance from this yoke is one of the keynotes of the gospel, ensuring deliverance from a repressive tutelage that restricted and convicted at every turn.

It is a direct consequence of this parenthetical nature of the law that even some of the most fundamental elements of the Mosaic code were transitional. The Aaronic priesthood was transitional. The sacrificial system was transitional. The temple and its centralized worship were transitional. The purity laws were transitional.

23. C. E. B. Cranfield, *A Critical and Exegetical Commentary on the Epistle to the Romans,* vol. 1 (Edinburgh: T. & T. Clark, 1975), p. 292.

It is in this context that we have to evaluate Jesus' action in abolishing the distinction between clean and unclean foods. It was but one detail in a much more radical shake-up signaling the end of an era. The age of Moses was over.

As far as the food laws were concerned,[24] there can be little doubt that they served as boundary markers between Israel and the Gentiles. In Leviticus 11, for example, the regulations about "the living things which you may eat among all the beasts that are on the earth" (v. 2) are specifically linked (v. 45) to the imperatives of separation: "For I am the LORD who brought you up out of the land of Egypt to be your God; you shall therefore be holy, for I am holy." The link is equally clear in Deuteronomy 14:2-3: "For you are a people holy to the LORD your God, and the LORD has chosen you to be a people for his own possession, out of all the peoples that are on the face of the earth. You shall not eat any abominable thing." At the same time, the dietary laws were not merely symbolic. They also contributed to the effect they were intended to symbolize, as J. E. Hartley points out: "Close adherence to these regulations guarded the Israelites from following the immoral customs of their neighbours and from incorporating pagan rites into their worship of Jahweh. The dietary laws in particular made it difficult for Israelites to fellowship at the same table with their neighbours and blocked their participation in festivals to foreign gods."[25]

The rescendment of the dietary laws is thus closely linked to the abolition of the distinction between Jew and Gentile and the incorporation of both into the one new covenant Church. As we have seen, this is established at the very commencement of the Gentile mission as recorded in Acts. Peter's vision clearly silenced his scruples about eating Gentile food (Acts 10:15). It also implied that the Gentiles themselves were *kosher.* The outworking of this is seen in Ephesians 2:14-22. Christ broke down the dividing wall between Jews and Gentiles, did so precisely by abolishing those external ordinances which were meant to keep the Jew distinct from the Gentile, and incorporated both into his one Body. The Christian Jew

24. On the food laws, see further the excursus, "Ritual Purity," in John E. Hartley, *Leviticus,* Word Biblical Commentary 4 (Dallas: Word, 1992), pp. 140-47.

25. Hartley, *Leviticus,* p. 144. Cf. J. I. Packer, *Honouring the Written Word of God* (Carlisle: Paternoster, 1999), p. 116: "the law was meant to act as 'a wall of partition' (Eph. 2:14) between Jew and Gentile, keeping the Jews from the pagan ways of surrounding nations and isolating them for the moral and spiritual training that God planned to give them."

would no longer be defiled by sitting at a Gentile table or by accidentally touching something a Gentile had handled in the marketplace.

As N. T. Wright points out, the temple, the Sabbath, the food laws, and circumcision "formed the boundary fence around the people of Israel, the nation of the Jews."[26] Without these, Israel loses her uniqueness. Wright goes on, correctly, to argue that what Jesus was doing was "revolutionising the God-given marks of Israel's uniqueness."[27] *His* followers, the New Israel, would be clearly distinguished not only from Gentiles but from Jews. No longer, however, would what was distinctive be a matter of external observances. Nor would they be based on what J. I. Packer calls "a casuistry of abstinence."[28] The boundary markers would now be much more radical. The New Israel would be characterized not by worshipping in the Jerusalem temple but by worshipping in spirit and in truth (John 4:24), not by pedantic observance of rules and regulations but by love of enemies and prayer for their persecutors (Matt. 5:44), and not by avoidance of unclean foods but by avoidance of malice and hypocrisy (1 Cor. 5:8).

Implicit in this, as Wright[29] again points out, is a more fundamental demarcation still: "the clash between Jesus and his Jewish contemporaries, especially the Pharisees, must be seen in terms of *alternative political agendas* generated by *alternative eschatological beliefs and expectations.*" In the last analysis, this is a clash over the nature of the Jewish hope, and that, in turn, is a fundamental disagreement over the vision of the Law and the Prophets: over the nature of Messiahship. The kingdom envisaged by the Pharisees focused on the symbols of Jewish uniqueness: "sabbath, food taboos, ethnic identity, ancestral land, and ultimately the Temple itself."[30] Jesus was not calling into question either the hope of Israel or their special place in the divine purpose, but he was reinterpreting it. The kingdom of God would consist of a righteousness greater than that of the scribes and Pharisees: one not obsessed with boundary markers but with those "universal horizons"[31] implicit in God's promise that in Abraham all the nations of the earth would be blessed (Gen. 22:18; Matt. 28:19), and one

26. N. T. Wright, *Jesus and the Victory of God* (London: SPCK, 1996), p. 388.
27. Wright, *Jesus and the Victory of God,* p. 389.
28. Packer, *Honouring the Written Word of God,* p. 124.
29. Wright, *Jesus and the Victory of God,* p. 390.
30. Wright, *Jesus and the Victory of God,* p. 390.
31. Watson, *Text and Truth,* p. 315.

where the citizens would be more concerned with what God saw in secret than with what men saw in public (Matt. 6:4).

Jesus and Biblical Criticism

What credit is due to Jesus' pronouncements on questions that lie within the domain of biblical criticism? "Do His words," asked Charles Gore, "foreclose certain critical positions as to the character of Old Testament literature?"[32] In particular, does his attribution of Psalm 110 to David (Matt. 22:43), Exodus and Deuteronomy to Moses (Luke 12:37; Matt. 19:7-12), and Isaiah to Isaiah (Matt. 15:7) have to be taken into account in discussing the authorship of these books?

Gore himself certainly did not think so. The historical Jesus, he said, "willed so to restrain the beams of his Deity as to observe the limits of the science of his age,"[33] and the same restraint applied to his historical knowledge. His references to questions of literature and criticism are vague and indefinite, and he clearly had no more intention of anticipating modern biblical criticism than he had of anticipating modern physics. In both departments he abode by the conditions of his *kenosis* and never drew on his unveiled omniscience.[34]

From the standpoint of Christian orthodoxy this is as powerful a justification as can be offered for a biblical criticism untrammeled by dominical pronouncements. However, is Gore's reasoning cogent?

It is certainly true that dominical pronouncements by themselves would not rule out biblical criticism, since such pronouncements would always be open to validation by critical means. If, for example, Moses wrote Deuteronomy, the evidence for his authorship could not be limited to a saying of Jesus. There would be internal evidence in the book itself and external evidence in the surrounding history. Both of these would be the

32. C. Gore, ed., *Lux Mundi: A Series of Studies in the Religion of the Incarnation,* 12th ed. (London: John Murray, 1891), p. 264. The words quoted are from Gore's own contribution, "The Holy Spirit and Inspiration."

33. Gore, *Lux Mundi,* p. 264.

34. Gore, *Lux Mundi,* p. 265: "the utterances of Christ about the Old Testament do not seem to be nearly definite or clear enough to allow of our supposing that in this case He is departing from the general method of the Incarnation, by bringing to bear the unveiled omniscience of the Godhead, to anticipate or foreclose a development of natural knowledge."

province of the critical scholar; and if we were certain that Jesus had indeed pronounced Moses the author of Deuteronomy, the critical vindication of this position would in effect be a department of apologetics, driven by a Christological agenda.

It is also true that it is seldom wise to quote any man's opinion on a question he never faced. For example, if John Calvin never consciously addressed the question of the extent of the atonement, it is perilous to quote his opinion on it. Similarly, if Jesus never reflected on the authorship of the Pentateuch or the unity of Isaiah, we must be extremely careful about ascribing to him definite views on such questions.

Linked to this is the possibility that all Jesus' references to the authors and titles of Old Testament books were ad hominem. Just as his contemporaries thought the sun "rose," so they assumed that the Pentateuch was from "Moses" and the Psalms were from "David," and to have spoken of "the author of the Pentateuch" would have been unpardonable pedantry.

This is not, however, what either Gore or modern biblical scholars are claiming. Their position is that Jesus genuinely shared the belief of all his Jewish contemporaries that Moses wrote the Pentateuch. That belief was, they say, mistaken, and Jesus shared in the mistake.

It is absurd to think that this has no Christological implications and that the Christian scholar can simply take it in his stride. The Christian scholar cannot lightly assume that Jesus was wrong, and, when he finds himself examining questions on which Jesus also held opinions, he cannot easily dismiss these opinions as merely antiquarian. Nor can the Christian scholar treat the Bible as merely part of the ordinary sequence of human literature, or treat the literary questions relating to it as he would the literary questions relating to any other book. Jesus gave the Old Testament an endorsement he gave to no other literature, and every scholar has to come to terms with that endorsement. Is the Old Testament canonical or is it not? Are its "commandments" (even the least of them) binding or are they not?

This is not to deny that the Bible *is* human literature or that its human authors went through the same psychological processes of composition as any other authors. They researched their material, wrestled over word selection, agonized over structure and arrangement, compared and collated documents, edited and revised their work, and experienced triumph and despair. In these respects they were no different from any modern poet or journalist. According to Jesus, however, their product was different. It was the word of God. The scholar who believes that knows that he is standing on holy ground. The scholar who disbelieves it will despise the book for daring to claim it.

Yet the most serious problem remains: the sheer scale of the difference between the historical Jewish view of the Scriptures (endorsed by Jesus) and the modern critical view. It is not a matter of a few differences on minor questions of date, authorship, and sources. There is no serious problem in documentary sources as such, nor in the idea that some parts of the Pentateuch are not in their current form Mosaic, nor even in the idea that the present text of Deuteronomy is the result of "generations of use within public worship in ancient Israel."[35] Even the problem of pseudepigraphy, serious though it is, we might overcome.

However, the scale of the Reuss-Graf-Kuenen-Wellhausen revolution dwarfs such details. Not only were Jesus and the Jews wrong, they were monumentally wrong. Books that claimed to date from the Exodus were in fact later than the Exile. Works that claimed to be from the pen of Moses were in fact as late as Ezekiel. 1 Samuel, which was thought to describe the situation long after the giving of the law, in fact describes Israel as she was generations *before* the torah. The Pentateuch, which purports to be the foundation of Israel's life and religion, was in fact its copestone, taking its place at the center of national life only when the days of Israel's glory lay far behind her. It is as if some future generation of historians were to discover that the Magna Carta and *habeas corpus* dated from the end of the third millennium.

Behind this lies something even more disturbing. If the prevailing consensus is correct, Jesus was completely mistaken as to the fundamental nature of Israel's religion. He believed that for the duration of her history Israel was under the tutelage of Yahweh, undergoing a process of education through cumulative divine revelation. God taught her "line upon line." Moses laid the foundation, giving Israel a detailed account of her origins and history, as well as a corpus of laws to live by. Elijah and Elisha saved this heritage when it was threatened with extinction by the priests of Baal. Isaiah, Jeremiah, Hosea, and the other great prophets refined and purified it.

But all this, we are now told, is myth. The real explanation of Israel's religious history is that it was an evolutionary development, driven not by divine but by natural forces. To begin with, the religion was polytheistic:

35. See Duane L. Christensen, *Deuteronomy 1–11*, Word Biblical Commentary 6A (Dallas: Word, 1991), p. lxii.

little better than animism. Then it evolved into local centers dedicated to the worship of Yahweh, before attaining, finally, the rigid liturgical forms laid down after the Exile. The Levitical Code, far from being the point of departure of Israel's history, was in fact its culmination: its codification in rules and taboos that represented the final triumph of priestly legalism over the radical spirituality of the prophets.

Jesus suspected none of this. He did not detect the strands of animism in Israel's early history. He did not realize that Leviticus was a betrayal of ethical monotheism. He was blind to the double narratives that prove composite authorship. He was totally unaware of the contradictions that demonstrate that Moses did not write Deuteronomy.

Gore's thesis was that Jesus' lack of awareness of critical issues could be explained quite simply by his *kenosis.* Its plausibility depended on one thing: the unimportance of the details on which he was ignorant. To be unaware of the composite nature of Isaiah was no more culpable than to be unaware of DNA.

Yet that was not the point criticism had reached. It required us, even then, to believe that Jesus was taken in by a national myth no more plausible than that of Romulus and Remus.

Any approach to the Old Testament that has such serious Christological implications should surely give us pause. It should also, precisely because of these implications, inspire a believing criticism that takes the canonical nature of Scripture as seriously as humanist scholarship takes its mythological status. Christianity cannot afford to be intimidated by the assumption that "only a completely profane interpretation of the (Old) Testament, that is, one that leaves out of consideration every normative meaning, can make any claim to be scholarly."[36]

Jesus and the New Testament

So far, we have focused only on Jesus' attitude to the Old Testament. Yet what of his role in connection with the New? In the nature of the case he could not give it the same endorsement as he gave to the Old. Nor did he ever refer to the future writings that his disciples would compose and that

36. W. G. Kummel, *The New Testament: The History of the Investigation of Its Problems* (London: SCM, 1973), p. 203. Kummel repudiates the assumption.

would be added to the canon. It would be a mistake, however, to assume either that the New Testament was a development unforeseen by Jesus or that he himself took no part in its formation.

For one thing, he is the direct author of major parts of it in the sense that they consist of his sayings. This is most obviously true of the Gospels, but dominical sayings are also recorded in the book of Acts (Acts 1:5-8) and in 1 Corinthians (1 Cor. 7:10). The Letters to the Seven Churches (Rev. 2:1–3:22), in all probability, also come into this category. The authenticity of virtually every one of these sayings has, of course, been challenged. Assuming the challenges to have been rebutted, the New Testament enables us to hear the voice of Jesus as surely as the Old enables us to hear Jeremiah and Isaiah.

Jesus was also aware that he could not, personally, teach his disciples all they needed to know. The reason was not in him, however, but in them: "I have yet many things to say to you, but you cannot bear them now" (John 16:12). Two factors were involved in this. One was that, prior to the denouement, events such as the crucifixion made little sense. The other was that prior to Pentecost the disciples lacked insight. Much of what Jesus had to tell them would have to wait, therefore, until after his death. This clearly implies that neither Jesus' own sayings nor the Synoptic Gospels as a whole exhaust what Christians have to learn. It also implies that Jesus' later teaching would have to be subject to special arrangements. These special arrangements are described in John 14:26 and John 16:13-15. In essence, Jesus will continue to "say things" through the Paraclete. He it is who will bring back to the mind of the disciples all the things Jesus said to them (John 14:26). He will teach them everything about Jesus and give them detailed instructions for the new age. Above all, he will glorify Christ, not least by leading such writers as Paul and John into a Christology far more complex and profound than was possible during Jesus' lifetime.

The link between Jesus (the Lord) and the Paraclete (the Spirit) is a close one. Not only does the Spirit come in Jesus' name (John 14:26) and therefore as his representative, but the Lord is the Spirit (2 Cor. 3:17, 18). This explains why we are invited by Luke to see the book of Acts as a continuation of what Jesus "began to do and teach" (Acts 1:1). Behind the ministry of the apostles and behind the work of the Holy Spirit there lay the ongoing work of Jesus after he was taken up (Acts 1:2). The sending of the Spirit is his act (Acts 2:33). The calling of Saul of Tarsus is his act (Acts 9:5). The conversion of Lydia is his act (Acts 16:14).

Furthermore, the production of the New Testament is his act — not merely a record of his acts or a witness to his acts, but itself one of the redemptive acts of the risen Lord; one of the things he does for the salvation of his people.

The clearest linguistic expression of this is Paul's concept of tradition *(paradosis)*. Over against human tradition *(ho paradosis tōn anthrōpōn)* Christ creates his own divine tradition. Human or rabbinical tradition went back to "the men of old." Apostolic tradition went back to Christ himself. He was its source. This is certainly Paul's understanding, as appears in 1 Corinthians 11:23: "For I received from the Lord what I also delivered to you." These words clearly imply "a chain of tradition which *begins* with the Lord."[37] Paul makes the same point from a wider perspective in Galatians 1:1, 12, "where he implicitly acknowledges that he would not be an apostle if he had not received the gospel *directly* from Christ":[38] "For I did not receive it from man, nor was I taught it, but it came through a revelation of Jesus Christ" (Gal. 1:12). Precisely for this reason, the tradition is normative: "keep away from any brother who is living in idleness and not in accord with the tradition that you received from us" (2 Thess. 3:6). For the same reason, too, the Thessalonians are urged to take a firm hold of "the traditions which you were taught by us, either by word of mouth or by letter" (2 Thess. 2:15).

This is not a tradition in addition to or an alternative to Christ. It is the continuance and completion of Christ's prophetic ministry: the postresurrection form of his teaching. Nor is it an open-ended process destined to last as long as the Church itself. On the contrary, apostolic tradition represents "the faith which was once for all delivered *(paradotheisę)* to the saints" (Jude 3). With the Messiah the last word is spoken. After the Son there is silence.

The process of tradition forming is not, then, passed on to the Church. It belongs exclusively to the period of the incarnation.[39] The Christian community lives forever subject to the apostolic tradition that called it into being and with which God closed his canon. We may, indeed must, expound it. We may not add to it. Nor may we give to our own expositions

37. O. Cullmann, *The Early Church* (London: SCM, 1966), p. 62. The words quoted are from an essay entitled "The Tradition."

38. Cullmann, *The Early Church*, p. 78.

39. Cullmann, *The Early Church*, p. 78.

the force of revelation. Christ still speaks, and speaks eloquently, but only in Scripture, the living, life-giving word.

If they do not listen to the Law and the Prophets and to the Apostolic Tradition, neither will they listen though one go to them from the dead.

"Let God Be Proved True": Paul's View of Scripture and the Faithfulness of God

Drake Williams

The relationship between Paul and the Jewish Scriptures has long been considered an important concern for understanding the ideas that Paul conveys in his letters. Current research continues to focus on questions like the following. Why does the wording of his Scripture citations differ from that of the known versions of the day?[1] What is the role of less explicit Scripture references like scriptural allusions and echoes in his letters?[2] What role does Scripture play in Paul's ethics?[3] Does Paul use Scripture in relation to its context?[4] What is the relationship between Paul's interpreta-

1. For example, C. Stanley, *Paul and the Language of Scripture: Citation Technique in the Pauline Epistles and Contemporary Literature,* Society for New Testament Studies Monograph Series 69 (Cambridge: Cambridge University Press, 1992).

2. For example, R. B. Hays, *Echoes of Scripture in the Letters of Paul* (New Haven: Yale University Press, 1989). See the discussion of Hays's book in C. A. Evans and J. A. Sanders, eds., *Paul and the Scriptures of Israel,* Studies in Scripture in Early Judaism and Christianity 1 (Sheffield: Sheffield Academic Press, 1993), pp. 1-96.

3. For a good summary of the debate, see the discussion of the source of Paul's ethics in B. S. Rosner, ed., *Understanding Paul's Ethics: Twentieth-Century Approaches* (Grand Rapids: Eerdmans; Carlisle: Paternoster, 1995), pp. 5-10, 25-71.

4. See the discussion about the way Paul does or does not apply Scriptures in relation to their context in G. K. Beale, ed., *The Right Doctrine from the Wrong Texts? Essays on the Use of the Old Testament in the New* (Grand Rapids: Baker, 1994).

tion of Scripture and contemporary Jewish interpretation of that Scripture?[5] Does Paul use a particular hermeneutical principle to interpret the Scriptures?[6] While these questions are of great value, this article will pay attention to a supposition that lies behind these questions and one that has received far less attention: What is Paul's conception of Scripture? In other words, how does he view Scripture? As Brian S. Rosner has noted, this concern is one that is a presupposition for these other areas of inquiry but remains largely unexplored.[7]

This study will examine Paul's conception of Scripture in relation to a particular theme, the faithfulness of God. To explore this connection between the faithfulness of God and Paul's conception of Scripture, this essay will examine his writings in two ways. It will first examine portions of Paul's writing where he presents the faithfulness of God to the Jewish people in relation to the Scriptures. This will mean an examination of portions of the book of Romans where Paul explains his perception of the Scriptures in relation to God's dealings with the people of Israel. Second, this article will survey some of the ways in which Paul uses Scripture in his correspondence with his readers. While this brief study could not possibly examine every Scripture text that Paul employs, it will consider the implications of some of the ways in which Paul introduces some scriptural texts, applies those texts in polemical situations, applies Scripture to himself, and uses Scripture to introduce new teaching. From this survey conclusions can also be drawn regarding Paul's perception of the Scriptures in relation to the faithfulness of God.

5. For example, B. S. Rosner, *Paul, Scripture, and Ethics: A Study of I Corinthians 5–7*, Arbeiten zur Geschichte des antiken Judentums und des Urchristentums 22 (Leiden: Brill, 1994); C. A. Evans, "Listening for Echoes of Interpreted Scripture," in *Paul and the Scriptures of Israel*, ed. C. A. Evans and J. A. Sanders, Studies in Scripture in Early Judaism and Christianity (Sheffield: Sheffield Academic Press, 1993), pp. 47-51; R. Longenecker, "Who Is the Prophet Talking About? Some Reflections on the New Testament Use of the Old," *Themelios* 13 (1987): 4-8.

6. See the helpful discussion in S. J. Hafemann, *Paul, Moses, and the History of Israel*, Wissenschaftliche Untersuchungen zum Neuen Testament 81 (Tübingen: J. C. B. Mohr [Paul Siebeck], 1995), pp. 16-29, 452-58.

7. B. S. Rosner, "'Written for Us': Paul's View of Scripture," in *A Pathway into the Holy Scripture*, ed. P. E. Satterthwaite and D. F. Wright (Grand Rapids: Eerdmans, 1994), p. 82.

God's Faithfulness, Scripture, and the Jewish People

In examining the relationship between Paul's view of Scripture and his understanding of the faithfulness of God, the most likely places to begin are explicit instances in his writing where he connects the faithfulness of God with the Scriptures. In three passages in Romans, Paul particularly refers to the Scriptures and the faithfulness of God. From an examination of these texts in Romans, some conclusions can be drawn about Paul's perception of Scripture.

Romans 3:1-4

Romans 3:1-4 is the first passage that will be considered.[8] It is of particular importance in this discussion of Paul's perception of the faithfulness of God and Scripture since these verses contain a reference to both. Moreover, it is also an important part of the epistle to the Romans since many key ideas from the epistle are found within these verses and the four subsequent verses (Rom. 3:5-8).[9] Thus, it is a good place to begin considering Paul's view of Scripture and the faithfulness of God to his people. Romans 3:1-4 reads:

> Then what advantage has the Jew? Or what is the value of circumcision? Much, in every way. For in the first place the Jews were entrusted with the oracles of God. What if some were unfaithful? Will their faithlessness nullify the faithfulness of God? By no means! Although everyone is a liar, let God be proved true, as it is written, "So that you may be justified in your words, and prevail in your judging."[10]

This text indicates that the Scriptures are the benefit that has been given to the Jew. This Paul indicates in Romans 3:2 when he says that the Jews have been given the oracles of God *(ta logia tou theou)*. Although one

8. I am thankful to Dr. Bruce Winter for stressing the importance of this passage.

9. Note how W. S. Campbell sees Rom. 3:1-8 as the structural center of the epistle. W. S. Campbell, "Romans III as a Key to the Structure and Thought of the Letter," *Novum Testamentum* 23 (1981): 22-40. Note how the questions in Rom. 3:1-8 provide a link with Romans 6–7 and 9–11.

10. All Scripture citations within this essay are from the NRSV.

scholar believes that Paul is speaking particularly of the promises of God,[11] these oracles are best understood to be the Scriptures. Although Paul does not use the word *ho logos* in the singular or the plural on other occasions, the phrase *ta logia* should be considered to be the Scriptures in 3:2 since other texts from the Septuagint, the New Testament, and early Jewish literature use this word to refer to the Scriptures.[12] The surrounding context also affirms that Paul is speaking of the entire corpus of Scripture rather than a portion of it. Thus far in Romans Paul appears to be referring more broadly to the Scriptures and not focusing specifically on the promises (Rom. 1:2; cf. 2:12-29). It is only later in Romans that he appears to distinguish different portions within the corpus of Scripture (9:4-5). Thus for Paul in 3:2, the oracles of God, the Scriptures, are the gifts given to God's people.

Possessing these Scriptures is a great benefit. Certainly Paul states this fact plainly when he answers the question "What advantage has the Jew?" with the statement "Much in every way" (Rom. 3:1-2). This great benefit of being entrusted with the Scriptures is magnified further by the way Paul distinguishes this benefit from other possible ones.

From the broader context of Romans 3, being entrusted with the Scriptures is the sole benefit of being a Jew. Although it appears that Paul will delineate many advantages in being a Jew since he uses the phrase *prōton men* in 3:2,[13] he only mentions one advantage in 3:1-4, the possession of the Scriptures. This fact stresses the importance of the benefit since it is the only one that is presented in what is expected to be a lengthy list of

11. S. K. Williams, "The Righteousness of God in Romans," *Journal of Biblical Literature* 99 (1980): 267.

12. Cf. Deut. 33:9; Ps. 12:6 (LXX 11:7); 18:30 (LXX 17:31); 107:11 (LXX 106:11); 119:11 (LXX 118:11); 119:38 (LXX 118:38); 119:41 (LXX 118:41); 119:50 (LXX 118:50); 119:58 (LXX 118:58); 119:67 (LXX 118:67); 119:76 (LXX 118:76); 119:82 (LXX 118:82); 119:103 (LXX 118:103); 119:116 (LXX 118:116); 119:123 (LXX 118:123); 119:133 (LXX 118:133); 119:140 (LXX 118:140); 119:148 (LXX 118:148); 119:158 (LXX 118:158); 119:162 (LXX 118:162); 119:169 (LXX 118:169); 119:170 (LXX 118:170); 119:172 (LXX 118:172); 138:2 (LXX 137:2); 147:15 (LXX 147:4); Isa. 5:24; Acts 7:38; Heb. 5:12; 1 Pet. 4:11; Wis. 16:11. In Philo see *Praem.* 1; *Vit. Cont.* 25. In Josephus see *J.W.* 6.311. J. D. G. Dunn, *Romans 1–8,* Word Biblical Commentary 38A (Dallas: Word, 1988), p. 131. D. J. Moo, *The Epistle to the Romans,* New International Commentary on the New Testament (Grand Rapids and Cambridge: Eerdmans, 1996), p. 182; D. R. Hall, "Romans 3.1-8 Reconsidered," *New Testament Studies* 29 (1983): 185.

13. Moo, *Epistle to the Romans,* p. 182.

benefits. The next benefit that he lists for the Jews will be found later in Romans 9.

The great value of being entrusted with the Scriptures is magnified further by the context into which Paul states this blessing. The blessing of possessing the Scriptures is the sole benefit that is declared to be of advantage to the Jew following Paul's portrayal of the sinfulness of all of humankind. Thus far, in Romans 1:18–2:29 Paul has portrayed the condemnation of all people, both Gentile and Jew, before God due to their sinful nature. Gentiles are condemned since they have suppressed the truth of God as is seen in creation (1:18-19). Jews are likewise condemned when they perform the same acts as Gentiles (2:3-4). When Jews disobey the law that has been given to them, they dishonor God and are worthy of his punishment (2:17-21). When Paul chooses to distinguish the Jews from the rest of humankind and its sinful ways, however, the Scriptures alone appear to give the Jews unique status (3:1-4). Whether the Jews disobey the Scriptures or not, having the Scriptures is seen to be of great benefit. From the way Paul presents Romans 1–3, the great advantage for sinful humankind is the possession of the Scriptures.

It is this benefit that Paul will connect with the theme of the faithfulness of God in Romans 3:1-4. The theme is prominently displayed in these four verses and is connected to the Jewish blessing of possessing the Scriptures. This can be seen from the way Paul connects 3:2 with 3:3. Paul moves immediately and directly from the benefit of possessing the Scriptures to the discussion of God's faithfulness. Indeed, the idea of faithfulness can also be seen within 3:2-3 from the play on the concept of *pistis.* The verbs *pisteuō* and *apisteō* appear in these verses along with the nouns of *apistia* and *pistis.*[14] The repetition of this concept emphasizes the importance of the faithfulness of God in this passage.

Of course, this strong association between the faithfulness of God and the possession of the Scriptures is not new to Paul. The Jewish people also considered their custody of the Scriptures as an indication of God's blessing and faithfulness (cf. Deut. 4:8; Pss. 33:4; 147:19-20; Jer. 32:41; Lam. 3:23; Hos. 2:20; *Pss. Sol.* 8:28).[15] It is likely that Paul is continuing to affirm this connection that was made within Jewish thinking in Romans 3:1-4.

There are many reasons to believe that Paul would have continued to

14. Dunn, *Romans 1–8,* p. 131.

15. Moo, *Epistle to the Romans,* p. 184.

hold to such a Jewish understanding of the possession of the Scriptures and the faithfulness of God. From his own testimony in Philippians 3:4b-6, Paul clearly implies that his family upheld distinctive Jewish characteristics: circumcision on the eighth day; membership in the people of Israel, and of the tribe of Benjamin; and a Hebrew born of Hebrews (cf. 2 Cor. 11:22).[16] As a self-described "Hebrew of Hebrews" before his conversion (Phil. 3:5), Paul likely received exposure to Jewish teaching about the Scriptures at an early age. The normal, first-century, Jewish experience would have meant exposure to the Scriptures at home and in the synagogue (Josephus, *Ag. Ap.* 2.178, 204; Philo, *Leg.* 210; *m. 'Abot* 5:21). The goal of this instruction would have been to instill an accurate knowledge of the Scriptures (4 Macc. 18:10-19; Josephus, *Ag. Ap.* 2.175, 178).[17] There is no reason to expect that Paul's upbringing was any different than this.

Many other scholars studying Paul are also noticing the Jewish influence in his writing. His letters have a large amount of Scripture that witnesses to his gospel.[18] They also are similar to early Jewish doctrine and ethical instruction in many places.[19] Even when he explains or defends his calling, his Jewish heritage has been noted to exert an influence within his explanation.[20] It is, therefore, likely that Paul would have maintained many Jewish understandings about Scripture. This would have included a Jewish understanding about the connection between Scripture and the faithfulness of God.

God's faithfulness to his people is seen in a second way in Romans 3:1-4.

16. J. B. Lightfoot, *St. Paul's Epistle to the Philippians,* The Epistles of St. Paul 3.1 (London: Macmillan, 1868), p. 144.

17. Rosner, *Paul, Scripture, and Ethics,* p. 12.

18. D. A. Koch, *Die Schrift als Zeuge des Evangeliums: Untersuchungen zur Verwendung und zum Verständnis der Schrift bei Paulus,* Beiträge zur historischen Theologie 69 (Tübingen: J. C. B. Mohr [Paul Siebeck], 1986), pp. 322-53.

19. For example, M. N. A. Bockmuehl, *Revelation and Mystery in Ancient Judaism and Pauline Christianity,* Wissenschaftliche Untersuchungen zum Neuen Testament 2.36 (Tübingen: J. C. B. Mohr [Paul Siebeck], 1990), pp. 227-30; P. J. Tomson, *Paul and the Jewish Law: Halakha in the Letters of the Apostle to the Gentiles,* Compendia rerum iudaicarum ad novum testamentum 3.1 (Assen: Van Gorcum, 1990), pp. 264-69; Rosner, *Paul, Scripture, and Ethics,* pp. 177-80.

20. Cf. 2 Cor. 11:22–12:13; Gal. 1–2; Phil. 3:5. K. W. Niebuhr, *Heidenapostel aus Israel: Die jüdische Identität des Paulus nach ihrer Darstellung in seinen Briefen,* Wissenschaftliche Untersuchungen zum Neuen Testament 62 (Tübingen: J. C. B. Mohr [Paul Siebeck], 1992), pp. 179-84.

God's great faith*ful*ness in entrusting his people with the Scriptures is greater than the faith*less*ness of the people who are entrusted with those Scriptures. He states this plainly in 3:3-4 in his response to his question "Will their faithlessness nullify the faithfulness of God?" Paul answers "no" emphatically by employing the phrase *mē genoito* (3:4). This phrase indicates in strong terms that God will be faithful despite the faithlessness of his people.[21]

In 3:1-4, Paul also indicates God's faithfulness to the Jews in another way. Not only does Paul state that God is faithful to Israel by entrusting them with the Scriptures, but he also indicates God's faithfulness to the Jewish nation through his use of Scripture in 3:1-4. The scriptural texts that Paul uses are worth further investigation to see how they may add understanding to the relationship between the faithfulness of God and Scripture.

Paul uses two references from the Psalms within Romans 3:1-4 that draw further attention to his perception that the Scriptures are a faithful and reliable record of God's ways with his people. Both texts from the Psalms help to draw attention to the faithfulness of God to his people in the statement "although everyone is a liar, let God be proved true." The first part of this phrase is either a citation from or an allusion to Psalm 116:2 (LXX 115:2). This can be seen from the strong resemblance between the phrase *(pas anthrōpos)* in the Psalms and the phrase "everyone is a liar" *(pseustēs)* in Romans 3:4b. Since this phrase *(pas de anthrōpos pseustēs)* is related to the Psalms and forms part of the assertion "Although everyone is a liar, let God be proved true," and since the entire assertion is related to the citation of Psalm 51:4 [LXX 50:6] in Romans 3:4b, the other portion of the phrase "let God be proved true" *(genesthō de ho theos alēthēs)* is also related to the Psalms.

When God's truthfulness *(alētheia)* is considered in relation to the Psalms, it emphasizes the faithfulness of God. God's truthfulness *(alētheia)* is regularly connected with God's faithfulness within the Septuagint version of the Psalms. This is seen by the predominant translation for the Hebrew word "truth" *('emet)* in the Septuagint portion of the Psalms by the Greek word *alētheia,* which means faithfulness.[22] This suggests that God's

21. For other Pauline uses of *mē genoito* see Rom. 3:6, 31; 6:2, 15; 7:7, 13; 9:14; 11:1, 11; 1 Cor. 6:15; Gal. 2:17; 3:21; 6:14.

22. For example, Ps. 36:5 (LXX 35:6); 40:10 (LXX 39:11); 88:11 (LXX 87:12); 89:1, 2, 5, 8, 14, 24, 33, 49 (LXX 88:2, 3, 6, 9, 25, 34, 50); 92:2 (LXX 91:3); 96:13 (LXX 95:13); 98:3 (LXX 97:3); 100:5 (LXX 99:5); 119:30, 75, 86, 90, 138 (LXX 118:30, 75, 86, 90, 138); 143:1 (LXX 142:1). Ps. 33:4 (LXX 32:4) is the exception. Dunn, *Romans 1–8,* p. 133.

truthfulness is connected with his faithfulness. Whether Paul's readers would have grasped this connection between truth and faithfulness as portrayed in the Psalms or not, it appears that Paul is drawing a further connection between God's truthfulness presented in the Scriptures and God's faithfulness. From Paul's perspective God's truthfulness and faithfulness in entrusting the Jewish people with the Scriptures is not undermined by the faithlessness of those who possess them.

Finally, the strong connection in Paul's mind between the faithfulness of God and the Scriptures that he has given to his people can be seen in Paul's choice of the citation of Psalm 51:4 (LXX 50:6) in Romans 3:4. God's faithfulness is highlighted by the particular scriptural text that Paul chooses. He uses a citation from Scripture to assert that God is reliable and true despite the unreliability of humankind.

Psalm 51:4 (LXX 50:6) is found within Psalm 51 (LXX 50), which is a penitential psalm involving the confession of sin and a plea for God's mercy. The superscription of this psalm places it within the familiar context of 2 Samuel 11 and 12 when Nathan the prophet confronted King David concerning David's sin with Bathsheba. Psalm 51 (LXX 50) clearly speaks of human guilt and failing. Verses 1-4 (LXX vv. 3-6) read:

> [To the leader. A Psalm of David, when the prophet Nathan came to him, after he had gone in to Bathsheba.] Have mercy on me, O God, according to your steadfast love; according to your abundant mercy blot out my transgressions. Wash me thoroughly from my iniquity, and cleanse me from my sin. For I know my transgressions, and my sin is ever before me. Against you, you alone, have I sinned, and done what is evil in your sight, so that you are justified in your sentence and blameless when you pass judgment.

While there are many places within Psalm 51 (LXX 50) and throughout the tradition in 2 Samuel 11–12 that concern confession of sin, Paul cites Psalm 51:4 (LXX 50:6), the one text within this tradition that concerns God's blamelessness in his judging. Anyone who was familiar with the psalm or its surrounding tradition from 2 Samuel 11–12, however, would have clearly heard the echoes of David's sin, his confession to God, and his plea for mercy along with Paul's citation.[23] By isolating this one

23. Hays, *Echoes of Scripture,* p. 49.

scriptural citation that focuses on God's faithfulness in adhering to his ways, Paul emphasizes the faithfulness of God in the midst of human sin.[24] From this Scripture context, God is faithful to judge his servants when they sin because of his word.[25] By using this particular verse from within Psalm 51 (LXX 50) and the tradition of confession, Paul emphasizes again the faithfulness of God (this time to judge) despite the sinfulness of humankind who knew his ways and possessed the Scriptures.

Thus, from Romans 3:1-4, Paul sees the faithfulness of God to his people as related to the Scriptures in two ways. First, Paul considers God to be faithful to his people by entrusting them with the Scriptures. As E. Käsemann has stated of 3:2b-3, "In good OT fashion God's truth is his reliability. . . ."[26] Since the Jews possessed the Scriptures, Paul declares that these witness to God's faithfulness to his people. Second, Paul's view that God's faithfulness and reliability are related to the Scriptures is underscored by the scriptural texts that he chooses to support his argument. These texts indicate that God is faithful to his people even despite human faithlessness.

Romans 9:6-29

Paul's belief that God's faithfulness is related to the Scriptures can be seen in other passages within Romans. As in Romans 3:1-4, a connection between the faithfulness of God and the Scriptures is displayed in 9:6-29, a passage where Paul explains the history of Israel. He introduces this history with the statement in 9:6: "It is not as though the word of God had failed." The theme of God's faithfulness and the Scriptures resurfaces in 9:14, which reads: "What then are we to say? Is there injustice on God's part? By no means." This statement is made in relation to the Scriptures since Paul cites Exodus 33:19 in Romans 9:15. Thus, it is worth examining

24. Moo, *Epistle to the Romans,* pp. 179-80; Hall, "Romans 3.1-8 Reconsidered," pp. 186-88.

25. Hall, "Romans 3.1-8 Reconsidered," p. 188. See other places in the Old Testament where this idea was upheld: Neh. 9:32-33; Lam. 1:18. Cf. 2 Chron. 12:6; Ezra 9:15; Dan. 9:14; *Pss. Sol.* 2:15.

26. E. Käsemann, *Commentary on Romans,* trans. G. W. Bromiley (Grand Rapids: Eerdmans, 1980), p. 79.

Paul's understanding of the faithfulness of God and its relation to the Scriptures in Romans 9:6-29 in some detail.[27]

In 9:6-29 Paul indicates that God's faithfulness to his people can be seen from his explanation of the Jewish nation's history in relation to the Scriptures that God gave them. Paul declares that the word of God *(ho logos tou theou)* has not failed (9:6).[28] While one scholar suggests that this phrase indicates Paul's gospel,[29] this word of God refers to the word of God as the Jews would have understood it, the Scriptures. This can be seen from Paul's sequence of thought in 9:4-5, in which he referred to the law and the covenants that are found within the Scriptures. Moreover, Paul primarily refers to the Scriptures throughout the remainder of Romans 9 rather than to his gospel.[30] In fact, within chapter 9 he does not appear to refer to his gospel apart from the Scriptures. Thus, despite the great sorrow and agony that he has for many of his own Jewish people who have not trusted the Scriptures (9:1-5), Paul believes that the Scriptures have not failed his fellow Jews (9:6). Paul finds God's word to be faithful.

Paul then puts God's faithfulness, as it is found in the word of God, on display in the remainder of Romans 9.[31] This is seen by the large number of Scripture citations that fill his argument. This fact indicates God's faith-

27. Note the connection between Rom. 3:3 and 9:6. Dunn, *Romans 1–8,* p. lxiii.

28. Although the verb *ekpiptō* can have the meaning "fall" or "fall away from" (in a physical sense: Acts 12:7; 27:17, 26, 29; Jas. 1:11; 1 Pet. 1:24), it can also have the meaning of become weakened (Sir. 34:7; 1 Cor. 13:8 [v. 1]). Moo, *Epistle to the Romans,* p. 572.

29. E. Güttgemanns, "Heilsgeschichte bei Paulus oder Dynamik des Evangeliums? Zur structurellen Relevanz von Röm 9-11 für die Theologie des Römerbriefs," in *Studia Linguistica Neotestamentica,* Beiträge zur evangelischen Theologie 60 (Munich: Kaiser, 1971), pp. 40-41.

30. Moo, *Epistle to the Romans,* pp. 572-73. See also Num. 23:19; Ps. 119:89; Isa. 31:2; 55:10-11. J. D. G. Dunn, *Romans 9–16,* Word Biblical Commentary 38B (Dallas: Word, 1988), p. 539.

31. Note the number of scholars who see the point that Paul makes in Rom. 9:6 extending through portions of Romans 9: J. W. Aageson, "Scripture and Structure in the Development of the Argument in Romans 9–11," *Catholic Biblical Quarterly* 48 (1986): 268; W. S. Campbell, "The Freedom and Faithfulness of God in Relation to Israel," *Journal for the Study of the New Testament* 13 (1981): 28; Hays, *Echoes of Scripture,* p. 64. Dunn sees the point of Rom. 9:6 extending through Romans 11 (*Romans 9–16,* p. 539). While not commenting specifically on Scripture, note that J. C. Beker sees the faithfulness of God to the Jewish nation as the priority within Romans (J. C. Beker, "The Faithfulness of God and the Priority of Israel in Paul's Letter to the Romans," in *Christians among Jews and Gentiles,* ed. G. W. E. Nickelsburg, with G. W. MacRae [Philadelphia: Fortress, 1986], pp. 10-16).

ful dealings with his people. His argument shows that he believes that God's dealing with Israel and the nations in the present age is fully consistent with God's prophetic promises found in Scripture.

To prove that the word of God has not failed, Paul supports his argument with stories from Scripture that portray the selective quality of God's grace. He begins by citing Genesis 21:12 in Romans 9:7b: "It is through Isaac that descendants shall be named for you." This supports the claim that not all of Abraham's seed are true descendants (Rom. 9:7a).[32] Paul then continues to explain this rationale of the promise made to Abraham by supporting his next statement in 9:8 with a loose quotation of Genesis 18:10, 14. These texts, then, are the first of an intertextual web in Romans 9:6-29 that explains God's ways from the Scriptures.[33]

Throughout the remainder of Romans 9:6-29, Paul uses Scripture texts to support his argument on the election and choosing by God. His illustrations are drawn from throughout the Scriptures. He uses Jacob and Esau as examples of God's election, citing Genesis 25:23 and Malachi 1:2-3 in Romans 9:12-13. He then uses Moses and Pharaoh as examples of God's selectivity, citing Exodus 33:19 and 9:16 in Romans 9:15 and 9:17, respectively. He supports the assertion that God has the right to do what he pleases, citing Isaiah 29:16 in Romans 9:20 and Jeremiah 18:3-6 in Romans 9:21.[34]

Paul then explains his view of the current status of the people of God and of Israel from the Scriptures. He cites Hosea 2:23 and 1:10b in Romans 9:25-26 to support the fact that God has called people not only from the Jews but also from the Gentiles. Romans 9:25-26 states,

> As indeed he says in Hosea, "Those who were not my people I will call 'my people,' and her who was not beloved I will call 'beloved.'" And "in

32. Note that the NRSV does not clearly distinguish this translation. It renders Rom. 9:7a as "not all of Abraham's children are his true descendants." Paul's point, however, is that Abraham has many children *(tekna)* but not many of them belong to his seed *(sperma).*

33. Hays, *Echoes of Scripture,* p. 65. See W. R. Stegner and E. E. Ellis, who argue that Rom. 9:6-29 is a midrash (W. R. Stegner, "Romans 9:6-29 — A Midrash," *Journal for the Study of the New Testament* 22 [1984]: 37-52; E. E. Ellis, *Prophecy and Hermeneutic in Early Christianity: New Testament Essays,* Wissenschaftliche Untersuchungen zum Neuen Testament 18 [Tübingen: J. C. B. Mohr (Paul Siebeck), 1978], p. 219). See also J. W. Aageson, "Scripture and Structure," pp. 268-73.

34. Besides Jer. 18:1-6 see the theme of the potter and the clay in other places in Scripture, such as Isa. 41:25; 45:9; 64:8; Sir. 33:10-13. Hays, *Echoes of Scripture,* pp. 65, 206.

the very place where it was said to them, 'You are not my people,' there they shall be called children of the living God."

Thus, Paul finds proof of the Gentiles' incorporation into the people of God within the canon of Scripture, just as he found proof of the election of God's people from within Israel in Scripture.

He finds the predictions of Israel's remnant status in the Scriptures, too. Without stating Israel's condition himself, he boldly declares that Israel's remnant status is foretold in the texts of Isaiah 10:22-23 (Rom. 9:27-28) and Isaiah 1:9 (Rom. 9:29). From Paul's perspective Isaiah 10:22-23 cries out *(krazei)* concerning Israel's remnant status and predicts *(proeirēken)* Israel's future remnant status.[35]

These references to the remnant close the intertextual web that started in Romans 9:7 with God's election and the promised seed. From all of these scriptural texts that have formed the structure of Paul's argument in Romans 9:6-29, it can be concluded that Paul explains the current status of the Jewish people from the Scriptures. The selective operation of God's will is a truth deeply imbedded in Israel's canonical texts.[36] The inclusion of the Gentiles is found in Scripture, and the remnant status of Israel is also found there. Thus, it can be concluded from Paul's presentation in Romans 9:6-29 that he believes that the Scriptures have not failed. The Scriptures, according to Paul, have been a faithful representation of God's will and his ways as seen in his dealings with his people.

Romans 11

In Romans 11 Paul brings to a conclusion his discussion of the faithfulness of God and his people. In Romans 11:1 Paul reopens the issue of the faithfulness of God in relation to his people by asking: "I ask, then, has God rejected his people?" What is striking for our purposes is that within the remainder of Romans 11 Paul once again answers the question of God's faithfulness to his people by appealing directly and indirectly to the Scriptures.

Paul answers his rhetorical question in Romans 11:1 by responding

35. Dunn, *Romans 9–16,* p. 572.
36. Hays, *Echoes of Scripture,* p. 68.

with scriptural texts and language. In Romans 11:2 he states, "God has not rejected his people whom he foreknew." This phrase echoes 1 Samuel 12:22 and Psalm 94:14 (LXX 93:14) since Paul uses a significant number of vocabulary words from those texts *(ouk, apotheomai, laos, autos)*. There is also a thematic agreement between Romans 11:2 and these texts.[37] The change in verb tense from the future (*apōsetai* in 1 Sam. 12:22 and Ps. 94:14) to the aorist (*apōsato* in Rom. 11:2) indicates Paul's confidence that God has not abandoned his people despite their present disobedience (Rom. 10:21).[38]

What follows in support of Romans 11:2 is more references to the Scriptures substantiating Paul's belief that God is faithful. He begins in Romans 11:2b by questioning whether his readers are familiar with the Scriptures, stating, "Do you not know what the scripture says of Elijah, how he pleads with God against Israel?" Paul then continues to cite particular portions of Scripture in his argument. In Romans 11:3-4 Paul cites portions of the Elijah narratives (1 Kings 19:10, 14, 18) to support God's faithfulness and justify the current situation of the remnant of Israel and the idea of election. God was faithful to Israel in her apparent hopeless state by preserving a remnant at the time of Ahab and Jezebel. By citing such a text now, Paul indicates that God will be faithful in the midst of the nation's present disobedience (Rom. 9:5). As D. J. Moo rightly states, "No more than the defection of Israelites to the worship of Baal in Elijah's time could the widespread Jewish indifference to the fulfillment of God's promises in Paul's day invalidate God's faithfulness to Israel and thereby cause his word to 'fall.'"[39]

Even the current manner in which God has gone about disciplining the Jewish nation is found faithfully recorded in the Scriptures. This is exhibited in Romans 11:7-10:

> What then? Israel failed to obtain what it was seeking. The elect obtained it, but the rest were hardened, as it is written, "God gave them a sluggish spirit, eyes that would not see and ears that would not hear, down to this very day." And David says, "Let their table become a snare and a trap, a stumbling block and a retribution for them; let their eyes be darkened so that they cannot see, and keep their backs forever bent."

37. Hays, *Echoes of Scripture*, pp. 69-70.
38. Dunn, *Romans 9–16*, p. 636.
39. Moo, *Epistle to the Romans*, p. 677.

Paul cites the three divisions of the Hebrew canon: the Law (Deut. 29:4), the Prophets (Isa. 29:10), and the "Writings" (Ps. 69:22-23). By appealing to all three sections of Scripture, Paul indicates in strong terms that God's hardening of Israel was faithfully recorded and is now occurring.

Thus, as in other portions of Romans (9:6-29), Paul exhibits the faithfulness of God in connection with the Scriptures and perceives that God's ways of election and the disobedience of Israel are faithfully recorded within the Scriptures. Thus, according to Paul, despite God's hardening of Israel he is faithful to his elect and will not forsake his people.

From these accounts within portions of Romans it is fair to assume that Paul considered the Scriptures and the faithfulness of God to the Jewish nation to be connected. Paul believes God faithfully entrusts Israel with the Scriptures. He believes God's faithfulness in entrusting Israel with the Scriptures is not undermined by their faithlessness. Rather, Paul finds God's faithfulness to Israel greater than humankind's faithlessness. He even finds God's election, preservation, and hardening of Israel faithfully recorded within the Scriptures.

God's Faithfulness, Scripture, and Paul's Readers

Paul's perception of the Scriptures and the faithfulness of God is not only seen in relation to the Jewish people. His perception of the Scriptures can be found in other places in his writings. While a large majority of the following passages that will be considered do not explicitly state the relationship between the faithfulness of God and the Scriptures as the texts just considered from Romans, there are implications that can be drawn from the way that Paul presents Scripture or uses Scripture. The following sections will consider some of the ways and contexts in which Paul presents Scripture texts to his readers, and then will draw some conclusions about Paul's view of Scripture and the faithfulness of God.

Presentation of Scripture Citations

Paul introduces Scripture in many ways within his writings. Sometimes he uses introductory formulae such as *kathōs gegraptai* and *gegraptai gar.* At other times he simply uses a conjunction like *gar* or *de,* or no introductory formula at all. While many facets of Paul's introduction of Scripture are left to be explored, at times the way in which Paul introduces scriptural citations indicates his understanding of Scripture.[40]

One introductory formula that likely reveals Paul's understanding of Scripture is his use of the present tense of the verb *legō* when introducing Scripture in his letters. He uses this verb to introduce what Scripture says (Rom. 9:17; 10:11; 11:3; cf. 1 Tim. 5:18), what David says (Rom. 4:7-8; 11:9-10), what Moses says (Rom. 10:19), what Isaiah says (Rom. 10:16; Rom. 15:12), and what God says (Rom. 10:1; 2 Cor. 6:2). Romans 4:3 is particularly noteworthy in that Genesis 15:6 is introduced by the question, "What does the scripture say?" From these introductions, it can be concluded that Paul believes that what was written in Scripture in the past still speaks to his audience.

That Paul sees Scripture as still faithfully speaking to his readers can also be seen by his addition of the phrase *legei kyrios* for no apparent reason into some of his citations. Paul uses this phrase in three places (Rom 12:9, citing Deut. 32:35; 1 Cor. 14:21, citing Isa. 28:11; and 2 Cor. 6:17, citing Isa. 52:11).[41] While there is debate whether this phrase was due to early Christian prophets[42] or whether it reflects that the speaker is God,[43] the phrase does indicate Paul's perception of these texts. Paul believes that what the prophets spoke long ago is what God speaks today. This is especially true of Isaiah 28:11 in 1 Corinthians 14:21, which takes the text from the prophet Isaiah as a statement of God. 1 Cor. 14:21 reads, "In the law it is written, 'By people of strange tongues and by the lips of foreigners I will speak to this people; yet even then they will not listen to me,' says the Lord *(legei kyrios)*."

Thus, from the ways in which Paul presents scriptural texts, two conclusions can be drawn. First, Paul considers what Scripture said in the past to be still relevant. Second, from Paul's perspective Scripture of old is still faithfully representing God's will and his ways to his readers.

40. Much of this section is derived from Rosner, "Written for Us," pp. 88-90. His ideas will be developed further in light of the issue in this essay, the faithfulness of God.

41. In two other places (Rom. 14:11 and 2 Cor. 6:18), the same addition appears as "part of a brief excerpt from a specific portion of the LXX" (Stanley, *Paul and the Language of Scripture,* p. 173).

42. E. E. Ellis, *Paul's Use of the Old Testament* (Edinburgh: Oliver and Boyd, 1957; reprinted Grand Rapids: Baker, 1981), pp. 107-12.

43. D. Aune, *Prophecy in Early Christianity and the Ancient Mediterranean World* (Grand Rapids: Eerdmans, 1983), pp. 339-46.

Application in Polemical Situations

Not only does the way in which Paul introduces some scriptural texts betray his belief in the faithfulness of God, but the way in which he applies Scripture to his readers in polemical situations also indicates that he sees Scripture to be faithfully recounting God's ways to his readers. While every instance can not be considered in depth, this section will examine contentious situations in Galatia and in Corinth and consider the general characteristics of Paul's use of Scripture in these situations.

Paul uses Scripture to argue with opponents from very different backgrounds. In Galatians he argues with people who come from a Jewish background. In the main body of his argument Paul appeals to Scripture in Galatians 3:6-14 to correct the false understanding of his Jewish opponents with respect to Abraham and his descendants. He cites an overwhelming number of texts to correct their view regarding membership in God's family (cf. Gen. 15:6 in Gal. 3:6; Gen. 12:3; 18:18 in Gal. 3:8; Hab. 2:4 in Gal. 3:11; Lev. 18:5 in Gal. 3:12; Deut. 27:26 in Gal. 3:13). He refers to the promise that God gave Abraham from Genesis 13:15; 17:8; and 24:7 in Galatians 3:16. He appeals to a scriptural allegory at the end of his main argument in Galatians 4:21-31 to validate the main portion of his argument in Galatians 3–4. He cites Isaiah 54:1 in Galatians 4:27 and Genesis 21:10 in Galatians 4:30. Furthermore, a large number of scriptural echoes are found within the body of Galatians. Indeed, in a recent commentary on Galatians, Ben Witherington commented on the amount of Scripture found within Galatians: "If we were to take into account not only the quotations of Scripture by Paul in Galatians, but also the echoes of Scripture, we would discover what a very large role Scripture actually plays, often beneath the surface in all of Paul's arguments."[44] Thus, in the most polemical letter of Paul's writing, where he even skips the customary thanksgiving portion of the letter to leap into his argument, Paul uses a great deal of Scripture in his argument. In confronting his opponents who have been influenced by Jewish thinking, Paul uses the Scriptures and scripturally based argumentation to a large extent to correct their ways.

It is also intriguing to note how Paul uses Scripture in an argument with those who come from an entirely different background and have en-

44. B. Witherington, *Grace in Galatia: A Commentary on St. Paul's Letter to the Galatians* (Grand Rapids: Eerdmans, 1998), p. 223.

tirely different problems. Paul uses Scripture citations and scripturally based argumentation in his confrontation with the Corinthians, those who have been substantially influenced by a Greco-Roman worldview.[45] In a context where there are misunderstandings about wisdom, boasting, and workers, Paul uses a large amount of Scripture to bolster his argument. He cites Isaiah 29:14; Job 5:13; and Psalm 94:11 (LXX 93:11) in 1 Corinthians 1:19 and 3:19-20 to refute Corinthian wisdom. He cites Jeremiah 9:24 (LXX 9:23) in 1 Corinthians 1:31 in his argument against human boasting. All of these citations in 1 Corinthians 1–3 are also used in the context of refuting the Corinthian trust in human leaders (1 Cor. 1:12; 3:21-23).

His use of Scripture as a corrective tool within 1 Corinthians continues into the ethical sections of the letter. For example, he cites Deuteronomy 17:7 in 1 Corinthians 5:13 in his exhortation to exclude the man found in an incestuous relationship. He also cites Genesis 2:24 in 1 Corinthians 6:16 in his discussion of sexual immorality. One scholar has noted that many of Paul's exhortations regarding civil litigation, sexual immorality, divorce, and remarriage in 1 Corinthians 5–7 can be "reliably traced back into the Scriptures."[46] Later on in 1 Corinthians 10:1-11, Paul also uses portions of the Exodus in his argumentation. Following his brief retelling of some of these events, he states in 1 Corinthians 10:6: "Now these things occurred as examples for us, so that we might not desire evil as they did." In 1 Corinthians 10:11 he reinforces this conclusion by stating that the Scriptures were "written down to instruct us."[47] In other words, from

45. See the writings of A. D. Clarke, *Secular and Christian Leadership in Corinth: A Socio-Historical and Exegetical Study of I Corinthians 1–6,* Arbeiten zur Geschichte des antiken Judentums und des Urchristentums 18 (Leiden: Brill, 1993); D. Litfin, *St. Paul's Theology of Proclamation: 1 Corinthians 1–4 and Greco-Roman Rhetoric,* Society for New Testament Studies Monograph Series 79 (Cambridge: Cambridge University Press, 1994); B. W. Winter, *Philo and Paul among the Sophists: A Hellenistic-Jewish and a Christian Response,* Society for New Testament Studies Monograph Series 96 (Cambridge: Cambridge University Press, 1996); B. Witherington, *Conflict and Community in Corinth: A Socio-Rhetorical Commentary on I and II Corinthians* (Grand Rapids: Eerdmans, 1995).

46. Rosner, *Paul, Scripture, and Ethics,* p. 177. Note also that Tomson sees Jewish teaching in 1 Cor. 8–10 (Tomson, *Paul and the Jewish Law*).

47. Note what G. Fee says with regard to this text in Paul's writing: "In these statements, one can sense Paul's view of Scripture that both the historical and the inscripturated narrative are not simply history or isolated texts in Scripture; rather behind all these things lies the eternal purposes of the living God . . ." (G. Fee, *The First Epistle to the Corinthians,* New International Commentary on the New Testament [Grand Rapids: Eerdmans, 1987], p. 458).

Paul's perspective the events of the Exodus were written for the ethical instruction of the Corinthians, so that they would keep away from idolatry, immorality, and grumbling. Thus, in his confrontation with opponents from a Gentile background, Paul also uses many Scripture citations, echoes, and stories as a corrective measure.

So, what difference does this make for the connection between the faithfulness of God and Scripture in Paul's mind? While Paul does not use Scripture to refute every situation in these letters, he at least views Scripture as a faithful representation of God's will and his ways to rebuke his opponents. This conclusion is strengthened further by the fact that Paul uses scripture texts and themes to confront audiences from entirely different backgrounds and to deal with entirely different issues.

Application to His Calling and Ministry

Perhaps the greatest indication that Paul believes that the Scriptures are a faithful representation of God's will and his ways can be seen in the way that he applies the Scriptures to himself, as an evaluation of his calling and his ministry. After all, it is one thing to apply Scripture to others and another thing to apply it to oneself. Paul repeatedly applies Scripture texts to his own calling and ministry in a number of his writings.

Paul applies Scripture to his own ministry when he writes in 1 Cor. 4:6: "I have applied all this to Apollos and myself for your benefit, brothers and sisters, so that you may learn through us the meaning of the saying, 'Nothing beyond what is written,' so that none of you will be puffed up in favor of one against another." While this phrase "Nothing beyond what is written" is a difficult one, it seems most natural to consider it, as Morna D. Hooker did, to refer to Scripture. In particular she believes that the phrase refers to the citations of Isaiah 29:14 in 1 Corinthians 1:19; Jeremiah 9:23-24 in 1 Corinthians 1:30-31; Job 5:13 in 1 Corinthians 3:19; and Psalm 94:11 in 1 Corinthians 3:20.[48] The implication is that Paul views his own conduct in the ministry to be in agreement with these Scriptures.

Later on, in 1 Corinthians 9:9-10, Paul applies Scripture to his own ministry when he writes,

48. M. D. Hooker, "'Beyond the Things Which Are Written': An Examination of I Cor. IV.6," *New Testament Studies* 10 (1963): 127-32.

> For it is written in the law of Moses, "You shall not muzzle an ox while it is treading out the grain." Is it for oxen that God is concerned? Or does he not speak entirely *(pantōs)* for our sake? It was indeed written for our sake, for whoever plows should plow in hope and whoever threshes should thresh in hope of a share in the crop.

Although there are many controversies in the interpretation of this section, it is plain that Paul applies an obscure text in the Torah (Deut. 25:4) to his work in the Corinthian situation. Even this obscure text still speaks by all means *(pantōs)*. Moreover, it appears that Paul seems to elevate the importance of this text in supporting his argument, using the phrase *pantōs ē kai* in 1 Corinthians 9:8 to stress the importance of the argument from Scripture over the argument from common experience (1 Cor. 9:7), justice (1 Cor. 9:12-13), temple practice (1 Cor. 9:13), and the Lord's command (1 Cor. 9:14).[49] From the appeal to Scripture in these two places in 1 Corinthians, it can be said that Paul considers Scripture to be a faithful rule for the evaluation and conduct of his ministry.

While Paul cites Scripture in the two previous passages in 1 Corinthians 4:6 and 9:9-10, scholars have also noted that Paul uses Scripture in less explicit ways to view his calling and ministry. There are many other sections of Paul's writing where scholars find that Paul has applied scriptural ideas to his calling and ministry. For example, in 1 Corinthians 9:15-18 K. O. Sandnes has noticed that Paul applies the ideas of preaching under compulsion (Jer. 4:19; 20:7-9; Amos 3:7-8), as well as the self-directed woe of the prophets (Isa. 6:5; Jer. 15:10; 45:3) to his ministry. Sandnes also sees Paul portraying an understanding of his mediatory message as prophetic in 2 Corinthians 4:6.[50] In Galatians 1:6-10, R. E. Ciampa has noticed that Paul represents his current role to the Galatians as akin to Moses' prophetic ministry (Exod. 32:8; Deut. 9:12, 16).[51] Some scholars have noticed that the reorientation of Paul's life and his servant prophetic calling strongly suggest a prophetic understanding in relation to the Scriptures

49. Rosner, *Paul, Scripture, and Ethics,* p. 192.

50. K. O. Sandnes, *Paul — One of the Prophets? A Contribution to the Apostle's Self-Understanding,* Wissenschaftliche Untersuchungen zum Neuen Testament 2.43 (Tübingen: J. C. B. Mohr, 1991), pp. 117-45, 154-71.

51. R. E. Ciampa, "What Does the Scripture Say? An Analysis of the Presence and Function of Scripture in Gal. 1–2," Ph.D. diss., Aberdeen University, 1996, pp. 58-67. Cf. Deut. 13:1-2. Sandnes, *Paul — One of the Prophets?* pp. 72-73.

(Gal. 1:15-16).[52] S. J. Hafemann has noted that Paul employs in 2 Cor. 2:16 *hikanos* terminology from Exodus 4:10 reminiscent of Moses' prophetic model.[53] While there is more evidence to be gathered on this front, it appears that scriptural texts form a backdrop for Paul's calling and ministry.

So, what difference does this make in the connection between the faithfulness of God and Scripture in Paul's mind? From the number of texts that Paul uses in reference to himself and his ministry, it can be inferred that he considered Scripture as a faithful guide for his own calling and ministry.

Application to the Future

One final area of Paul's writing that can be considered here is the amount of Scripture that is found in Paul's explanation of the future. While Paul employs Scripture and scriptural themes in other portions of his gospel teaching,[54] he clearly illustrates his understanding of the faithfulness of Scripture when he explains the future.

When Paul introduces teaching about the future resurrection in 1 Corinthians 15, he refers to a number of Scripture citations to lead the way,[55] using Scripture to support or convey his argument. For example, in 1 Corinthians 15:25-27 the subjection of evil powers is supported by Paul's ref-

52. B. Lindars, *New Testament Apologetic: The Doctrinal Significance of the Old Testament Quotations* (London: SCM, 1961), p. 223; Sandnes, *Paul — One of the Prophets?* pp. 64-65; Ciampa, "What Does the Scripture Say?" pp. 91-102; S. Kim, *The Origin of Paul's Gospel*, Wissenschaftliche Untersuchungen zum Neuen Testament 2.4 (Tübingen: J. C. B. Mohr [Paul Siebeck], 1984), pp. 91-96.

53. Hafemann, *Suffering and the Spirit*, pp. 98-101, 220.

54. For example, U. Mell, who considers the importance of the new creation theme from Isaiah in Gal. 6:15 and 2 Cor. 5:21 (U. Mell, *Neue Schöpfung: Eine traditionsgeschichtliche und exegetische Studie zu einem soteriologischen Grundsatz paulinischer Theologie*, Beihefte zur Zeitschrift für die neutestamentliche Wissenschaft 56 (Berlin: Walter de Gruyter, 1989). See also James M. Scott, who sees the Old Testament background centered upon 2 Sam. 7:14 as the key for understanding Paul's idea of "adoption as sons" (James M. Scott, *Adoption as Sons of God: An Exegetical Investigation into the Background of ΥΙΟΘΕΣΙΑ in the Pauline Corpus*, Wissenschaftliche Untersuchungen zum Neuen Testament 2.48 [Tübingen: J. C. B. Mohr (Paul Siebeck), 1992]).

55. A. Robertson and A. Plummer, *A Critical and Exegetical Commentary on the First Epistle of St. Paul to the Corinthians*, International Critical Commentary (Edinburgh: T. & T. Clark, 1911), p. 376.

erence to Psalm 8:7 and 110:1.[56] In 1 Corinthians 15:33 he cites Isaiah 22:13 to illustrate the hopelessness of God's people if there is no resurrection. In 1 Corinthians 15:45 Paul appeals to Genesis 2:7 to aid in his explanation of the new body that believers will receive.

What is most striking in 1 Corinthians 15, however, is the way Paul explains the mystery of being changed at the last trumpet. While Paul uses mystery language in a variety of portions of his letters, this is one of only two occasions where Paul uses the term "mystery" to disclose new teaching to his readers.[57] In 1 Corinthians 15:51-55 Paul communicates to his readers new teaching regarding their future at the resurrection of the dead. He states,

> Listen, I will tell you a mystery! We will not all die, but we will all be changed, in a moment, in the twinkling of an eye, at the last trumpet. For the trumpet will sound, and the dead will be raised imperishable, and we will be changed. For this perishable body must put on imperishability, and this mortal body must put on immortality. When this perishable body puts on imperishability, and this mortal body puts on immortality, then the saying that is written will be fulfilled: "Death has been swallowed up in victory." "Where, O death, is your victory? Where, O death, is your sting?"

Paul introduces this new teaching by relating it to the Scriptures. He cites Isaiah 25:8 and Hosea 13:14 in 1 Corinthians 15:54-55. This new disclosure about the future of a believer has thus been couched in scriptural reasoning.[58]

So what difference does this make concerning Paul's perception of God's faithfulness in relation to the Scriptures? From his use of Scripture in his discussion of the future in 1 Corinthians 15, he indicates that Scripture has been his faithful guide to the new teaching regarding the future.

56. T. Moritz notes the similar tradition of Ps. 8:7 and 110:1 in Eph. 1:21-23 (T. Moritz, *A Profound Mystery: The Use of the Old Testament in Ephesians*, Supplements to Novum Testamentum 85 [Leiden: Brill, 1996], pp. 9-22).

57. The other is Rom. 11:25-27. Bockmuehl, *Revelation and Mystery*, p. 170.

58. Bockmuehl, *Revelation and Mystery*, p. 174.

Conclusion

From an examination of explicit portions of Paul's letters that connect the faithfulness of God to the Scriptures and from a broad survey of portions in his letters that point out noteworthy ways that Paul uses Scripture, it is fair to say that Paul views Scripture as a faithful representation of God's ways with his people. According to Romans 3:1-4, Paul states clearly that God's faithfulness is seen by the fact that God entrusted Israel with the Scriptures. Despite Israel's sinfulness, God's faithfulness was not undermined. According to Romans 9:6-29 and Romans 11, God's ways of electing, hardening, and preserving his people are found within the Scriptures. Paul thus considers the Scripture with which Israel was entrusted as faithfully representing their current condition. Implications of Paul's perception of Scripture for his readers can be found in the way he presents Scripture, applies it to his opponents in a polemical situation, applies it to his calling and ministry, and uses it for new teaching. In his presentation of Scripture, Paul often indicates that Scripture still speaks the same message today as it did years ago. In his application to his opponents and to himself he implies that Scripture is a faithful corrective and guide. In his use of Scripture to explain the future, he implies that Scripture is a faithful friend, leading his readers to a better understanding. Thus, from an examination of these explicit texts we can conclude that Paul believes that "the word of God has not failed," that God is proved faithful *(alētheia).*

God and Scripture in Hebrews

David Peterson

The central thrust of Hebrews is the challenge to respond appropriately to the voice of God in Scripture and to Christian exhortation derived from Scripture. Although the writer is clearly absorbed with expounding a distinctive Christology, soteriology, and eschatology, *theology is in the service of exhortation* in the structure of this book. For example, the first main section, which concerns God's ultimate revelation in the person and work of the Son (1:1-14), concludes with an exhortation to pay closer attention to what has been heard from Christ (2:1-4). The next section, which begins to explore his redemptive achievement (2:5-18), is followed by an exhortation not to miss out on the enjoyment of the inheritance he has secured for those who trust him (3:1–4:13). Fundamental to the writer's theology is the notion of God's faithfulness to his promises (e.g., 6:9-20; 7:20-22; 8:6; 9:15; 10:23; 11:6, 8-16; 13:5-6). These promises are recorded in what we call the Old Testament, and they are shown to have been fulfilled in Christ. God's faithfulness becomes the basis for every appeal "to realize the full assurance of hope to the very end" (6:11, NRSV).

Within the framework of alternating exposition and exhortation, the writer's argument is based on a series of scriptural explications. This is one of several features leading many contemporary scholars to characterize Hebrews as a sermonic discourse or homily in a written form, rather than as an epistle.[1] Thus, for example, George Caird argues that Hebrews falls

1. Cf. W. L. Lane, *Hebrews 1–8*, Word Biblical Commentary 47A (Dallas: Word, 1991), pp. lxix-lxxv.

into four sections, each having as its core an Old Testament passage that declares the ineffectiveness and symbolic or provisional nature of the old covenant's religious institutions. All other scriptural references are ancillary to these four (Psalms 8, 95, 110 and Jeremiah 31), which control the drift of the argument.[2] Richard Longenecker modifies Caird's approach by insisting that the catena of quotations in 1:5-13 constitutes a fifth major biblical "portion."[3] William Lane proposes that Habakkuk 2:3-4 and Proverbs 3:11-12 form the basis of two key sections of exhortation at the end of Hebrews, thus extending Caird's approach in the other direction.[4]

Old Testament Citations and Allusions in Hebrews

There are many direct quotations from the Old Testament in Hebrews, identified by an introductory formula (as in 1:5), and even more indirect quotations or allusions, without an introductory formula (as in 11:5). There are also summaries of Old Testament material (as in 1:1; 10:1-4) and mere references to an Old Testament name or topic "that are as important for understanding and describing the author's hermeneutics as are quotations and allusions."[5] Scholars differ on the number of explicit quotations, but there are about thirty-eight, based on twenty-seven Old Testament passages (a number of texts are cited more than once).[6] There are eleven quotations from the Pentateuch, one from the historical books, eighteen from the Psalms, one from Proverbs, and seven from the prophetic books,

2. G. B. Caird, "The Exegetical Method of the Epistle to the Hebrews," *Canadian Journal of Theology* 5 (1959): 44-51. S. Kistemaker (*The Psalm Citations in the Epistle to the Hebrews* [Amsterdam: van Soerst, 1961], p. 101) insists that the argument of Hebrews 8–10 is based on Psalm 40:6-8 rather than Jeremiah 31:31-34. However, the latter is more central to the argument of the section and the former is used in a supportive role.

3. R. N. Longenecker, *Biblical Exegesis in the Apostolic Period* (Grand Rapids: Eerdmans, 1975), pp. 174-85.

4. Lane, *Hebrews 1–8*, pp. cxiv-cxv, citing the unpublished work of J. Walters.

5. M. Barth, "The Old Testament in Hebrews: An Essay in Biblical Hermeneutics," in *Current Issues in New Testament Interpretation*, ed. W. Klassen, W. Snyder, and G. F. Snyder (London: SCM, 1962), p. 54.

6. Longenecker, *Biblical Exegesis*, pp. 164-70. Lane, *Hebrews 1–8*, p. cxvi, counts 31 explicit quotations and 4 implicit quotations, a minimum of 37 allusions, 19 instances where OT material is summarized, and 13 more where a biblical name or topic is cited without reference to a specific context.

of which three are from Jeremiah 31:31-34. At least fifty-five allusions have been identified: forty-one from the Pentateuch, two from the Psalms, one from Proverbs, and eleven from the prophetic books (of which seven are from Isaiah).

Longenecker observes that from the Pentateuch the writer drew "the basic structure of his thought regarding redemptive history, quoting some eleven times from ten different passages and alluding to forty-one others." From the Psalms he derived "primary support for his Christology, quoting some eighteen times from eleven different passages and alluding to two others."[7] Noncanonical texts are not cited, but allusions to such material have been detected at certain points in the argument. Although Hebrews cites some Old Testament texts used elsewhere in the New Testament (Gen. 21:12; Deut. 32:35; 2 Sam. 7:14; Ps. 2:7; 110:1; Hab. 2:4), nineteen or twenty of the passages quoted are not cited elsewhere.

The writer of Hebrews appears to have regarded the Greek Version of the Old Testament as authoritative, and some scholars have argued that "he nowhere shows any immediate knowledge of the Hebrew text."[8] Longenecker, who takes this view, acknowledges that six references cannot be explained as originating from the LXX (either A or B texts) and proposes that a now extinct septuagintal version based on Hebrew readings also now extinct must have been used.[9] It certainly appears as if Greek translations of the Old Testament were in the process of being standardized in the first century and that New Testament quotations are not always from the Greek translation that eventually formed a part of the official text.[10]

The Inspiration and Authority of the Written Word

It is important to observe how distinctive is the manner of introducing Old Testament citations in Hebrews. In the majority of cases God himself

7. Longenecker, *Biblical Exegesis,* p. 167. 2 Sam. 7:14; Deut. 32:43 (LXX); Isa. 8:17-18 are the only portions apart from Psalms used to explicate the person of Christ.

8. B. F. Westcott, *The Epistle to the Hebrews,* 3rd ed. (London: Macmillan, 1914), p. 481.

9. Longenecker, *Biblical Exegesis,* p. 169.

10. Cf. G. Howard, "Hebrews and Old Testament Quotations," *Novum Testamentum* 10 (1968): 208-21, who argues that the quotations in Heb. 1:6; 2:13a; 2:17; 5:6; 13:5 agree with the Hebrew against the Greek version. Lane (*Hebrews 1–8,* pp. cxvii-cxviii) highlights the issues in this debate.

is the speaker through the person of the prophet or psalmist (e.g., 1:5, 6-12, 13; 4:3-5, 7; 5:5-6; 6:13-14; 7:17, 21; 8:5, 8-12; 10:30; 12:26; 13:6). In four quotations from three passages the words are attributed to Christ (2:12-13; 10:5-7), suggesting that these verses find their true or ultimate meaning in what he says and does. In three quotations from two passages the Holy Spirit is the speaker (3:7-11; 10:15-17), though the same passages are also more generally attributed to God at 4:7 and 8:8-12, respectively. In four instances the human authors are mentioned: Moses (9:20; 12:21), David (4:7, God "saying through David"), and "someone" (2:6, Greek *tis*).

In many cases the words of Scripture are introduced by the writer as being spoken in the present (e.g., 3:7-11; 8:8-12; 12:5-6). He makes no distinction between the word written and the word spoken, and he treats the words of human authors as the words of God. In this way the writer expresses his belief in the divine inspiration of the Old Testament documents and in God's intention to continue speaking through them to his people. For example, God can use Psalm 95 to sustain faith in Christ and the promise of sharing in his "rest" (Heb. 3:7–4:13). Through Proverbs 3:11-12, God can teach his children under the new covenant how to respond to the discipline of suffering, literally addressing each one as "my son" (Heb. 12:5-6). The same Spirit who inspired the human authors to write the words of God in the first place continues to illuminate, challenge, encourage, and warn through those definitive words once given. For all generations of believers, the written record is the voice of God, and "as a necessary consequence the record is itself living. It is not a book merely. It has a vital connexion with our circumstances and must be considered in connexion with them."[11]

There is nothing really parallel to this general mode of quotation in the other books of the New Testament. The apostle Paul, for example, prefers to introduce citations with an expression like "as it is written" (e.g., Rom. 1:17; 2:24; 1 Cor. 1:19; 2:9, Greek *gegraptai*), but Hebrews never follows this pattern. The writer characteristically uses some form of the verb "to speak" (Greek *legein*) with God as subject.[12] When the verb "to speak" is used in introductory formulas by other New Testament writers, it is usu-

11. Westcott, *Hebrews,* p. 477.

12. Cf. Westcott, *Hebrews,* pp. 477-78; Lane, *Hebrews 1–8,* p. cxvii. Westcott notes a partial correspondence with Hebrews in the way Scripture is quoted in the epistles of Clement and Barnabas.

ally combined either with the name of the prophet (e.g., "Isaiah says," Rom. 10:16; "David says," Rom. 11:9) or with Scripture ("Scripture says," Rom. 4:3; 9:17). When God is the subject, as is rarely the case, the reference is to words spoken to someone like Moses (e.g., Rom. 9:15) or to Israel in a specific context (e.g., Rom. 9:25). The closest parallel to Hebrews would be a passage like 2 Corinthians 6:2, where God's words to Israel in Isaiah 49:8 are taken to be directly applicable to the Corinthians, as if they were written to the Corinthians.[13]

Bishop Westcott, whose commentary contains a valuable excursus on this topic, notices that in connection with this belief in the present, personal voice of God in the Old Testament "there is no indication of any anticipation of a written N.T."[14] However, the issue is not as simple as he makes out. The message that was "declared at first through the Lord" and was "attested to us by those who heard him" (2:3) may have come to the writer of Hebrews and his readers in some written form.[15] Even more significantly, it appears that the writer expects his readers to respond to his own message with as much care and diligence as to the Scriptures (compare 5:11–6:12 with 3:7–4:13). Hebrews itself is a "word of exhortation" based on the Scriptures, drawing out their meaning in the light of the Christ event and applying them to the situation of the readers. It is a document that calls upon the readers to hear the voice of God warning and encouraging them in the present, and to respond (cf. 12:25-29). The writer apparently had some confidence that God would use his efforts to transform the situation he addressed (cf. 6:1-3).

13. Cf. the discussion of Paul's usage in the contribution to this volume by Drake Williams.

14. Westcott, *Hebrews*, p. 478

15. Cf. H. W. Attridge, *The Epistle to the Hebrews* (Philadelphia: Fortress, 1989), pp. 66-67. There is certainly scholarly debate about the meaning of "the basic teaching about Christ" in 6:1 (Greek *ton tēs archēs tou Christou logon*). In its context, does this expression refer to certain basic credal statements about Christ or to something more? Was this transmitted in an oral or written form?

Listening to the Voice of God: The Writer's Sustained Appeal

Revelation and Redemption in Christ

Hebrews begins with the claim that the God who spoke long ago "to our ancestors in many and various ways by the prophets" has "in these last days" spoken to us again "by a Son" (1:1-2, NRSV). God is not silent or unknowable. He has spoken definitively through his chosen agents "in many and various ways," a fact that suggests that his self-communication was in multiple portions and in diverse forms. It is clear from what follows that the writer of Hebrews identified these portions and forms of revelation with the Jewish Scriptures and that he viewed the whole as "one vast prophecy, in the record of national fortunes, in the ordinances of a national Law, in the expression of a national hope."[16]

Whatever unity of purpose or content there was in this revelation "long ago," Hebrews implies a contrast with the singularity and finality of God's eschatological speech "in one who is Son."[17] Nevertheless, it is the same God who speaks in both dispensations, and the salvation that he accomplishes through the Son is said to have been anticipated or foreshadowed in the provisions of the former revelation (8:5; 9:8-10; 10:1). Hebrews will allow no differentiation of authenticity or trustworthiness between the revelation in the prophetic Scriptures and the revelation in the Son.[18] Indeed, the Scriptures are regularly used to illuminate and explain the full significance of Christ and his work.

The superiority of God's revelation in the Son has to do with his identity and role in God's redemptive plan (1:2-4). God speaks through his Son not only in word but also in deed, "in the entirety of the Christ-event, providing for humanity atonement for sin and an enduring covenant relationship."[19] There is also a finality about the revelation through the Son since it comes (literally) "at the end of these days," inaugurating the eschatological

16. Westcott, *Hebrews,* p. 493.

17. Paraphrase of the Greek expression in 1:2 without an article *(en huiǭ).* Suggested by Westcott, *Hebrews,* p. 7.

18. It is true that the writer characterizes God as speaking formerly "on earth" and now "from heaven" (12:25), but in both cases the words are God's. Moreover, there is a common purpose in this speech, namely, to motivate his people to offer "an acceptable worship with reverence and awe" (12:26-29).

19. Attridge, *Hebrews,* p. 39.

era towards which the prophetic Scriptures pointed. The character of Christ as Son, which is first proclaimed in 1:2b-3a, is then expounded by means of a series of citations that compare him to the angels and their role in God's plan (1:5-13).[20] The nature of his redemptive work, which is first announced in 1:3:b, is not explored until 2:5-18.

The climax of this first section of the argument is a warning to "pay greater attention to what we have heard so that we do not drift away from it" (2:1). The reference here is to the message "declared at first through the Lord" and then attested to the writer and his readers "by those who heard him," "while God added his testimony by signs and wonders and various miracles, and by gifts of the Holy Spirit, distributed according to his will" (2:3-4). In some extracanonical Jewish writings, angels were portrayed as intermediaries in the giving of the law at Sinai.[21] This tradition is appropriated by the writer to make the point that the revelation delivered by the Son is even more significant. The salvation proclaimed and effected by the Son enables believers to experience in advance "the powers of the age to come" (6:4-5) by being sanctified, cleansed, and perfected as beneficiaries of the new covenant (10:10-18). Failure to hold fast to the message that brings the messianic salvation can only mean experiencing the eschatological judgment of God (cf. 10:26-31).

In 2:5-18, attention turns to the nature of the salvation that was accomplished by Christ. His actual words are not quoted, but his teaching about "the time" being fulfilled and the kingdom of God being "at hand" (Mark 1:15 par.) finds expression in the eschatological framework that Hebrews provides in this passage. The writer's subject is "the world to come" (2:5) and the way Christ brings "many children to glory" (2:10). This happens when the Son of God fulfills Psalm 8:4-6, becoming "for a little while lower than the angels" but then "crowned with glory and honor because of the suffering of death" (2:9). The way in which Christ's death and heavenly exaltation benefits believers begins to be explored (2:10-18), though much more remains to be said as the writer's argument unfolds in chapters 5–10.

20. Cf. J. W. Thompson, "The Structure and Purpose of the Catena in Hebrews 1:5-13," *Catholic Biblical Quarterly* 38 (1976): 352-63; S. Motyer, "The Psalm Quotations of Hebrews 1: A Hermeneutic-free Zone?" *Tyndale Bulletin* 50 (1999): 3-22.

21. For example, *Jubilees* 1:27, 29; 2:1; 5:1-2; Josephus, *Ant.* 15.5.3. Cf. Gal. 3:19; Acts 7:30, 38, 53.

The Danger of Missing Out on the Inheritance Promised by God

In Psalm 95:7-11, David warned his own generation against hardening their hearts in unbelief and rebellion against God, taking as an example the behavior of those Israelites who left Egypt under the leadership of Moses. The writer of Hebrews expounds these verses at some length (3:7–4:13) because he views Christians as being in a similar situation. Redeemed by Christ, we have been promised an inheritance or "rest" at the end of our spiritual pilgrimage. Nothing must be allowed to weaken our faith in this promise and cause us to turn away from God as the Israelites did in the wilderness.

The land of Canaan, or the situation of being free from enemy oppression in that land, was viewed in the Old Testament as the "rest" granted to Israel by God (e.g., Exod. 33:14; Deut. 3:20; 12:9-10; Josh. 21:43-4; 1 Kings 8:56). Yet, when Psalm 95 was written, the Israelites were already established in Canaan. Our writer reasons that David's warning about missing out on God's rest must refer to something beyond the material inheritance outlined in the Mosaic covenant (Heb. 4:6-8). Using the Jewish hermeneutical principle called *gezerah shawah,* Hebrews interprets the "rest" (Greek *katapausin*) of Psalm 95:11 in terms of Genesis 2:2, where the related verb "rested" *(katepausen)* is found.[22]

The rest that God promises his people is a share in the "sabbath" of his own rest. This rest was the sequel to his "works" in creation, according to Genesis 2:2. By implication, the fall made it impossible for those cast out of the Garden of Eden to share in God's rest. However, God's redemptive "works" in the time of Moses (cf. Ps. 95:9) allowed Israel to enjoy an earthly inheritance that was an anticipation of the ultimate, eschatological rest. The true rest was achieved by Jesus Christ when he entered into the divine presence, as a consequence of his sacrificial death, and it opened the way for us to follow (cf. 6:20; 9:11-12; 10:19-21).

God's rest is equivalent to the "heavenly homeland" (11:16), the "heavenly Jerusalem" (12:22), the "unshakable kingdom" (12:28), and

22. For Jewish hermeneutics in the first century note Longenecker, *Biblical Exegesis,* pp. 19-50. *Gezerah shawah* means "verbal analogy from one verse to another; where the same words are applied to two separate cases it follows that the same considerations apply to both" (p. 34).

other descriptions of the Christian's inheritance in this book. From one point of view, that rest already exists for us in the heavenlies and can be "entered" now, by faith (4:3; 12:22). From another point of view, we seek "the city that is to come" (13:14; cf. 2:5). Thus, the imagery of the rest is best understood as "a complex symbol for the whole soteriological process that Hebrews never fully articulates, but which involves both personal and corporate dimensions."[23]

It is significant that the writer's most explicit theology of "the word of God" is set forth in this context (4:12-13). His reference could be to the gospel, which is described in verse 2 as "the message they heard" (Greek *ho logos tēs akoēs*). The gospel brings the promise of salvation as well as the warning of judgment (cf. 2:1-4). However, since Psalm 95 functions as the voice of God in the immediate context, calling the readers to faith and warning them about hardening their hearts, the word of God written in Scripture is more likely to be the reference in 4:12-13 (Greek *ho logos tou theou*).[24] In language recalling Isaiah 55:11, the word of God is said to be "living and active," implying that it achieves the purpose for which it is uttered by God. The metaphor of the "two-edged sword" is used to paint what initially appears to be a rather frightening picture. God's word penetrates to the deepest recesses of our being, opening us up and judging "the thoughts and intentions of the heart." It is the "critic" (Greek *kritikos*) by which all are judged. Indeed, confronted by the word of God, we are confronted by God himself, and "before him no creature is hidden." When the writer says "all are naked and laid bare to the eyes of the one to whom we must render an account," the image is that of an animal with its head thrown back and neck bare, ready to be sacrificed! The final day of reckoning is anticipated when the word of God exposes us. In the final analysis, then, this passage suggests that God can use the negative or judging function of his word to help us in pursuing the journey of faith, since it can deliver us from hardness of heart and unbelief.

23. Attridge, *Hebrews,* p. 128. Attridge (pp. 126-30) helpfully compares the exegesis of Hebrews with Jewish applications of the notion of sabbath rest to the new creation or to the state of the dead.

24. Cf. Lane, *Hebrews 1–8,* pp. 102-3. Of course it is true that the Psalm actually offers in a written form the promise of rest and a warning of judgment that the gospel gives in an oral form.

Holding Fast to Our Confession

As the writer moves towards the central section of his argument, he introduces an exhortation in 4:14-16 that finds its echo in 10:19-25, in an expanded form. These exhortations stress the importance of holding fast to the "confession" (Greek *homologia*) about Jesus as Son of God, who is also the high priest who has "passed through the heavens" (4:14; 10:23; cf. 3:1).[25] In the flow of the argument, this is necessary if believers are not to fall by the wayside and miss out on the final rest of God. Allied to this continued confession of Christ and his saving work, readers are urged to keep on drawing near to God through Christ as heavenly high priest, to receive "mercy" and find "grace to help in time of need" (4:16; 10:19-22). In the inclusion formed by these parallel exhortations, the exposition of Christ's priestly and sacrificial work offers the greatest possible encouragement to persevere in faith, hope, and love (cf. 6:9-20; 10:24-39).

Aaron's high-priestly work under the Mosaic law is then compared with the role given to the Messiah in Scripture and carried out by Jesus in his earthly ministry and heavenly exaltation (Heb. 5:1-10). Here the importance of Psalm 110:4 is first signaled, but its full significance is not disclosed until chapter 7. Meanwhile, there is serious warning about paying attention to what the writer is about to teach and a challenge to receive the "solid food" that will lead them to maturity and faithful perseverance, instead of apostasy (5:11–6:12). As the readers are urged to respond to the writer's word with as much diligence as they are challenged to respond to Scripture in 3:1–4:13, the impression is given that he sees himself to have an authority from God that can only be ignored at their peril. In effect, this is a claim to be writing New Testament Scripture.

The basis of Christian hope is not wishful thinking about the future but *the solemn promise of God.* As far as Hebrews is concerned, there is fundamentally only one divine promise in Scripture. It was first given to Abra-

25. It is possible that this confession is "a firmly outlined, liturgically set tradition by which the community must abide" (O. Michel, "*homologeō*," in *Theological Dictionary of the New Testament,* vol. 5, ed. G. Kittel and G. Friedrich, trans. and ed. G. Bromiley [Grand Rapids: Eerdmans, 1967], p. 215). More cautiously, V. H. Neufeld (*The Earliest Christian Confessions* [Leiden: Brill, 1963], pp. 134-35) argues that the confession known to the readers was essentially that "Jesus is the Son of God" and that the words "apostle" and "high priest" (3:1) are "not part of the content of the *homologia* but refer to offices mentioned in the author's comparison between Jesus and Moses."

ham in Genesis 12:1-3 and then repeated at various stages to the forefathers of Israel in different forms (e.g., Gen. 15:1-21; 26:2-4; 28:13-15; Exod. 3:6-10). God promised to multiply the descendants of Abraham, making them into a great nation, establishing them in their own land, and blessing them so that they might become a source of blessing to all nations. On one particular occasion, God confirmed the truthfulness of this promise with an oath (cf. Gen. 22:16). Hebrews notes that Abraham was encouraged by this to wait patiently for what was promised. God began to fulfill his promise in Abraham's lifetime, but the ultimate blessing came in the person of Jesus the Messiah.

In human affairs, "an oath given as confirmation puts an end to all dispute" (6:16). So God inspired the use of this pattern of speech in Scripture to make the unchanging nature of his promise abundantly clear (6:17). He accommodated himself to human weakness by employing "two unchangeable things in which it is impossible that God would prove false" (6:18). His promise and his oath give the greatest possible encouragement to his people to put their trust in him. It is clear from what follows that Christians who have fled to take hold of the hope offered to them in Jesus are the ultimate heirs of what was promised to Abraham (cf. Gal. 3:26-29). With this argument, Hebrews shows how much the Christian hope and the motivation for godly living (6:9-12) is tied to a belief in the faithfulness of God as expressed in Scripture (6:13-20). There is no other way of knowing the divine promises apart from God's word written. To impugn that revelation, with its assurances of divine inspiration and authority, is to deny the trustworthiness of God. According to Hebrews, God stands by what has been written in his name, and he expects his people to do the same.

In 6:18-20 the writer anticipates 7:20-22, where it is argued that the promise of Psalm 110:4 ("you are a priest forever, according to the order of Melchizedek") establishes the eternal validity of the Messiah's priesthood. Like the foundational promise to Abraham and his offspring, this promise is prefixed by a divine oath ("The Lord has sworn and will not change his mind"). These two promises are closely linked in *form* but also in their *intention.* With the provision of the eternal priesthood "according to the order of Melchizedek," God reveals how he will secure for his people an inheritance where they may enjoy his presence forever. To put it another way, the promise to Abraham finds its ultimate fulfillment in the saving work of Christ (cf. 11:13-16, 39-40).

The notion of Christ's high-priestly work is progressively drawn into the argument from the end of Hebrews 6 to explain how Christians can have "strong encouragement" (6:18) to seize the hope set before them. Jesus' sacrifice and entrance into the "inner shrine behind the curtain" guarantee our acceptance and entrance into God's presence (6:19-20; cf. 9:11-15, 24; 10:19-23). Living with God in his heavenly sanctuary is another way of expressing the hope of an eschatological inheritance. Cultic imagery is used in the central section of Hebrews to show how Jesus Christ has already realized that hope for us.

Abraham's encounter with Melchizedek, the priest-king of Salem (Gen. 14:18-20), is briefly analyzed in Hebrews 7:1-10, in preparation for the exposition of Psalm 110:4 and its application to Jesus in the rest of that chapter. Once again, a text from Genesis is used in a supportive and explanatory way, this time to assist in outlining the writer's Christology. The writer perceives that the biblical representation of Melchizedek corresponds in certain decisive ways to the person and work of Christ, so that in the record of Scripture he is "made to resemble" (Greek *aphōmoiōmenos*) the Son of God (7:3).[26] To some extent, the significance of Genesis 14 was noted by the author of Psalm 110, who linked together David's inheritance of Jerusalem with the promise of a share in the royal priesthood of Melchizedek. As far as Hebrews is concerned, Psalm 110 is a prediction about the Messiah (cf. 1:13; 5:5-6), with verse 4 signifying such imperfection in the whole system of priesthood descended from Aaron that there is need for "a better hope through which we approach God" (7:11-19).

The rest of Hebrews 7:20–10:19 is designed to show how the high-priestly work of Jesus provides that "better hope." The *eternity* of his priesthood is established by his resurrection and heavenly exaltation: "he holds his priesthood permanently, because he continues forever" (7:24). This is really "the main point" of the promise about a royal priesthood "according to the order of Melchizedek" (cf. 8:1). The practical implications of the writer's use of Psalm 110:4 are then revealed in 7:25. Jesus is able "for all time to save those who approach God through him, since he always lives to make intercession for them." The idea of "approaching," "drawing near," or "coming" to God is prominent in Hebrews (cf. 4:16; 7:19; 10:1, 22;

26. It is appropriate to read the passive in the strict sense here and to understand that "God is the sculptor who lets a sign of primitive times correspond to the event of the End time" (O. Michel, *Der Brief an die Hebräer,* 13th ed., Meyer Kommentar [Göttingen: Vandenhoeck & Ruprecht, 1975], p. 263).

11:6; 12:18, 22). It is a cultic way of expressing what it means to be in a genuine relationship with God. The Old Testament priesthood and sacrificial system only imperfectly provided for such a relationship (8:1-5; 9:1-10; 10:1-4), but Jesus is able to "perfect" those who would draw near to God by inaugurating the new covenant way of approach (10:14-18).[27] Christians can look to Jesus for help at every stage in their earthly pilgrimage, because "he always lives to make intercession for them" (cf. Rom. 8:34; 1 John 2:1-2). The image of the heavenly intercessor is used to emphasize Christ's willingness and ability to go on applying the benefits of his once-for-all sacrifice (cf. 2:18; 4:14-16; 10:19-22).

In 7:26-28, the claim is made that, as a faultless high priest, Jesus sacrificed for the sins of God's people "once for all, when he offered himself" (7:27; cf. 9:12; 10:10 [Greek *ephapax*]; 9:26, 28 [Greek *hapax*]). Unlike the high priests of Judaism, he does not need to offer sacrifices day after day, first for his own sins, and then for those of the people. The perfection of his sacrifice is associated with the perfection of the victim. Jesus himself was "perfected" as high priest (7:28; cf. 2:10; 5:9) by means of his obedient life, his sacrificial death, and his entrance into the heavenly presence of God (as vv. 26-27 suggest).[28]

The Foundational Promise of the New Covenant

The oath confirming the eternal priesthood of the Messiah in Psalm 110:4 makes Jesus "the guarantee of a better covenant" (Heb. 7:22). This introduces the next main section of the argument, where Jeremiah 31:31-34 is the key text. It is quoted in full in Hebrews 8:8-12 and quoted again in an abbreviated form when the section is ended (Heb. 10:15-17). The writer has already linked the promise to Abraham with the promise to the Messiah in Psalm 110:4 (Heb. 6:13-20). By means of his sacrifice and heavenly exaltation, Jesus is now shown to be the "mediator" of a new covenant (Greek *mesitēs,* 8:6; 9:15; 12:24), making possible the ultimate fulfillment of the promise to Abraham. As "guarantee" of the new covenant (Greek

27. Cf. D. G. Peterson, *Hebrews and Perfection* (Cambridge: Cambridge University Press, 1982), pp. 126-67.

28. For a "vocational" reading of the perfecting of Christ in Hebrews cf. Peterson, *Hebrews and Perfection,* pp. 1-125.

engyos, 7:22), Christ's eternal priesthood vouches for the fact that the blessings of that covenant are readily available. The "better covenant" (7:22) is the basis for the Christian's "better hope" (7:19).

The prophecy of Jeremiah is initially cited in Hebrews for a negative purpose. The writer's introductory and concluding remarks (8:7-8a; 8:13) stress the imperfect and provisional character of the covenant made with Israel at the time of the Exodus from Egypt. Although Scripture speaks about God making a covenant with Abraham (e.g., Gen. 15:18; 17:2), Hebrews restricts the notion of covenant to the disposition made at Sinai (Exodus 19–24) and to the new covenant of Jeremiah 31:31-34. Attention is first drawn to the *blame* contained within the prophetic oracle (8:9), which finds fault with the recipients. However, our writer also suggests that the very prediction of a second or "new" covenant would not have been made "if that first covenant had been faultless" (8:7). In speaking of a new covenant through Jeremiah, God "has made the first one obsolete. And what is obsolete and growing old will soon disappear" (8:13).

Hebrews does not simply argue that what is new must be superior to what is old. The contrasts in 8:1-6 show that the writer viewed the old covenant largely in terms of its provisions for worship. The levitical priesthood served in a sanctuary that was only "a sketch and shadow of the heavenly one" (8:5; cf. 10:1). This claim, which is backed up with a citation from Exodus 25:40, assumes that everything prescribed by God in the Mosaic law was intended to be a "pattern" or model (Greek *typos*) of what was to come with the work of Christ. Consequently, he is "a minister in the sanctuary and the true tent that the Lord, and not any mortal, has set up" (8:2). Although this perspective has sometimes been described as a modified form of Platonic idealism, our writer's distinction between the earthly and the heavenly is eschatologically controlled rather than philosophically inspired.[29]

The negative evaluation of the old covenant is continued in 9:1-10. The writer stresses the earthly nature of the Mosaic sanctuary and its ritual (vv. 2-5) and goes on to describe its weakness as a means of relating to God (vv. 6-10). The very existence of such a sanctuary, with its two divisions and rigid regulations of approach, "witnessed constantly to the aim of man and to the fact that he could not as yet attain it. He could not penetrate to that innermost sanctuary to which he necessarily looked, and from

29. Cf. Lane, *Hebrews 1–8,* pp. 206-8. Contra Attridge, *Hebrews,* pp. 219-24.

which blessing flowed."[30] A particular weakness of the old covenant is then emphasized in 9:9-10. In the worship of the earthly sanctuary, gifts and sacrifices are offered that are not able to (literally) "perfect the worshipper with respect to conscience" (Greek *kata syneidēsin teleiōsai ton latreuonta*). The following verse explains this failure in terms of the external operation of the cultus — they are "regulations for the body" — and in terms of its provisional status — being in force "until the time comes to set things right." Those who sought to draw near to God through the provisions of the Mosaic law were not "perfected" because the system was unable to deal effectively with the problem of a guilty conscience (9:9) or "consciousness of sin" (10:2, Greek *syneidēsin hamartiōn*).

The writer's positive use of the promises of Jeremiah 31:31-34 must be understood in this context. Jeremiah predicted a profound transformation of the members of the chosen people, issuing in an authentic knowledge of the Lord. The basis of this change would be a divine act of mercy towards them: "*for* I will be merciful towards their iniquities, and I will remember their sins no more." Hebrews notes the foundational importance of this last promise to the whole notion of a new covenant.[31] When the passage from Jeremiah is quoted again in 10:16-17, the focus is on the last verse of the oracle and this interpretative comment is added: "where there is forgiveness of these, there is no longer any *offering for sin*" (10:18). The fulfillment is proclaimed in priestly and sacrificial terms because Hebrews sees the work of Christ as the reality towards which the Old Testament cult and Jeremiah's prophecy were both pointing.

From Hebrews 9:11 to 10:18, the writer's purpose is to show how that definitive offer of forgiveness is made possible by the shedding of Christ's "blood." Against the background of Mosaic regulations, this terminology indicates that his death is a sacrifice for sins and the means by which the new covenant is inaugurated (9:12, 14, 15; 10:19-22, 29; 12:24; 13:20; cf. 9:18-22). By a single act of obedience, he fulfills and replaces the entire sacrificial system of the old covenant, as envisaged in Psalm 40:6-8 (Heb. 10:1-10). It is his unblemished self-offering in death that makes his sacrificial blood so effective (Heb. 7:27; 9:14). The Day of Atonement ritual is

30. Westcott, *Hebrews,* p. 252.

31. This is clear from the structure of Jer. 31:31-34 itself, in which the last promise of v. 34 is linked to the preceding promises by "for, because" (Hebrew *kî*, Greek *hoti*). Cf. Heb. 8:12. This point is made in a different syntactic manner in Heb. 10:15-17, with the preface in v. 15 highlighting the importance of what follows in v. 17.

particularly in view in Hebrews 9:11-14, as the writer seeks to show how the weaknesses of the Mosaic system have been overcome by the work of Christ. His death and heavenly exaltation accomplish what the yearly activity of the high priest could not, since they achieve "an eternal redemption" (9:12) and can "purify our conscience from dead works to worship the living God" (9:14). The writer can thus declare that "by a single offering he has perfected for all time those who are sanctified" (10:14).

Believers can now draw near to God in the heavenly sanctuary "with a true heart in full assurance of faith, with our hearts sprinkled clean from an evil conscience and our bodies washed with pure water" (10:22; cf. 4:16; 7:25; 12:22-24). With such language, Hebrews appears to proclaim the fulfillment of the promise of Jeremiah 31:33 about the renewal of the heart of God's people, with all that flows from such a miracle. The writer's presentation may also have been colored by the prophecy of Ezekiel 36:25-27, with its expectation of "a new heart" and "a new spirit," made possible by God sprinkling his people with clean water to purify them from all their idols. Only when the heart is set free from the burden of unforgiven sin can it be renewed in faith and sincerity towards God, thus providing the immediate and spontaneous fidelity to God that was foretold by these prophets.[32] The fulfillment of Jeremiah's promise about a definitive forgiveness of sins is therefore central to the exposition of God's faithfulness in Hebrews.

Since the writer is concerned to show how the original promises to Abraham find their fulfillment, and since the notion of an inheritance for God's people is critical to the provisions of the old covenant, it is not surprising to find the new covenant linked to the prospect of an "eternal inheritance." Christ is the mediator of a new covenant "so that those who are called may receive the promised eternal inheritance, because a death has occurred that redeems them from the transgressions under the first covenant" (9:15). Redemption from sin is necessary if we are to enjoy the ultimate inheritance promised by God. Even though the old covenant provided a system of cleansing and renewal for those who lived in the earthly inheritance of Canaan, it was only the sacrifice of Christ that secured the redemption necessary for life in God's presence forever (cf. 12:22-24).

32. I have argued this case more fully in "The Prophecy of the New Covenant in the Argument of Hebrews," *Reformed Theological Review* 38 (1979): 74-81.

A Final Call to Faithfulness

With the exposition of Christ's work in cultic terms completed, the need to respond to such teaching with persevering faith dominates the argument from 10:19 to the end of the book. In 10:23 the encouragement to "hold fast to the confession of our hope without wavering" is explicitly based on the conviction that "he who has promised is faithful." The writer has done everything to demonstrate the trustworthiness of God, specifically as it is related to the fulfillment of Scripture, and wants his readers to live in the light of this belief. A number of key texts are quoted and expounded in these chapters (e.g., 10:30, 31, 37-38; 12:5-6, 26; 13:5, 6), and allusions to other texts abound. Hebrews 11 stands in the middle of this section, with its catalog of examples from the Old Testament. These are not merely designed to demonstrate the faith that pleases God but to show how God's saving purposes for his people were actually advanced by those who believed his promises. Here, the promise to Abraham and the patriarchs returns to center stage (11:8-22). Either side of this chapter is the call to express faith in terms of patient endurance (10:32-39; 12:1-12).

The writer appears to allegorize when he notes that Abraham "looked forward to the city that has foundations, whose architect and builder is God" (11:10). The expansion of this idea in 11:13-16, with reference to all the patriarchs, makes it clear that our writer had in mind a heavenly homeland or inheritance. In other words, he claims that the true goal of the faithful, even in patriarchal times, was the heavenly Jerusalem, "the city of the living God" (12:22). This notion has its parallels in Jewish apocalyptic expectations of a new Jerusalem, prepared from the creation of the world.[33] Hebrews has already anticipated such a claim with the teaching about entering into the "rest" that God established "at the foundation of the world" (4:3). So, as with the doctrine of creation, the teaching of Genesis on the subject of an inheritance for God's people is interpreted *in the light of its fulfillment in Christ.*

This is not an arbitrary way of treating the Old Testament. The writer discerns that the oft-repeated promise of an inheritance, with the challenge to live by faith until it is realized, establishes a *pattern of relationship*

33. Cf. Attridge, *Hebrews,* p. 324, especially n. 38. Attridge observes that the imagery in 11:13-16 is rooted in the patriarchal narratives, "but it clearly bears the imprint of their metaphorical application in Hellenistic Judaism and early Christianity" (p. 328).

between God and his people. This is also the pattern for Christians under the new covenant. The patriarchs function more effectively as exemplars of faith for Christians when this similarity of life situation is observed. Moreover, Hebrews wants to stress that all those who died in faith, without receiving what was promised, are "perfected" together with us through Christ (11:39-40; cf. 9:15; 12:23). So, "if the New Testament writers are not misguided in portraying them as the ancestors of the family of faith, their essential blessings must be of the same order as the blessings enjoyed by their spiritual children under the new covenant."[34]

In 12:18-29 there is a climactic appeal to heed the one who "warns from heaven." This passage also highlights the eschatological tension in the argument of Hebrews.[35] When Israel gathered at Mt. Sinai to hear the voice of God, it was a terrifying occasion (12:18-21; cf. Exodus 19), moving the people to beg that "not another word be spoken to them." Christians, however, have come by faith to "Mount Zion and to the city of the living God, the heavenly Jerusalem," where God, "the judge of all," is in the midst of "a festal gathering," comprising angels and the perfected saints of all generations (12:22-24). The scene is one of covenant conclusion, "modelled on the Sinai definitive pattern,"[36] but the locus is actually the final encounter with God in the new Jerusalem, which is the hope of the eschatological prophets in the Old Testament. The emphasis is on acceptance because of Jesus, "the mediator of a new covenant," and his "sprinkled blood," which "speaks a better word than the blood of Abel."

With the words "you have come" in 12:22,[37] the writer implies that believers are now already part of that heavenly scene. This is a vivid way of saying that we have secured the promised eternal inheritance through faith in Jesus and his work. To some extent we can enjoy its benefits in advance

34. F. F. Bruce, *The Epistle to the Hebrews* (London: Marshall, Morgan & Scott, 1964), p. 299. Bruce (pp. 297-99) compares the way Philo treats the patriarchal narratives.

35. Cf. C. K. Barrett, "The Eschatology of the Epistle to the Hebrews," in *The Background of the New Testament and Its Eschatology,* ed. W. D. Davies and D. Daube (Cambridge: Cambridge University Press, 1954), pp. 363-93.

36. Cf. W. J. Dumbrell, "The Spirits of Just Men Made Perfect," *Evangelical Quarterly* 48 (1976): 154-59.

37. *Proselēlythate* in 12:22 is the perfect tense of the verb that is used in the present tense in 4:16; 7:25; 10:22. The perfect stresses the idea of having *already arrived,* whereas the present tense stresses the need to *keep on approaching God* in his heavenly sanctuary through Christ by faith. In other words, there is the need to realize continually through prayer the benefits of having drawn near to God definitively in Christ.

of literally coming into God's presence. In view of this assurance, the stern warning in 12:25-29 is rather unexpected. Yet the writer's point is that the God who spoke at Sinai ("who warned them on earth") continues to call us from the heavenly Jerusalem ("who warns us from heaven").

No artificial distinction is to be made between the God of the Old Testament and the God of the New! Since God continually speaks to us of forgiveness and acceptance through the gospel about his Son, we must not refuse him. If the Israelites did not escape God's condemnation when they turned away from him, how much less will we (cf. 2:1-4)? When God spoke from Sinai, the whole mountain trembled violently (Exod. 19:18). Haggai 2:6 promises that, when it is time for the final judgment and the end of this world order, God will shake "not only the earth but also the heavens" (12:26). All that will remain is "what cannot be shaken" (12:27), namely, the kingdom that Christ shares with those who continue to trust in him (12:28).

The writer's assurance about sharing in God's unshakable kingdom is coupled with a further warning about apostasy, to challenge the readers to go on heeding the voice of God through the gospel and the Old Testament Scriptures (cf. 3:7–4:13), and thus to live a life of gratitude and acceptable worship (12:28-29).

The Hermeneutical Achievement of Hebrews

Much more could be said about the writer's particular use of key texts or the eschatological framework through which he interprets Old Testament narratives or legal material. His underlying conviction about the inspiration of Scripture leads him to believe that God was preparing his people for the person and work of Christ in all that he said to Israel and did on their behalf. The God who speaks so powerfully today through the gospel and calls people to share with him in his eternal kingdom and presence is the same God who spoke to the patriarchs and made them promises long ago. Everything else in Scripture, including the cultic provisions of the Mosaic law, is seen to have had an immediate application to the original recipients, as well as having an ultimate application to Christ and to those whom he has "perfected," "in these last days." There is a unity and shape to Scripture that gives point and purpose to the various sections within it. Yet the aim of this "word of exhortation" is not simply to develop a Christian hermeneutic or to develop an integrated biblical theology. The writer's abiding concern is to urge his readers to discern and heed the voice of God in Scripture appropriately.

It is sometimes argued that the writer's use of the Old Testament is too much influenced by the Alexandrian school of Jewish Platonists, and more particularly by Philo. The assumption is that this approach should not be imitated by Christians today! However, at the end of a massive comparison of the two, Ronald Williamson concludes that Hebrews differs radically from the outlook and attitude of Philo. "Neither in his basic judgement about the essential character of the Old Testament, nor in his chief method of scriptural exegesis does the Writer of Hebrews appear to owe anything to Philo."[38] Caird has also insisted that Hebrews was in reality "one of the earliest and most successful attempts to define the relations between the Old and New Testaments, and that a large part of the value of the book is to be found in the method of exegesis which was formerly dismissed with contempt."[39] The writer believed that the old covenant had been "superseded and fulfilled but not abrogated. It contained a genuine foreshadowing of the good things to come, not a Platonic illusion of ultimate reality."[40]

However, Caird rightly points out that in Hebrews "part of the validity of the Old order is its constant disclaimer of finality": the writer's interest is in the confessed inadequacy of the old order. "The epistle seeks to establish its main thesis, that the Old Testament is not only an incomplete book but an avowedly incomplete book, which taught and teaches men to live by faith in the good things that were to come."[41] As noted earlier in this chapter, Caird argues that Hebrews falls into four sections, each having as its core an Old Testament passage that declares the ineffectiveness and sym-

38. R. Williamson, *Philo and the Epistle to the Hebrews* (Leiden: Brill, 1979), p. 538.

39. Caird, "Exegetical Method," p. 45. Longenecker (*Biblical Exegesis,* p. 164) proposes that Hebrews "should not automatically be classed as an example of hellenistic Christian argumentation and hermeneutics, but is to be viewed in continuity with early Christian exegetical procedures and in conformity with common Jewish exegetical practices, even though it employs these in its own highly individualized fashion."

40. Caird, "Exegetical Method," p. 46. Cf. F. F. Bruce, *The Time Is Fulfilled* (Exeter: Paternoster, 1978), pp. 77-94.

41. Caird, "Exegetical Method," p. 49; Motyer ("The Psalm Quotations," p. 21) similarly concludes that the writer looks for the tensions, even the contradictions, between texts, which allow him to assert that "Jesus is the fulfilment, the answer to the puzzle," and paradoxically, "to reinstate the Old Testament as 'the word of God' witnessing in its 'partial and fragmentary' way (1:1) to the Son who is the final Word."

bolic or provisional nature of the old covenant religious institutions. All other scriptural references are ancillary to these four (Psalms 8, 95, 110 and Jeremiah 31), which control the drift of the argument. Other scholars such as Richard Longenecker and William Lane have endorsed this approach and developed it in various ways.

Graham Hughes has investigated more extensively the hermeneutical method of Hebrews and related this to the situation of the original recipients, particularly as this is portrayed in 5:11–6:20. The writer addresses them as he does because they "have not attained the level of Christian maturity at which deep and sustained reflection on the meaning of the Word of God takes place."[42] He is concerned that they should be motivated to press on in their Christian lives by hearing correctly the Word of God. Hughes makes the interesting observation that in the theological-Christological sections, where the meaning of the death of Jesus is explored, the eschatological viewpoint is a realized one, but in the paraenetic passages Hebrews assumes a futurist aspect. Thus, "in the theologically oriented passages ('realized eschatology') the discontinuity with the old covenant is written large; in the exhortatory passages ('futurist eschatology') the continuity between old and new covenant is such that one might almost think the Christian era had never dawned."[43] The bipolarity of Christian existence has become "a hermeneutical screen which has been placed across the O.T. Scriptures" by the writer of Hebrews "to let them speak to different elements within the Christian experience." This is described as "the hermeneutic of eschatological existence," and in the concluding chapter of his book Hughes relates this hermeneutical technique to modern problems in the field of biblical interpretation.

The aim of this chapter has been to build on the insights of such scholars and to show more precisely how the various sections of Hebrews and their underlying scriptural themes link together. The hortatory thrust of Hebrews is grounded in the writer's presentation of the faithfulness of God in Scripture and its outcome in the person and work of Christ. Readers are urged to respond to God's faithfulness with persevering faith, sincere expressions of love, and grateful obedience.

42. G. Hughes, *Hebrews and Hermeneutics* (Cambridge: Cambridge University Press, 1979), p. 50.

43. Hughes, *Hebrews and Hermeneutics,* p. 70.

Paul's Literal Interpretation of "Do Not Muzzle the Ox"

David Instone-Brewer

Summary

Paul appears to use an allegorical method to interpret the Old Testament on a few occasions. All of these have been shown to be typological or literal interpretations except for his teaching from the text "Do not muzzle the ox," which he interprets as "Do not neglect to pay Christian ministers." However, in the eyes of a first-century Jew this is a literal interpretation because it was assumed that wherever the law said an "ox," it meant any kind of animal or human servant. This means that Paul nowhere used the allegorical method.

Does Paul Use Allegory?

Paul uses typology to interpret the Old Testament on many occasions, but he also appears to use allegory on a few occasions. Others have shown that his apparent allegories are either typology or literal interpretations, with the one exception of the text "Do not muzzle the ox." I will argue that this too is a literal interpretation.

This essay is adapted from "1 Corinthians 9.9-11: A Literal Interpretation of 'Do Not Muzzle the Ox,'" *New Testament Studies* 38 (1992): 554-65.

The difference between these three methods of interpretation can be illustrated by one of the texts where Paul appears to interpret allegorically: "the rock which followed — which was Christ" (1 Cor. 10:4).

A typological interpretation of "the rock which followed" would argue from a comparison between the rock and Christ: for example, just as God cared for the Israelites by providing water from a miraculous rock that followed them, in the same way God cares for his Church by providing refreshment from Christ, who is always with us. This is based on the assumption that God works in similar ways in similar situations, and that Scripture is likely to highlight these similarities.

An allegorical interpretation would argue from a spiritual or hidden equivalence between the rock and Christ; for example, when Scripture tells us that the rock followed Israel through the wilderness, it also teaches us that Christ keeps especially close to the believer when he travels through times of spiritual dryness. This is based on the assumption that Scripture has hidden truths that can be fathomed by the initiate or a spiritually minded person.

A literal interpretation would argue from an actual equivalence between the rock and Christ; for example, the rock was a preincarnate appearance of Christ who followed Israel in this guise through the wilderness and provided water when they needed it. This is based on the strange fact that the same rock was reported in more than one place — at Sinai (Exod. 17:6), at Kadesh (Num. 20:11), and perhaps also at Beer (Num. 21:16-18).[1]

At first glance Paul appears to imply an allegorical equivalence, because he says "the rock was Christ." Yet comparisons with traditional Jewish interpretations suggest that Paul had a literal equivalence in mind. Traditional Jewish sources preserve all three types of interpretation.

A typological interpretation:

> "Wherever Israel may turn, God will go with her in order to provide water for his people."[2]

1. Rabbinic literature preserves legends that link this well with the rock. This is seen most fully in *t. Sukk.* 3:11 and *Num. Rab.* 1:2. These probably represent a later development, but the concept of a rock that followed Israel through the wilderness is attested to by the first-century author Pseudo-Philo (*Bib. Ant.* 10:7, "a well of water followed them," and 1:15, "the water of Mara followed them in the desert 40 years").

2. *Mek. Exod.* 17:6. This is a relatively late source that preserves some early traditions. It is impossible to decide if this tradition dates back to the first century.

An allegorical interpretation:

> "The Rock of flint is the Wisdom of God from which he feeds the souls that love him."[3]

A literal interpretation:

> "the living well . . . which had been hidden . . . which was dug by the fathers of the world, Abraham, Isaac and Jacob, the princes who were of old."[4]

The last interpretation literally identifies the rock with a well that the patriarchs had dug and that had remained hidden in the meantime. This interpretation developed into a detailed legend about a well in the shape of a rock that followed Israel through the wilderness. Although it is unlikely that Paul referred to this legend,[5] it is likely that Paul had something like this in mind when he says that the rock "followed them."

A literal acceptance of the Old Testament text entailed belief that the rock moved because it was reported in more than one place. The modern reader would assume that the two place names indicated an error of some kind or that there were two similar rocks, but an ancient reader would assume that this pointed to a great miracle. This, together with the fact that the rock was identified with wisdom[6] and with God,[7] made a literal theophany seem logical and inevitable to a first-century mind. A literal interpretation is also suggested by Paul's use of the past tense when he says "the rock *was* Christ" instead of "the rock *is* Christ," which would be expected

3. Philo, *Leg. Alleg.* 2:21. See also Wisd. of Sol. 2:4, where Wisdom is associated with the giving of "water out of a flinty rock."

4. *Tg. Onq.* Num. 21:18. This is a late collection of Targum interpretations that can contain early material. It is likely that this interpretation is relatively early because the Well Midrash at Qumran (CD 6:3ff.) appears to be a response to it. The main thrust of the Qumran exposition is to identify the "princes" who dug the well, and the main point of the Targum story is that these princes were the patriarchs.

5. It was probably not fully developed till after Paul, and many details would not fit in with Paul's interpretation. See E. E. Ellis, "A Note on First Corinthians 10:4," *Journal of Biblical Literature* 76 (1957): 53-56.

6. See n. 4.

7. God is frequently called the Rock in the Old Testament: e.g., Gen. 49:24; Deut. 32:4, 15, 18, 30, 31; Pss. 18:31; 62:2; 78:35; 89:26; 95:1.

in an allegory.[8] For these reasons most commentators accept that Paul used a literal interpretation of the rock texts, although his idea of "literal" may be very different from ours.

Another text that appears to be an allegory is Galatians 4:22-31, which Paul himself called "allegorizing." However, several commentators have pointed out that this is actually a complex typology and not an allegory in a strict sense.[9] This is not too surprising because allegory had not yet become popular in the rabbinic Judaism in which Paul claims to have been trained. By the first century it was very popular in Alexandria, where it is exemplified by Philo, and it was starting to appear in Qumran and other sectarian literature, but allegory did not infiltrate rabbinic Judaism till after A.D. 70[10] and did not have much influence till Akiva in the mid-second century. In Galatians 4 Paul may have been trying to show that he could compete with the likes of Apollos, whose Alexandrian style of teaching seemed to impress so many people (Acts 18:24; 1 Cor. 3).

However, concerning 1 Cor 9:9-11[11] there is general agreement that Paul is interpreting allegorically. A. T. Hanson admits: "it is technically allegory, for there is no integral connection between a clergyman and an ox."[12] Even J. Jeremias, who regards Paul as conforming to Hillelite exegesis

8. See, e.g., A. Robertson and A. Plummer, *A Critical and Exegetical Commentary on the First Epistle of St. Paul to the Corinthians,* The International Critical Commentary (Edinburgh: T. & T. Clark, 1914), p. 185; and G. D. Fee, *The First Epistle to the Corinthians,* New International Commentary on the New Testament (Grand Rapids: Eerdmans, 1987), p. 407.

9. A. T. Hanson, *Studies in Paul's Technique and Theology* (London: SPCK, 1974), p. 161; F. F. Bruce, "Abraham Had Two Sons — A Study in Pauline Hermeneutics," in *New Testament Studies — Essays in Honor of Ray Summers in His Sixty-Fifth Year,* ed. H. L. Drumwright and C. Vaughan (Waco, Tex.: Baylor University Press, 1975), p. 83; O. Michel, *Paulus und seine Bibel* (Darmstadt: Wissenschaftliche Buchgesellschaft, 1972), p. 110; Leonhard Goppelt, *Typos: The Typological Interpretation of the Old Testament in the New,* ed. and trans. Donald H. Madvig (Grand Rapids: Eerdmans, 1981), p. 139.

10. In my survey of early rabbinic exegesis, of the approximately one hundred examples of exegesis that could be dated before A.D. 70, not one used allegory, or even attempted to interpret anything other than the plain meaning of the text; see D. Instone-Brewer, *Techniques and Assumptions in Jewish Exegesis before 70 CE* (Tübingen: J. C. B. Mohr [Paul Siebeck], 1992).

11. Other important studies not otherwise cited include: J. T. Noonan, Jr., "The Muzzled Ox," *Jewish Quarterly Review* 70 (1980): 172-75; G. M. Lee, "Studies in Texts: 1 Corinthians 9.9-10," *Theology* 71 (1968): 122-23.

12. A. T. Hanson, *The Living Utterances of God: The New Testament Exegesis of the Old* (London: Darton, Longman and Todd, 1983), p. 136.

in every other instance, regards 1 Cor. 9:9-11 as an example of Hellenistic Jewish allegory.[13] G. D. Fee disputes that allegory is the correct term,[14] arguing that "Paul does not speak to what the law *originally meant*, . . . [but] what it *means*, that is, with its *application* to their present situation" (his italics). Like R. C. H. Lenski[15] and others, he suggests that Paul has derived a general principle from the law, but he does not present a convincing methodology by which Paul did this except to say that it is "analogical."[16] W. C. Kaiser Jr. claims that Paul's interpretation is literal, saying that Paul did not "resort" to allegory because his interpretation was already implicit in Deuteronomy 25:4,[17] though he too fails to present Paul's methodology.

Paul's Interpretation of Muzzling the Ox

In 1 Corinthians 9:9-11, Paul cites his text and then presents an exegesis with four stages:

> In the Law of Moses it is written: "You shall not muzzle a threshing ox."
> 1. Is God concerned with oxen? [No]
> 2. Is it not surely/altogether *(pantōs)*[18] said for us? [Yes]
> 3. Certainly it was written for us because:

13. J. Jeremias, "Paulus als Hillelit," in *Neotestamentica et Semitica: Studies in Honor of Matthew Black,* ed. E. Ellis and M. Wilcox (Edinburgh: T. & T. Clark, 1969), p. 89.

14. Fee, *The First Epistle to the Corinthians,* p. 407.

15. R. C. H. Lenski, *The Interpretation of St. Paul's First and Second Epistles to the Corinthians* (Minneapolis: Augsburg, 1937), pp. 361-62.

16. Fee, *The First Epistle to the Corinthians,* p. 408.

17. W. C. Kaiser, Jr., "The Current Crisis in Exegesis and the Apostolic Use of Deuteronomy 25.4 in 1 Corinthians 9.8-10," *Journal of the Evangelical Theological Society* 21 (1973): 3-18.

18. H. St. J. Thackeray pointed out (in *The Relation of St. Paul to Contemporary Jewish Thought* [London & New York: Macmillan, 1900], p. 194) that *pantōs* could be translated "surely," as in the Vulgate *(utique* instead of *omnino).* He claimed that Paul used *pantōs* in this sense in every instance except 1 Cor. 9:22. Although he may have spoiled his case by overstating it, this is a valuable suggestion that has been taken up by many scholars. It is especially valuable because it appears to remove the implication that Paul is denying the plain meaning of the text. However, it still leaves the question as to why Paul wrote in such a dangerously ambiguous manner. In the present exegesis, *pantōs* can be read as either "surely" or "altogether."

He who ploughs should plough in hope,
and he who threshes [should thresh] in hope that he will partake.

4. If we sowed spiritual things for you, much more should we reap material things from you.

Paul used the timeless technique of arguing from what is accepted towards that which he wished to prove. Stages 1-3 all have parallels in rabbinic legislation and would have met with approval. Point 4 is the conclusion when these are accepted.

1. *Does the provision "do not muzzle the ox" demonstrate God's great love for oxen?*

Any rabbinic Jew would immediately answer, "No: it states a command that we should obey."

In the early days of synagogue worship, before the wording of the services had a fixed form, there was need for guidelines concerning what could and could not be included in prayers. One of these guidelines was: "If a man said [in his prayer]: 'To a bird's nest do Thy mercies extend' [cf. Deut. 22.7] . . . they put him to silence."[19] It was forbidden to praise God for his compassion to animals as demonstrated in the Torah, in case it was felt that this detracted from the literal observance of the decree.[20] The law was not given to display God's character but to be obeyed.

Although Philo and Josephus cited the law of not muzzling the ox as an example of the humane character of the Law,[21] this was for teaching Gentiles. Gentiles were entitled to an explanation, but as far as an Israelite was concerned, it was sufficient that God had ordained it.[22]

Therefore Paul can ask, *Does this decree demonstrate that God cares for oxen?* and be confident that the answer is "No." However there is still doubt: If God did not give this decree for the sake of oxen, then why did he give it?

2. *Is the decree not altogether for man's benefit?*

A rabbinic Jew would answer: "Yes, the whole Law is given for man to obey, and to receive blessing through that obedience." This blessing would

19. *m. Ber.* 5.3; *m. Meg.* 4.9

20. The most likely reason for this is "because he presents the measures taken by the Holy One, blessed be He, as springing from compassion, whereas they are but decrees" (*b. Ber.* 33b; cf. *y. Ber.* 5.3).

21. Philo, *Virt.* 145-46; Josephus, *Ant.* 4.233 [8.21].

22. This is seen in the different reply that Yohanan b. Zakkai (late first century) gives to his disciples and to a Gentile concerning the red heifer (*Pesiq. R.* 14; *Num. Rab.* 19:8).

not be a reward for obedience but the blessing of knowing that they had obeyed God. It was the hypocrites who obeyed the Law in order to receive reward or to escape punishment.[23] Paul does not mean to deny the literal observance of this law because his continuing argument will depend on its literal interpretation. He points out, however, as any Jew would have done, that the law was not written for the ox to obey, but for people, and although this obedience would benefit the ox, this was insignificant compared to the benefit for the man who obeyed it.

In the age of animal rights and environmental politics this understanding is difficult to appreciate. However, older commentators had no difficulty understanding it. For example, Henry Alford argued in a very similar vein[24] (his italics):

> Every duty of *humanity* has for its ultimate ground, not the mere welfare of the animal concerned, but its welfare *in that system of which MAN is the head:* and therefore *man's* welfare. The good done to man's immortal spirit by acts of humanity and justice infinitely outweighs the mere physical comfort of a brute which perishes.

This attitude does not betray insensitivity towards animals but a realistic approach to the law. It is written for those who can read it, as Philo says: "The Law does not prescribe for unreasoning creatures, but for those who have mind and reason."[25] Luther puts it characteristically bluntly: "Oxen cannot read."[26] The decree is given altogether for man's benefit, who is far more important than an ox. Man benefits by obeying God, but as Paul (and the rabbis) go on to argue, man also benefits along with the ox by having the right to eat from the produce he labors over.

3. *Certainly it was written for us because "A laborer may partake of crops he ploughs or threshes."*

This is almost a paraphrase of a verse of Mishnah:

> These may eat [of the crop in which they labor] by virtue of what is enjoined in the Law: he who labours on what is still growing after the work

23. *y. Ber.* 9.7.

24. H. Alford, *The Greek Testament* (Chicago: Moody, 1958), 2:544.

25. Philo, *Spec. Leg.* 1.260

26. Quoted in Lenski, *Interpretation of St. Paul's First and Second Epistles to the Corinthians*, p. 361.

> is finished [i.e., from ploughing to reaping], and he who labours on what is already gathered before the work is finished [i.e., threshing]. (*m. B. Meṣ.* 7.2)

It seems likely that Paul had this specific ruling in mind, though in his day it would have existed as oral law rather than written tradition. His paraphrase divides up the ruling into the same two categories and the same order: first laborers working on crops that are planted (plowing), and then laborers working on crops no longer planted (threshing). He therefore appears to be quoting or referring to a well-known oral ruling. He preceded the quotation with a *hoti* that might be regarded as *recitativum,*[27] rather than with "it is written," which would have been normal for a written source.

Paul appears to emphasize the link between human laborers and oxen by naming the two activities in which both men and oxen are involved: plowing and threshing.[28] This is similar to the way in which a scriptural foundation was found for this ruling, which is recorded by later rabbis in the Talmud. First they found the reason why an ox has these rights, and then why men also have these rights.[29] Although the Talmudic exegesis

27. Weiss and then Conzelmann argued that the *hoti* of v. 10 is *recitativum* and that the rest of the verse is a quotation from an apocryphon. Most commentators replied as Robertson and Plummer (*First Epistle of St. Paul to the Corinthians,* p. 185) did, that "this is a most improbable construction: there is no such Scripture." It is unlikely that Paul knew this mishnah in any written form (except as private notes), so this is not a true *recitativum* linked with *egraphē,* but the construction does suggest that his readers would recognize the citation. See J. Weiss, *Der Erste Korintherbrief* (Göttingen: Vandenhoeck & Ruprecht, 1910), p. 237; H. Conzelmann, *1 Corinthians,* Hermeneia (Philadelphia: Fortress, 1975), p. 155.

28. See Philo, *Virt.* 145 [271]

29. The ruling states that a laborer may eat any crop that (a) is still planted and (b) is no longer planted. The Talmudic commentary discusses this at length (*b. B. Meṣ.* 87a-91b). Both halves of the ruling are derived from Scripture, and they are each applied to both human laborers and animals. First, the ruling that a human laborer may eat from a crop that is still planted is derived simply from Deut. 23:25-26 and then discussed (*b. B. Meṣ.* 87a-88b). Second, it is assumed from Deut. 25:4 that an animal may eat from a crop that is no longer planted. Then the Talmud continues: "We now know that man [may eat when employed upon] what is attached to the soil, and an ox of what is detached; whence do we know that man may eat of what is detached?" They cannot find a separate Scripture, so they argue by *qal waḥomer:* "It follows a *minori,* from an ox: if an ox, which does not eat of what is attached, may nevertheless eat of what is detached, then a man, who may eat of what is attached, may surely eat of what is detached!"

was probably added far later than the original ruling in the Mishnah, it is likely that this was a traditional exegesis. The Mishnah states that this ruling (unlike a great number of rulings) was based on the written law, so an exegesis did exist to substantiate the ruling though, as usual, the Mishnah omits this exegesis. This conforms to the style of early exegeses. It depends only on the plain meaning of the text and uses a common early argument called *qal waḥomer*, "from minor and major" ("if this major thing is allowed, then surely this minor thing is allowed as well"). There therefore is no reason to believe that this is not the exegesis envisioned by the Mishnah.

Stages 1-3 in Paul's exegesis have merely stated what was orthodox rabbinic thought. God's law is not to be used as a demonstration of his mercy to animals — it is to be obeyed. The law was written not for animals, but for man to obey. Obedience to a decree showing mercy to animals actually benefits the obedient man far more than the animal. Yet a human laborer also benefits from the law forbidding muzzling of oxen, because he too may eat from grain he threshes.

4. *If we worked on a spiritual crop, much more should we partake from a material crop.*

This is another *qal waḥomer* argument: If a laborer may eat of a valuable crop he is working on, then surely he is allowed to eat from a less valuable crop instead.

This is Paul's only new argument, and it is unanswerable. He has used the same exegetical technique accepted before at stage 3, and based it on the same texts. The technique of *qal waḥomer*, unlike some other exegetical techniques, could be used to derive a new legal ruling that had all the force of the original written law and, used properly, was virtually unquestionable. The only way in which his opponents could challenge Paul's argument would be to demonstrate some difference between the labor that Paul did and the labor intimated by Deuteronomy 23:25-26 or 25:4. Perhaps Paul had this defense in mind when he already established the similarity of the ministry to agricultural laboring at 1 Corinthians 3:5-8.

In this exegesis, Paul has derived from the law the right of a Christian worker to wages. He has based this on a literal interpretation of Deuteronomy 25:4 and on the contemporary understanding of the term "ox" in the law as a reference to all types of laborer, human and animal.

Possible Objections

There are three main objections to this exegesis that must be dealt with:

1. There are parallel texts in Philo and Aristeas that suggest that Paul is arguing for the use of allegory.
2. The rabbinic material is much later than Paul.
3. The exegesis ignores or goes beyond the plain meaning of Deuteronomy 25:4.

The texts in Philo and Aristeas that are often cited as parallels to "Does God care about oxen" are:

Philo, *Somn.* 1.93 (regarding Exod. 22:26-27):

> Do not those who feel that the Lawgiver feels all this concern about a cloak deserve, if not reproach, at least a reminder in such terms as "What are you saying, good sirs? Does the Creator and Ruler of the universe speak of Himself as compassionate in regard to so trifling a matter as a garment not returned to a debtor by a lender of money?"

Aristeas 144:

> Do not take the contemptible view that Moses enacted this legislation because of an excessive preoccupation with mice and weasels or suchlike creatures.

Philo and Aristeas go on to explain the allegorical meaning of the cloak and of weasels. Their attitude is similar to the modern legal maxim *de minimis non curat lex,* "the law takes no notice of trifles." If such trifles are present in the perfect law, then there must be some hidden meaning.

However, for the rabbis there was no matter too trifling for God, and if he decreed it, one should obey it, even if no reason could be found. Paul cannot have meant to imply that the literal meaning should be abandoned, because he depended on the literal meaning to prove that men, who were included in the term "oxen," should also be allowed to share the crop on which they labored.

A more likely understanding of Paul's phrase is, as argued above, that the law was written to benefit *man,* who obeys it. The man who, through obedience, shows mercy, gains far more than the one receiving the mercy.

The second objection, about the use of late rabbinic sources in New Testament studies, is a frequent and usually valid complaint. The dating of rabbinic material is still an inexact art, and the only safe route is to find validation in several different types of material, preferably including the LXX, Philo, Josephus, or possibly the Targumim. In most cases this is impossible because, unless the matter is frequently discussed, it is unlikely that enough sources will have survived.

The key discussion linking Deuteronomy 25:4 with a human laborer occurs only once as an anonymous exegesis in the Talmud.[30] It is likely, as argued above, that this is an accurate reflection of the exegesis referred to in the earlier Mishnah passage, but this Mishnaic ruling is also very difficult to date.

However, it is not necessary to show that Paul was alluding to this particular rabbinic ruling. It is only necessary to show that Paul's argument would be understood by contemporary Jews and that he was arguing in a way that would be acceptable to them. The fact that other Jews used very similar arguments suggests that this was so.

"Ox" Includes All Animal and Human Servants

The most important factor that underlies this argument in both Paul and the Mishnah and Talmud is the equivalence of the rights of human servants and oxen. In the Jewish world in general decrees that referred to an ox could be applied directly to a human servant.

There are two examples of this equivalence in exegeses that can, relatively securely, be dated before A.D. 70.

> An event happened when a slave of King Yannai killed a man. Simeon b. Shetah said to the Sages: Place your eyes on him and let him be judged. They sent to him: Your slave killed a man. He delivered him [the slave] to them. They sent to him: Come here yourself likewise. Torah says: *And warning is given to its owner* [Exod. 21:29] — the owner of the ox must come and stand with his ox. (*b. Sanh.* 19ab)

When the king sent his guilty servant to stand trial, Simeon sent a message that the king should come and stand with his "ox" (i.e., his ser-

30. *b. B. Meṣ.* 88b.

vant), as the Torah demanded (Exod. 21:29). This can be dated early because Josephus records the same event, although there are important differences in his account.[31]

The second example is a dispute between the Pharisees and the Sadducees. These disputes can generally be dated before A.D. 70 because the Sadducees lost virtually all their influence after the destruction of Jerusalem.[32]

> The Sadducees say: We protest against you Pharisees, for you say: My ox or my ass which has caused damage is liable [for compensation — Exod. 21:29-32], but my male or female slave which caused damage is not liable. Why is it that for my ox or my ass, for which I am not liable for commandments concerning them, I am liable for damages, but my male or female slave for whom I am liable for commandments concerning them [e.g., Exod. 21:20, 26-27], is it not logical that I am liable for damages? The Pharisees say: No, If you say [this] concerning my ox or my ass which have no understanding, will you say it concerning my male and female slaves which have understanding? If I anger them, they will go and burn the grain stack of another and I will be liable for compensation. (*m. Yad.* 4.7)

The argument concerns whether or not a master is liable for damage done by a servant. The details of the argument are not important here,[33] but it is significant that both Pharisees and Sadducees assumed the equivalence of "ox" and "servant." The Sadducean argument depended on this

31. He records that "Sameas stood up to King Herod after Herod's soldiers had slaughtered some untried bandits" (Josephus, *Ant.* 14.168-76 [9.4]). Although Josephus does not record that Herod first sent a soldier to stand trial, he does describe how Herod then brought with him a large band of soldiers into court. Both the Talmud and Josephus record how the rest of the Sanhedrin were cowed into submission, and all but Simeon/Sameas were subsequently killed (cf. *Ant.* 15.2-4 [1.1]). The record in the Talmud is clearly not as old as the event because enough time had elapsed for Herod to be confused with Alexander Jannaeus, who also had conflicts with the Sanhedrin. However, the core of the story is accurate, and the exegesis is unlikely to have been added later because it is integral to the story.

32. This exegesis is unlikely to be a later invention by the Pharisees, because they barely come out on top, mainly by having the last word. The exegetical argument of *qal waḥomer* used by the Sadducees is well constructed and based on the context of the main text, but the rebuttal by the Pharisees is based mainly on pragmatic issues.

33. For a detailed analysis of the argument see my *Techniques and Assumptions*, pp. 94-95.

equivalence, but they did not feel any need to substantiate it. The Pharisees did not dispute it, and even carried it further.

This debate represents just one of the multitude of debates that must have occurred concerning these verses because a large body of the law of tort is based on the equivalence of a man with a dangerous ox. The Mishnah tractate *Baba Qamma* (which deals with tort) starts with a definition of damages according to the four categories of damage dealt with in Scripture, the first of which is the ox.[34] This tractate is based on the same assumption as found in the Pharisee-Sadducee debate: that an ox that is known to be dangerous is equivalent to a human,[35] but not an ox that has previously been thought to be safe (for which no damages were liable — Exod. 21:28). This assumption is not explained or justified anywhere. It seems that "ox" was regarded as a standard legal term for a servant or laborer of any species. Even in the earliest strata of this tractate there is no interest in proving this equivalence, though exceptions to this general rule are noted.[36]

This equivalence of oxen and humans is also assumed in debates that involve the decree prohibiting muzzling. A wife was accused of stealing grain from her husband because she ate some grain that she was grinding, and R. Joseph (third century) defended her by saying: "The ox eats of his threshing."[37] Another woman, who was a childless widow, was being forced into a levirite marriage to her dead husband's brother, who was ugly or poor or both. R. Eliezer b. Azariah (end of first century) said that she should not be "muzzled" — that is, "gagged" or prevented from expressing her dissent regarding the marriage.[38] This exegesis is probably much older because the LXX and Targums allude to it.[39]

34. The four are: "the ox [Exod. 21:28-32, 35-36], the pit [Exod. 21:33-34], the tooth [which eats — Exod. 22:5 (MT 22:4)] and the fire [Exod. 22:6 (MT 22:5)]."

35. *m. B. Qam.* 3.8.

36. *m. B. Qam.* 3.10; 8.2.

37. *b. Git.* 62a.

38. *b. Mak.* 23a; *b. Yebam.* 4a. This argument is based on the exegetical technique *samuk,* i.e., exegesis together with the neighboring ruling, which in this case concerns levirate marriages (Deut. 25:5-6). L. Ginzberg ("The Allegorical Interpretation of Scripture," in *On Jewish Law and Lore* [New York: KTAV, 1955], pp. 127-50) and J. Bonsirven (*Exégèse rabbinique et exégèse paulinienne* [Paris: Beauchesne et ses fils, 1939], pp. 227-28) argued that Paul could have derived his ruling in 1 Cor. 9:9-11 from this exegesis alone.

39. The LXX translates using *phimoō,* which is to "gag" generally, instead of *kēmoō,* which Paul used and which means more specifically "to muzzle." The better MS evidence for

The third objection, that Paul's exegesis goes beyond the plain meaning of the text, is true only for the modern reader.[40] As far as Paul's contemporaries were concerned, an "ox" in Scripture implied any laborer, of any species of animal, including human.

With our historical-critical approach it is clear that the author of Exodus 21 did not have in his mind the vast body of tort that was finally derived from it. The Book of the Covenant was certainly not written with the assumption that "ox" meant anything other than "ox."

However, for Paul's contemporaries, the Torah was given by God to Moses. It was the perfect law, capable of ruling on every aspect of human life, with every decree perfectly interrelated with every other decree. They assumed that if the ox was named in a decree while other animals were not specified, this did not mean that the law had forgotten or neglected the others. Therefore, they reasoned that "ox" must be shorthand for "animal and human servants." This is similar to the way in which modern case law derives rulings from cases that are not identical but that are similar in significant details.

This equivalence of "ox" with all laborers is not just a legal nicety but lies at the core of the Jewish understanding of their law. Even when Josephus is speaking about the literal significance to oxen of the ruling "do not muzzle," he calls oxen "our fellow laborers *(syneirgasmenou)*."[41]

In conclusion, the understanding that "ox" in Scripture implied all laboring species was already well established by the time of Paul. It was a founding principle in the law of tort, and it is assumed in many other individual debates. Most significantly it is assumed by both sides in a Pharisee-Sadducee debate and by an exegesis dependent on Deuteronomy 25:4 that is witnessed to by the Targumim and possibly the LXX.

This exegesis is unique among Paul's exegeses, but not because it is an example of allegory, as others have argued. It is unique because it is the time when Paul derives a new law from Scripture. New laws, or *halakot,* are very common in rabbinic Judaism, but this is the only occasion when we

---

phimōseis is outweighed by the likelihood that *kēmōseis* would have been absorbed from the LXX. The Jerusalem and Palestinian Targumim read: "You shall not muzzle the mouth of the ox in the time of his treading out; nor the wife of the [deceased] brother, who would be mated with one smitten with an ulcer, and who is poorly related, shalt thou tie up with him."

40. Cf. M. D. Hooker, "Beyond the Things That Are Written? St Paul's Use of Scripture," *New Testament Studies* 27 (1980-81): 305.

41. Josephus, *Ant.* 4.233 (8.21).

see it in the writings of Paul. Here he mustered all his legal expertise, using legal terminology, quoting legal rulings, and employing legal exegetical techniques that a contemporary rabbi would have been proud of.[42] He prefaced this exegesis with "as it is written in the law of Moses" — a unique introductory formula for Paul.[43]

This exegesis represents a new halakah derived by Paul from the Torah in a thoroughly rabbinic way, which makes it all the more striking when he does not ask the Corinthians to obey it. E. P. Sanders pointed out that "Paul as a rule does not cite commandments . . . and *then* say that they should be obeyed."[44] Paul has argued like a Jewish legal expert, but he does not apply his conclusions like one. He has derived a ruling that carries all the force of the written law, but he does not demand obedience. He preached freedom from the law, so although he has demonstrated his rights under the law, he does not claim them.

42. D. Cohn-Sherbok, who regarded Paul's exegeses as thoroughly Pharisaic, said that nevertheless "certain aspects of rabbinic exegesis, such as the expansion of Scriptural law, are absent from the epistles" ("Paul and Rabbinic Exegesis," *Scottish Journal of Theology* 35 [1982]: 132). If my conclusions are correct, Paul is thoroughly Pharisaic in this respect too.

43. The exactly equivalent phrase ככתוב בתורה משה occurs in rabbinic sources, e.g., *b. Yoma* 35b, 66a.

44. E. P. Sanders, *Paul, the Law and the Jewish People* (London: SCM, 1985), p. 107.

HISTORICAL, SYSTEMATIC, AND PHILOSOPHICAL PERSPECTIVES

The Church Fathers and Their Use of Scripture

Gerald Bray

Summary

The Church Fathers wrote in a context in which ancient writings, especially those of Homer and Plato, were regarded as intellectual authorities. Not infrequently such texts were allegorized in order to update them or to make them morally acceptable to later generations. Christians used the Bible in a similar way, but they quoted Scripture with a frequency and an accuracy unparalleled in pagan literature. In spite of what many modern scholars think, they resorted to allegory only sparingly, and as time went on they developed special rules for its use. According to the Fathers, the Bible gave the Church its knowledge of God and provided principles that were meant to be applied as literally as possible. Only when the literal sense could not be applied for some reason was there recourse to other methods of interpretation. The Fathers were not always right in the conclusions that they drew, but this does not affect the validity of their presuppositions and methods, which have consistently proved their value in the history of the Church.

Introduction

For some curious reason, the attitude of the Church Fathers to Scripture has been relatively neglected in modern research. At the most fundamental level, the biblical commentaries that have come down to us from ancient times remain almost unknown even to most biblical scholars, and many of them have never been translated. Studies of patristic exegesis do exist,[1] but there are not many of them, and the work of some of the best expositors, like Ambrosiaster or Theodore of Mopsuestia, has been virtually ignored. This is unfortunate, because it is in the Fathers' exegesis, more than in any theoretical statements about the nature of the Bible, that we can see how they used the text and can determine from that what they really believed about it. In recent years there have been encouraging signs that interest in patristic exegesis is making a comeback,[2] but it is still too early to tell what impact this will have on the wider theological constituency.

Beyond what might be called "intentional" exegesis represented by commentaries and homiletical material, there is also an immense reservoir of patristic quotations from Scripture that can help us to understand how the Fathers used the Bible and what kind of text they understood it to be. These quotations have to be used with great care, of course, because the Fathers were in the habit of making casual allusions to Scripture whenever it came to mind in the course of their arguments, whether the passages in question had any real bearing on the issue or not. It would be easy to use examples of that kind as a way of discrediting their approach to the Bible, and this has sometimes been done, but it is unfair. What such allusions indicate is not that the Fathers were incapable of serious exegesis but that their minds were so steeped in the Bible that to quote it whenever the opportunity presented itself struck them as a perfectly natural thing to do. That in turn reflects a profound knowledge of Scripture that they would not have possessed if it had not been central to their faith. It is in this way, rather than in a literalistic reading of the quotes themselves, that we can measure the role the Bible played in the formation of their mental and spiritual outlook.

Defining the precise limits of the patristic period is difficult,[3] and it must always be remembered that the Fathers were very diverse in their interests, temperaments, and approaches to their faith. Although this diver-

1. See my *Biblical Interpretation: Past and Present* (Leicester: Apollos, 1996), pp. 77-115 for a general survey and bibliography.

2. Evidenced, e.g., in the *Ancient Christian Commentary on Scripture* series edited by T. C. Oden and being published by InterVarsity Press, U.S.A. (2001-).

3. For our purposes we take it to include everything up to the Council of Chalcedon in A.D. 451, though it should probably be extended to the time of Pope Gregory I "the Great" (590-604) or even later.

sity is important, it must not be allowed to obscure the underlying unity of their outlook, a unity that is particularly noticeable on the subject of Scripture. However different their interpretations may have been, and however often some of them may have strayed beyond the bounds of what has come to be regarded as orthodoxy,[4] *all* the Church Fathers, without exception, believed that the Bible was God's word written, and that it could therefore be fully trusted in everything that it affirmed to be true.

The Ancient Cultural Context

In historical terms, what we call the patristic period follows directly on the heels of that of the New Testament, and there is no clear break between them. Nevertheless, it is fair to say that it can be distinguished from the apostolic age by the fact that Greco-Roman culture, which played only a secondary role in the New Testament, came to dominate the Fathers' outlook. This was particularly true after the legalization of Christianity in the fourth century, but the phenomenon can be detected long before that. Even Justin Martyr (ca. 100-156), who was born in Samaria and who engaged in dialogue with the Jews of his day, was quite clearly a product of Hellenistic civilization, not of Judaism, either in its Palestinian or in its Diaspora form, and this sets him apart from the New Testament writers. There are many reasons for this, ranging from the growing marginalization of Judaism (beginning with the fall of Jerusalem in A.D. 70 and intensifying after the failure of the Bar-Kochba revolt in A.D. 142-45) to the fact that church leaders were increasingly drawn from the educated elite of Greco-Roman society, whose prejudices they often shared, whose concerns they wanted to address, and whose educational methods they naturally claimed as their own.

4. Orthodoxy is a complex notion in the patristic period, though everybody (including those regarded as heretics) believed that such a thing existed in principle. In general, most orthodox theologians today would make a distinction between those writers who were condemned later (e.g., Origen) for reasons that were not apparent during their own lifetimes, and those (e.g., Arius) who were condemned as they wrote and who were therefore consciously at odds with the Church. There is also a third category of writers (e.g., Pelagius) who were condemned in their own lifetimes but whose works were later "doctored" and recycled, under other names, as orthodox. It is generally regarded as fair to quote from the first and third types as representatives of the patristic tradition, but not from the second.

To what extent did their pagan cultural heritage influence what the Church Fathers believed and taught about the Bible? In many ways, of course, the Greco-Roman world was closer to contemporary Judaism than either are to the prevailing spirit of modern times, and this must be borne in mind when we judge how "distinctive" the Fathers were in their beliefs. For example, on the question of the divine inspiration of Scripture, it is not always fully appreciated that the Greeks and Romans were no strangers to the notion that literary works were divinely inspired, and they had much less difficulty with this idea than we might have today. Poetry, and particularly the epics attributed to Homer, were almost universally regarded as the work of some supernatural genius, and (to a surprising degree) the *Iliad* and the *Odyssey* even formed the basis of what passed for "theology" in the pagan Greek world. It is true that Homer's defects as a theologian were painfully apparent to Plato, who would have excluded all poets from his ideal republic, but the philosophers who followed him had to come to terms with the Greeks' attachment to their literary classics, and this included some acceptance of their "theology." On the whole, they resolved the difficulty by developing an allegorical interpretation of the texts, which looked for hidden meanings in them that would be more acceptable than those that appeared on the surface.

The allegorical method was subsequently adopted by Philo of Alexandria and applied by him to the Old Testament in an attempt to show that, underneath their "barbarous" exterior, the Jewish Scriptures were in effect the source from which Plato got all his best ideas.[5] Philo was a Jewish contemporary of Jesus and Paul, but there is no sign that he influenced the thinking of the New Testament writers. If there is any similarity between them (in the prologue to John's Gospel, for example, or the Epistle to the Hebrews), it must be regarded as coincidental. It was Clement of Alexandria, about A.D. 200, who took up Philo's allegories and introduced them into the Christian Church, where they have been a source of hermeneutical confusion ever since.

It is probably no exaggeration to say that the modern reluctance to take patristic (and medieval) biblical exegesis seriously is based to a large extent on the widely held conviction that it is mainly allegorical in nature. The Church Fathers undoubtedly did use allegory fairly often, and there are certain well-known instances in which they regarded it as the best

5. For one of the more sober accounts of this, see Augustine, *City of God* VIII, 11.

method to use in interpreting particular books or passages of the Bible. The parables of Jesus, for example, or the Song of Songs, were generally treated in this way, and the often bizarre results that allegory could give proved to be highly popular, particularly in medieval monasteries. Although that much is true, it does not mean that allegory was ever regarded as their standard method of interpretation by patristic exegetes. Even a cursory reading of ancient commentaries will reveal that it was only one device among many, and that normally its use was restricted to certain well-defined instances. Furthermore, the Fathers never accepted the idea that allegory could be a principle of biblical interpretation in its own right, but only that it was a way of discovering truths that were already known from the literal sense of other biblical texts.

The contrast between pagan and Christian writers on this point becomes clearer if we compare the actual use that the different groups made of their sacred literature. The ancient Greeks frequently quoted Homer in all sorts of contexts, but almost always as an embellishment to what they were saying in other ways — rather in the way that we today might quote Shakespeare to buttress a point. It is also true that they wrote commentaries on the Homeric epics, but these were mainly intended to explain the many obscurities that the Homeric dialect presented to Greeks of later generations. The best English comparison here is with Chaucer — without at least a glossary it is impossible for the average person to read and understand *The Canterbury Tales,* and some form of "commentary" is therefore essential. Although commentary of this kind on Scripture can certainly be found in the writings of the Church Fathers, the fact remains that they used the Bible and wrote about it in a way that had no real parallel in pagan Greco-Roman culture.

One comparison will suffice to illustrate this. Plotinus (ca. 204-70), who is generally regarded as the "founder" of Neoplatonism, mentions Plato relatively infrequently (about fifty times) and seldom quotes him directly, although modern scholars have detected up to 900 allusions to the Platonic corpus in his works.[6] Impressive as this may seem, it pales in comparison with his older contemporary Origen (ca. 185–ca. 254), who quotes Scripture so extensively and so exactly that he is often cited in critical edi-

6. M. L. Gatti, "The Platonic Tradition and the Foundation of Neoplatonism," in *The Cambridge Companion to Plotinus,* ed. L. P. Gerson (Cambridge: Cambridge University Press, 1996), pp. 10-37.

tions of the Greek New Testament as a witness for particular readings of the text. Given that it is possible (if unproved) that Origen and Plotinus studied under the same teachers at Alexandria and must have shared a similar outlook towards the authority of ancient sources, we can attribute this remarkable difference only to one of fundamental principle. It was not just the spiritual legacy of the Bible that mattered to Origen, but the very words of the text, because in his view every syllable came out of the mouth of God and enjoyed absolute authority over his mind and life. Plotinus did not feel that way about Plato (let alone about Homer), and the use he made of their writings bears that out.

More to the point, the Fathers' generally sober and literal approach to biblical exegesis stands in sharp contrast to the way in which the Greek philosophers read the "sacred texts" of ancient Hellenism. It would not be too much of an exaggeration to say that Plato, for example, did not believe a word that Homer said — which is why he wanted to expel all poets from his ideal republic. One might also say that later philosophers made up allegory as a way of accommodating poetic statements whose literal sense was morally or intellectually unacceptable to them. This is particularly clear in the commentaries that Porphyry (d. ca. 303), the disciple and successor of Plotinus, wrote on the Homeric epics, which became a model of allegorization for later Neoplatonists like Iamblichus and Proclus.[7]

The Christian approach to the Bible could not have been more different — something that is all the more remarkable when we consider that many of the Church Fathers, including Augustine, were strongly influenced by the Neoplatonists and were fully acquainted with their allegorizing tendencies. Yet in sharp contrast to them, the Fathers used allegory, if at all, only to clarify parts of the biblical text whose literal sense was obscure or appeared to be unworthy of God (like the treatment meted out to the Babylonian children in Psalm 13). Moreover, whether or not such a passage reflected God's character was not determined by the Fathers' own wishes in the matter but by clearly revealed statements elsewhere in Scripture. For example, the Bible states that God is good and that he hates nothing that he has made, but these statements are apparently contradicted by an incident like the destruction of the Babylonian children. It was in cases like these that allegory proved its worth by offering an interpretation of the text that was moral or spiritual — the children stood

7. See, e.g., R. T. Wallis, *Neoplatonism*, 2nd ed. (London: Duckworth, 1995), pp. 134-37.

for sins that had to be rooted out before they grew to the point where they became formidable enemies. Augustine states the position very clearly as follows:

> As well as the rule which warns us not to pursue a figurative expression as if it were literal, we must add a further one: not to accept a literal one as if it were figurative. We must first explain the way to discover whether an expression is literal or figurative. Generally speaking it is this: anything in the divine discourse that cannot be related either to good morals or to the true faith should be taken as figurative. Good morals have to do with our love of God and our neighbour, the true faith with our understanding of God and our neighbour.[8]

This solution enabled the Fathers to uphold the authority of difficult texts without contradicting what they knew to be true about God's character. They adopted it precisely because they did not regard themselves as free either to dispense with such texts altogether or to relegate them to a lower level of authority. If the literal sense was unacceptable for some reason, then it was clear to them that God was speaking to his people in another way, and it was up to the interpreter to determine, in the light of what he already knew, what that way was.

It is true that Christians quoted the Bible to illustrate points they were making, and that very often these quotations cannot be regarded as exegetically serious. It is also true that they wrote commentaries in order to explain the hard parts in the text (though few went to the trouble of learning Hebrew in order to do this). Once again, the results are comparable to what pagans achieved — sometimes they were right in their explanations, sometimes they were (pardonably) wrong, and sometimes they were just totally fanciful. As a matter of principle, however, the Fathers generally stuck to the literal interpretation of a text unless they had some reasonable ground for moving beyond it to one or more of the figurative senses that allegory encouraged. Moreover, when they did this, they were usually careful to respect the rule of exegesis that said that nothing should be "discovered" by figurative means that was not already plain from the literal sense of other biblical passages. This rule was expressed by saying that

8. Augustine, *On Christian Teaching* III, 33-34 (taken from the translation by R. P. H. Green [Oxford: Oxford University Press, 1997]).

the clearer parts of Scripture should be used to interpret the harder parts — a rule that has survived the collapse of allegory and remains valid today. For example, when Augustine interpreted the parable of the good Samaritan in a way that made the Samaritan a type of Jesus, the man lying by the wayside a type of the sinner to be saved, the inn a type of the Church, and so on, he was not inventing a gospel message that was unknown to his hearers. All he was doing was trying to show that the story of salvation, already perfectly familiar to them from the literal reading of the Gospels, could also be found in the parable by reading it along allegorical lines. Today everyone would agree that Augustine was mistaken in this attempt, but it would be most unfair to him to use such an example to dismiss his overall understanding of Scripture as primarily allegorical.

The real point of difference between ancient and (most) modern commentators is to be found in the ways in which they generally assess the relationship of the Old Testament to the New. It was standard practice in ancient times to look for typological and prophetic foreshadowings of the coming of Christ in the Old Testament, and so we find that the Fathers saw nothing wrong in regarding the epiphanies of angels, for example, as preincarnational appearances of the Son of God. This would not meet with general acceptance today, but neither is it fair to call it a figurative interpretation of the Bible. For the Fathers, believing that such incidents were a foretaste of the Messiah to come did not diminish the text's authority but enhanced it, by giving it an ongoing significance in the life of the Christian Church.

Modern exegetes may dislike such typological readings of the Old Testament, but if they are Christians, they still have to find some way of incorporating the Jewish Scriptures into the life of the Christian Church. It is no accident that most of the post-Enlightenment discussion about the nature and authority of the Bible has focused on the Old Testament because it still poses the most fundamental hermeneutical questions for Christian interpreters of Scripture. We may wish to dissent from the Fathers' resolution of this difficulty, but we should respect the fact that the problem they were dealing with is still alive and well in the Church today.

As far as the Fathers were concerned, the Old Testament may have lost some of its immediate applicability once Christ came and opened the way of salvation to the Gentiles, but this did not make it redundant. They understood that the New Testament did not start all over again from scratch but assumed a basic knowledge (and acceptance) of the Old Testament as a foundation on which it could build. Many things, like the doctrine of creation, were explained in the Old Testament and simply taken for granted in the New, so that a good knowledge of the Old remained essential for Christians. Even the apparently obsolete parts (like the Mosaic food laws) were there to teach the Church about the holiness of God in ways that the New Testament simply assumes. It is true that in the second century, Marcion rejected the Old Testament as a source of Christian doctrine, but almost everybody else regarded him as a heretic for this. In fact, it was very largely this felt need to retain the Old Testament, with all its obscurities and apparently inapplicable passages, which gave rise to patristic interpretation of the Bible in the first place.

Augustine explained the existence of the hard parts of Scripture by saying that God deliberately put them there in order to keep us awake and attentive to his voice. This may sound like an odd thing to say, but anyone who has read the Bible in another language will know what Augustine meant by this. When we read a text in a language familiar to us we actually skim over large parts of it, retaining only the essential drift of the message. In a foreign language, however, we have to pay close attention to every word, and so we pick up details that we would otherwise miss. This is what Augustine was getting at when he gave his justification for the existence of obscurities in the Bible. Careful and attentive reading of every syllable of the sacred text was essential for spiritual growth, and the hard parts of Scripture were put there in order to make sure that readers would give the text the kind of attention that it deserved. In his own words:

> No-one disputes that it is much more pleasant to learn lessons presented through imagery, and much more rewarding to discover meanings that are won only with difficulty. Those who fail to discover what they are looking for suffer from hunger, whereas those who do not look, because they have it in front of them, often die of boredom. In both situations the danger is lethargy. It is a wonderful and beneficial thing that the Holy Spirit organized the Holy Scripture so as to satisfy hunger by means of its plainer passages and remove boredom by means of its obscurer ones. Virtually nothing is unearthed from these obscurities which cannot be found quite plainly expressed somewhere else.[9]

9. Augustine, *On Christian Teaching* II, 13-15.

For Augustine, the harder parts of Scripture had another importance as well. If all that mattered was the general drift of the text, the obscurer parts would be superfluous and could be safely ignored. Yet Augustine believed that they were even more deserving of our time and attention than the clearer parts of Scripture because by puzzling over them we would master the ins and outs of God's word, and therefore of his will for our lives. To his mind, the hard parts of Scripture were tools for fine-tuning our spiritual perception, not excrescences that we can more or less do without.

Obviously, among these hard parts are all the passages that appear to be inconsistent, contradictory, or just plain wrong. Augustine recognized these problems, but he did not believe that they were deliberate. He was perfectly familiar with the claims made by many of the pagan enemies of Christianity, who believed that the Bible was full of errors and contradictions, and it was no secret that Christian apologists had been forced to contend with such opinions all along. Some of these supposed errors Augustine attributed to poor copying of the manuscripts and to bad translations of the originals, and he insisted that everyone do their textual homework in this regard before making any pronouncement on the meaning of particular passages of Scripture.

Beyond that, as we have already seen, Augustine argued that the Bible contained riddles that had been put there by God as intellectual hurdles designed to test how high our minds can jump. God's intention was not to produce a series of "leaps of faith" that fly in the face of the facts, but to help us to appreciate the many-sided character of his revelation. To the modern mind, this sounds highly implausible and a classic example of special pleading, but this judgment may be too hasty. It is not simply that there are plenty of perfectly sincere people who like to complicate things as a kind of mental game, though such people certainly exist. Crossword puzzle buffs know that the difficulty of a puzzle does not lie in the puzzle itself but in the nature of the clues that are given for solving it, and most people accept that the ability to decipher such obscure clues is a reasonable test of mental agility. Stretching the mind may go against the grain in modern education, but we should not therefore assume that it was not part of God's plan in revealing his will.

Far more dangerous are the people who want to make everything too simple, and who seek easy solutions to complex problems. This is a constant temptation to any monotheist, since monotheism is by definition "simple" in its understanding of ultimate reality. Yet it is also highly dangerous because overly simple solutions to complex issues may easily lead to rash decisions and result in inappropriate behavior, the effects of which cannot be undone. The mind of God may be clear, but it is also infinitely complex, and the man who claims to have understood it in any exhaustive sense is deluding himself. Modern theologians, who are usually all too ready to denounce "fundamentalists" for their supposed "simplicity," should be the first to recognize this. The danger was particularly serious in the ancient world, where it was all too obvious that most of the heresies that afflicted the Church were precisely this: oversimplifications of complex realities that could not be reduced to neat formulas as the heretics tried to do.

Yet Augustine's most profound justification for the existence of obscurities in the Bible came from his understanding that all personal relationships are both comprehensible and unfathomable at the same time. If this is true of human beings, how much more must it be true of our relationship with God as well? How, indeed, could it be otherwise, if God is truly greater than we are? According to Augustine, it would simply not make sense if we could fully understand him, even when he is speaking directly to us!

Scripture as Authority

Of course, none of these arguments would be valid if the underlying biblical text were simply wrong. If that were the case, it could be abandoned as easily as any pagan writing and would have no claim on our attention, let alone on our obedience. The utter trustworthiness of Scripture was a fundamental given without which the rest made no sense. After all, what would be the point in spending hours trying to solve a riddle that turned out to have no meaning? The literal sense of the Scriptures was therefore extremely important to the Fathers, as was its claim to divine origin. To them there was all the difference in the world between textual difficulties and errors — the Bible contained several of the former but none of the latter because it was given by the very mouth of God himself.

The key to understanding the attitude of the Church Fathers to the Bible is the trustworthiness that they attributed to the precise form that its literal sense took, even when they accepted that it must be interpreted figuratively. Divine inspiration was an important part of this, of course, but it was not enough by itself to make the Bible a uniquely authoritative guide to spiritual knowledge and experience. Many Christians believed that the hymns sung in Church were also divinely inspired,[10] but that did not give them the kind of prestige that was enjoyed by Scripture. It was the purpose for which the Bible was inspired, rather than the inspiration itself, that made the difference. This purpose was to convert the mind of the believer from his pre-Christian ways and instruct him in the will of God for his life. The two things went together, and any attempt to separate them was strongly condemned.

This can be seen quite clearly from the writings of Tertullian, for whom *doctrina* and *disciplina,* although they could both be used in their modern meanings, were also synonyms. Those who claimed to be giving the right teaching but who did not match this with right living were firmly rejected. Indeed, Tertullian did not think it improper to accuse those who (to his mind) were guilty of false teaching of living immoral lives, whether he had evidence for that or not. To him, it must have been so because the two things were so closely connected that if someone went wrong doctrinally, he would inevitably go wrong morally as well.

Tertullian is a particularly interesting case because, unlike most of his contemporaries, he regarded the New Testament as inadequate (in certain respects) for Christian living. He noted, for instance, that the Apostle Paul was prepared to allow the remarriage of widows under the age of sixty, something that he himself wanted to forbid.[11] If a modern theologian wanted to say that, he would probably try to argue either that Paul's authority was inferior to that of Jesus, or that the offending passage belongs to a deutero-Pauline corpus, which would make it a less important source. Either way, the aim of the exercise would be to relativize (and then discount) whatever authority the text might claim. What is so interesting about Tertullian, however, is that although minimizing the text's authority was certainly his goal, he did not adopt either of those methods for attaining it.

As far as Tertullian was concerned, the only way to get around a clear New Testament command was by relativizing it in much the same way that

10. Augustine seems to have believed this, as he tells us in his *Confessions.* Yet much as he was moved by the hymns sung in Church, it was not by them but by reading the Bible that he came to a personal knowledge of Christ as his Savior and Lord.

11. The whole argument is developed in his treatise *On Monogamy* 10-16.

Christians had already relativized the *Old* Testament. Such a procedure would not only do full justice to the divine inspiration of the Pauline text but would also affirm its absolute authority for believers *at the time it was written.* Yet just as the authority (in the sense of practical applicability) of many parts of the Old Testament lapsed at the coming of Jesus because he moved God's people on to a higher and fuller revelation that made those passages obsolete, so the coming of the Paraclete, as witnessed by the Montanist prophecies, made the New Testament concession to the weakness of the flesh equally outdated. As he put it:

> "Hardness of heart" reigned till Christ's time; let "infirmity of the flesh" be content to have reigned until the time of the Paraclete. The New Law [i.e., the New Testament] abrogated divorce . . . the New Prophecy [i.e., Montanism] abrogates second marriage, which is no less a divorce of the former marriage. But the "hardness of heart" yielded to Christ more readily than the "infirmity of the flesh" did. The latter claims Paul in its support more than the former claimed Moses, if indeed it can be said to be claiming him in support when it clings to his concession but ignores his basic principle. . . .[12]

The important point is that for Tertullian only direct divine intervention, bringing with it knowledge of a higher truth, was able to override the authority of the biblical text. Of course most of the Church disagreed with him in this particular instance, but it is important to understand on what basis they did so. They did not dissent from Tertullian's conclusion because they rejected his premise (i.e., that only a further revelation from God could make a part of the existing Scripture obsolete) but because they did not accept that the Paraclete had actually given such a revelation to Montanus, or to anybody else.

Furthermore, it is important to realize that Tertullian justified his position by claiming that Paul's original concession was a temporary measure designed to be superseded at some future point, an approach that paralleled the Christian view of the Old Testament. Just as Jesus had claimed that Moses tolerated divorce in spite of the fact that he knew that it was not

12. Tertullian, *On Monogamy* 14 (adapted from the translation by S. Thelwall in *Ante-Nicene Fathers* 4, ed. A. Roberts and J. Donaldson [Buffalo, N.Y.: Christian Literature Publishing Co., 1885]).

God's will, so Tertullian argued that the Apostle Paul similarly allowed remarriage even though he knew full well that God really wanted widows (and everybody else) to remain single. Tertullian could thus claim that he was not going beyond the New Testament but was merely pointing out that a specific concession to a particular weakness in special circumstances must not be allowed to overturn those general principles of spiritual conduct that are the *real* will of God for his people.

The belief that the particular must give way to the universal in cases of conflict between them was a commonplace of ancient thought, and we should not be surprised to see it invoked in the interpretation of Scripture. It was especially common in reading the Old Testament, and far more important than allegory as a device for interpreting it. The general line of argument, which can be found in Origen's commentary on Romans, for example, is that the covenant made with the Jews was a particular application of universal spiritual principles to a given historical nation. Because of that, it had features that were peculiar to it and could not be transferred without modification to other nations, or to the world in general. However particular the law of Moses was, it reflected universal principles that *could* be discerned and applied outside the immediate context. The fault of the Jews was that they mistook the form for the substance and gloried in the particular as if there were no underlying universal principles at all.

The Knowledge of God

The appeal to universal principles that underlie (and therefore give meaning to) particular texts and circumstances recorded in Scripture was an essential part of patristic apologetic because ultimately it was that appeal that allowed the Fathers to apply biblical passages of events from a remote past to their own context. The point is made quite clearly by Hippolytus as follows:

> There is, brethren, one God, the knowledge of whom we gain from the Holy Scriptures, and from no other source. For just as a man, if he wishes to be skilled in the wisdom of this world, will find himself unable to get at it on any other way than by mastering the dogmas of philosophers, so all of us who wish to practise piety will be unable to learn its practice from any other quarter than the oracles of God. Whatever

things, then, the Holy Scriptures declare, at these let us look, and whatever they teach, that let us learn, and as the Father wills our belief to be, let us believe. . . .[13]

Hippolytus compares the study of Scripture to the study of pagan philosophy, but it is important to notice one major difference between them. The philosophers were studied for their dogma, but Scripture was to be read for its practical teaching. Hippolytus did not mean by this that the Bible does not also contain what we might call "dogma" in the philosophical sense. Rather, he is making the point that the reading of the Bible leads to far more than mere head knowledge. The person who studies Scripture in the right way will learn from it what God's will is for his life. Every other aspect of its interpretation is ultimately tied to this, as Augustine reminds his readers:

> The student who fears God earnestly seeks his will in the Holy Scriptures. Holiness makes him gentle, so that he does not revel in controversy. A knowledge of languages protects him from uncertainty over unfamiliar words or phrases, and a knowledge of certain essential things protects him from ignorance of the significance and detail of what is used by way of imagery. Thus equipped, and with the assistance of reliable texts derived from the manuscripts, and with careful attention to the need for emendation, he should now approach the task of analyzing and resolving the ambiguities of the Scriptures.[14]

And again:

> The aim of its readers is simply to find out the thoughts and wishes of those by whom it was written down, and through them the will of God, which we believe these men followed as they spoke.[15]

Augustine evidently saw no contradiction between the human authors of the Bible and the will of God expressed in it because he believed that the former were acting on divine instructions as they wrote. There is no sug-

13. Hippolytus, *Against the Heresy of One Noetus* 9 (in *Ante-Nicene Fathers* 5, ed. A. Roberts and J. Donaldson [Buffalo: N.Y.: Christian Literature Publishing Co., 1886]).

14. Augustine, *On Christian Teaching* III, 1.

15. Augustine, *On Christian Teaching* II, 9.

gestion that they were merely dictation machines, suppressing their own thoughts as they transmitted the words of God, although this is sometimes the way in which the Fathers' belief in divine inspiration is caricatured. Instead, what we find is that the human authors of the text were consecrated to God's service beforehand, and that he used them accordingly to express his mind and will.

The proof of this was to be sought less in disputation than in the practical experience of a willing and obedient heart. It was because they lacked the latter that the Jews were unable to profit from their reading of the text, as Justin Martyr pointed out to the Jewish rabbi Trypho:

> If I undertook to prove this [i.e., the incarnation of the Son of God] by doctrines or arguments of man, you would not bear with me. But if I quote frequently the Scriptures, and so many of them, referring to this point, and ask you to comprehend them, you are hard-hearted in the recognition of the mind and will of God.[16]

The power of the Bible to implant the thoughts of God in the heart and mind of the hearer is clearly brought out by John Chrysostom:

> For if you want to learn how great the profit of the Scriptures is, examine yourself and compare what you become by hearing the Psalms with what you become when you hear a song of Satan. Contrast your feelings inside a church with your feelings inside a theatre, and you will see how different they are, even though you have only one soul. . . . [Scripture] is a soul's food, its ornament and its security, and not hearing it is famine and waste, for God says: "I will give them not a famine of bread, nor a thirst of water, but a famine of hearing the word of the Lord." . . . a word from the divine Scriptures softens the soul more than fire can, and renders it fit for all good things.[17]

Furthermore, the proof of the pudding was in the eating, as Augustine made quite plain:

16. Justin Martyr, *Dialogue with Trypho* 68 (in *Ante-Nicene Fathers* 1, ed. A. Roberts and J. Donaldson [Buffalo, N.Y.: Christian Literature Publishing Co., 1885]).

17. John Chrysostom, *Homilies on Matthew's Gospel* II, 10 (in *Nicene and Post-Nicene Fathers* 10, ed. P. Schaff [Buffalo, N.Y.: Christian Literature Publishing Co., 1888]).

> Anyone who thinks that he has understood the divine Scriptures or any part of them, but cannot by his understanding build up . . . love of God and neighbour, has not yet succeeded in understanding them.[18]

The danger of partial knowledge, to which Augustine refers here, was well known to the Fathers and greatly feared because in their view inadequate understanding was the root of heresy. Athanasius brought this out quite clearly in a pastoral letter that he wrote to the bishops of Egypt in 356. In that letter he reproached people like Marcion and Mani for having listened to the gospel but rejected the law, thereby leading their followers into beliefs that contradict the overall teaching of the Bible. Athanasius concluded his warnings about this with the following:

> But since Holy Scripture is of all things most sufficient for us, I recommend to those who desire to know more of these matters that they read the divine Word. . . .[19]

To know God one must know his will, and to know his will one must read the Scriptures. Moreover, to know his will correctly one must know the Scriptures fully, not picking and choosing from them only those parts that one happens to like or that one can accept on purely rational or historical grounds. The Scriptures possess a power that derives from their character, which is that they are the written expression of God's mind, as this was communicated to his faithful servants — the prophets and apostles who did the actual writing.

The Fathers had no difficulty in accepting this line of reasoning because ultimately they believed that there was no essential difference between the human authors of Scripture and any believing Christian. The link between them is one of obedient submission to the will of God. The prophets and apostles who obeyed God's voice were told to write the books of the Bible; we who hear and obey his voice are called to put the words of the Bible into practice in our lives and, by doing that, to discover what it is to know him. Difficulties in interpreting those words come from the text, but problems in understanding them can be overcome by learning the right method with which to approach them:

18. Augustine, *On Christian Teaching* I, 86.

19. Athanasius, *To the Bishops of Egypt* 4 (in *Nicene and Post-Nicene Fathers,* 2nd series, 4, ed. P. Schaff and H. Wace [Buffalo, N.Y.: Christian Literature Publishing Co., 1892]).

> The person who has assimilated the rules that I am trying to teach, when he finds a difficulty in the text, will not need another interpreter to reveal what is obscure, because he comprehends certain rules. . . . By following up various clues, he can unerringly arrive at the hidden meaning for himself, or at least avoid falling into incongruous misconceptions.[20]

For Augustine, as for all the Fathers, rule number one was that the prospective reader should love God with a pure and contrite heart, which was the essential context for understanding all the rest. Equipped with the right spirit of spiritual humility and guided by the inner logic of divine self-disclosure, the interpreter of the Bible would obtain the knowledge that he was seeking in spite of all the difficulties that the text presented to his mind. They could say this — and believe it — precisely because they looked beyond the details of the text to the principle that lay behind it, and principle was nothing less than the presence of God himself. This presence was not an accidental by-product of reading the Scriptures but their essential message. The truth of this proposition might perhaps be demonstrable by argument, but even if it were, this would not by itself convince anyone. Only those prepared to submit and experience the Scriptures for themselves would be able to come to an understanding of their truth, because then that truth would become real in their everyday experience. Those who enjoyed the fruit of that experience would need no further proof; those who did not enjoy it would never understand what Christians were talking about.

In the final analysis, the Fathers' teaching about Holy Scripture is not so much an explanation as a challenge to "taste and see that the LORD is good."[21] Whatever else may nowadays seem to be obsolete in their teaching, this remains as valid now as it was then, as those who have responded to the challenge can still testify.

20. *On Christian Teaching,* preface, 19.

21. Ps. 34:8.

The God of Unconditional Promise

Carl R. Trueman

The Reformation of the sixteenth century can be interpreted from a theological perspective in a variety of ways: as the discovery of assurance as a central aspect of Christianity; as a redefinition of notions of religious authority; as a reconstruction of the relationship between the institutional Church and the religious life of individuals; and as the religious dimension of the shift from a visual to a literary culture. Perhaps the most famous aspect of the theological Reformation, however, was the emphasis placed upon justification by grace through faith, as initially articulated by Martin Luther and then developed by subsequent Reformers such as Philipp Melanchthon and John Calvin. This, more than anything else, whether one agrees with it or not, stands out as perhaps the defining issue of the era.

Underlying the notion of justification by faith is a specific doctrine of God as he stands in relation to humanity. For the Reformers, faith in God is not an inexpressible or contentless existential encounter with the unknown but depends very much upon a particular notion of God and a particular notion of his revelation of himself to humanity. The point is made by John Calvin in his commentary on Hebrews with regard to Sarah, the wife of Abraham. Referring to the promise made to Sarah, Calvin says:

> Sarah's faith was this, — that she counted God to be true to his word, that is, to what he had promised. . . . We hence learn first, that there is no faith without God's word, for of his faithfulness we cannot be convinced until he has spoken. And this of itself is abundantly sufficient to confute

> the sophists respecting implicit faith; for we must ever hold that there is a mutual relation between God's word and our faith. But as faith is founded chiefly . . . on the benevolence or kindness of God, it is not every word, though coming from his mouth, that is sufficient; but a promise is necessary as an evidence of his favour. Hence Sarah is said to have counted God faithful who had promised. True faith then is that which hears God speaking and rests on his promise.[1]

The passage is important for a number of reasons. First, it makes it quite clear, in opposition to Catholic notions of implicit faith, that faith is a conscious human disposition that has a specific object and a specific content, that is, God's word. Faith is therefore not a self-sufficient entity: it is always faith *placed by the individual in God's word,* in the word that God has spoken to humanity. It is thus definitive of an interpersonal relationship. This is reflected in Calvin's theological epistemology, which also underscores the personal, relational nature of theology. The famous opening of the *Institutes,* with its assertion that knowledge of God and knowledge of ourselves are inseparable, makes it quite clear that who we consider ourselves to be and who we consider God to be cannot be isolated from each other.[2] That this knowledge is intimately connected with Calvin's notion of *pietas* (piety, godliness) serves further to underline the responsive, existential nature of knowledge.[3] True knowledge of God is always *Christian* knowledge of God and thus only exists on the basis of the bond of faith that binds the believer and triune Jehovah, that is, God as he has revealed himself to be towards us, together. In other words, human knowledge of God, or human faith in God, consists precisely in grasping God not as human beings speculate he is or should be but as he has manifested himself.[4] A bare theistic belief in the concept of God, or a trust in some non-Christian deity, is not in the same category as Christian faith and does not embody Calvin's ideal of *pietas.*

This point leads to the second significant aspect of the passage: faith has a specific object, that is, God's promise. A promise, unlike certain other statements, is by its very nature something that must involve an interpersonal relationship. As long as a promise is the immediate object of trust,

1. John Calvin, *Commentary on the Epistle to the Hebrews,* trans. John Owen (Grand Rapids: Eerdmans, 1949), p. 282.

2. Calvin, *Institutes* (1559) 1.1.

3. Calvin, *Institutes* 1.2.1.

4. Calvin, *Institutes* 1.2.2.

therefore, talk about faith in God cannot be reduced to the level of, say, bare belief in a factual proposition such as "All swans are white." Faith inevitably involves some element of cognition, but it cannot be reduced to mere cognition. In addition, promises require that certain conditions hold true for the faith invested in them to be done in a worthwhile and proper manner. First, the promiser must have the ability to deliver on his or her promise: the bankrupt who promises to give his creditors all that he owes them may well wish to do so, but his financial situation means that the promise is ultimately worthless and unworthy of faith. Second, in addition to the ability, the promiser must have the intention of delivering on the promise. The woman who promises to buy her child a present but who has no intention of doing so has made a promise that, again, is not worthy of trust because it is not backed up by the necessary disposition. In other words, that which makes the promise valid, which makes it worthy of trust or faith, is the person who promises, and whose ability and intention serve to make the promise good. A promise must carry with it certain implications about the one promising.

In his comment on Sarah, Calvin makes this point nicely: Sarah's faith is founded on the fact that she trusts the promise because she regards God himself, the one making the promise, as trustworthy. His promise reveals the benevolence upon which it is based, and thus faith in the promise is indistinguishable from faith in the promiser. The words of the promise are consistent with who God is, or, perhaps better, how God has chosen to be towards Sarah, and therefore the promise is good and her faith well founded. In other words, the promise is deemed trustworthy because the words of promise are themselves a revelation of who God is. It is this basic understanding of God's trustworthiness, tying his words to his disposition towards humanity, which lies at the heart of Reformation understanding of salvation; and it is this that is one of the key factors in focusing the Protestant theological tradition upon the phenomenon of Scripture. Faith in God's promise presupposes that God is who his promise reveals him to be, and thus it places God's revelation of himself right at the heart of the theological task. By identifying Scripture alone as the cognitive ground of theology, the Protestant Reformers then forged a basic connection between the trustworthiness of God and the trustworthiness of Scripture.[5]

5. On Scripture as the cognitive ground of theology, see Richard A. Muller, *Post-Reformation Reformed Dogmatics,* vol. 2 (Grand Rapids: Baker, 1993).

Scripture is trustworthy because the God behind Scripture is trustworthy; and faith depends upon being convicted of the revelatory and epistemological implications of this divine trustworthiness. Calvin states this clearly in *Institutes* 3.2.6:

> Now, therefore, we hold faith to be a knowledge of God's will towards us, perceived from his Word. But the foundation of this is a preconceived conviction of God's truth. As for certainty, as long as your mind is at war with itself, the Word will be of doubtful and weak authority, or rather of none. And it is not even enough to believe that God is trustworthy who can neither deceive nor lie unless you hold that whatever proceeds from him is sacred and inviolable truth.[6]

Here we have all the elements noted above, most importantly the requirement that assured faith demands a belief that the God behind revelation is trustworthy, that he is towards us precisely what his promise indicates that he is. Faith in God's trustworthiness thus has a *logical* (though one must stress not a *chronological*) priority when it comes to understanding what the Bible says.[7] Elsewhere in the *Institutes,* Calvin criticizes those who use God's apparent arbitrariness in the differences between the Old and New Testaments as evidence of his capriciousness or untrustworthiness. In essence, he argues, they divorce the outward trappings of God's historical actions from the fact that he is always righteous, just, and trustworthy; and these qualities should always provide the context and the foundation for understanding the activity of God.[8]

To highlight God's trustworthiness as a basic aspect of Reformation theology is not, of course, to suggest that the medieval Christian tradition, or the Catholic Reformation of the sixteenth century, argued that God was in any way *untrustworthy.* The increasingly voluntaristic theology of the late medieval period with its disjunction between God's absolute and his ordained power, and the Scotist distinction between archetypal and ectypal theology, no doubt helped not just to pave the way for the theology of Luther in the radical emphasis it came to place upon God's revelation as

6. Translation by Ford L. Battles in John Calvin, *Institutes of the Christian Religion,* vol. 1, ed. John T. McNeill (Louisville: Westminster; London: SCM, 1960).

7. Chronological priority would, of course, demand a knowledge of God prior to his revelation of himself.

8. Calvin, *Institutes* 2.11.14.

the sole source and criterion for knowledge of who he was, but also to formulate within the framework of the medieval Church a doctrine of God, who was trustworthy and reliable.[9] Nevertheless, it must also be remembered that Catholic notions of ecclesiastical authority, tradition, implicit faith, and the link between salvation and the penitential or sacramental system of the Church all served to create other theological foci that militated against the understanding of divine promise, of personal faith, and also of the kind of radical Scripture principle embodied in the magisterial traditions of the Protestant Reformation. Protestantism, with its emphasis upon God's *unconditional* promise of salvation, appropriated exclusively through the faith of the individual in God's word of promise rather than through the institutional Church, gave to God's word to humanity, and thus to Scripture, an exclusive importance in the understanding of God as trustworthy, which the medieval Church had not done.

This emphasis upon God's trustworthiness and its link to Scripture was further undergirded by the anti-Pelagian soteriology of the Reformers: because the promise was understood as absolutely unconditional, its fulfillment depended solely upon God's intention and action, not upon the sacramental action of the institutional Church (as in medieval Catholicism) or the believer (as in Anabaptism); as a consequence, the promise in itself had an exclusive and unmediated theological importance. Thus, it was solely the divine promise, not works, sacraments, or status in the institutional Church, which established the individual's standing before God; and the sole object of faith was not the Church in terms either of its dogma, authority, or sacramental system but simply the promise of God as given in Scripture. This is made most clear in Calvin's comments on infant baptism in *Institutes* 4.15.17:

> Now our opponents ask us what faith came to us during some years after our baptism. This they do to prove our baptism void, since it is not sanc-

9. God's absolute power referred to his ability to realize the set of all possibilities, providing that no logical contradiction was involved: for example, God could not make a triangle with four sides; his ordained power was that set of circumstances, and so forth, that he decreed would come into existence. Archetypal theology was God's own knowledge of himself, by definition necessary, infinite, perfect, and eternal. Ectypal theology was that which he chose to reveal to humanity. On these issues, see Heiko A. Oberman, *The Harvest of Medieval Theology* (Durham: Labyrinth, 1983); Richard A. Muller, *Post-Reformation Reformed Dogmatics,* vol. 1 (Grand Rapids: Baker, 1987).

> tified to us except when the word of promise is accepted in faith. To this question we reply that we indeed, being blind and unbelieving, for a long time did not grasp the promise that had been given us in baptism; yet that promise, since it was of God, ever remained fixed and trustworthy.[10]

Such a radical and one-sided emphasis upon God's gracious promise, as well as being inherently anti-Pelagian, also thrusts the notion of God's trustworthiness, that he is who he says he is, to the very center of the theological scheme and of the Christian's own life. This is scarcely surprising, as it constitutes the inevitable outcome of a theology that places faith and Scripture at the heart of its scheme.

Of course, while the promise of God is the center of faith, the Reformers held as basic to all theology that God is the one his words presuppose that he is. In Scripture, God is, after all, not only the promising God but also the commanding God; and divine trustworthiness extends to both categories of God's speech and determines the nature of the response to that speech. This point can be illustrated quite neatly from a number of passages in Calvin's commentaries.

Two good examples of this can be found in the *Commentary on Genesis:* in Calvin's discussion of the interchange between the serpent and the woman in Genesis 3, and in his comments on the narrative of Abraham. The former, of course, involves an instance of an approach to God's words that does not take them at face value, as a reliable guide to who God is and what he wills; the second provides a number of examples, supremely in the incident of the command to sacrifice Isaac, that demonstrate the priority of the promising God in the life of faith.

In his discussion of Genesis 3, Calvin sees the serpent's strategy as involving two different approaches to God's word of prohibition against the eating of the fruit. In the first instance, in Genesis 3:1, the serpent questions whether the command is really the word of God, on which Calvin comments:

> There are some who suppose that Satan expressly denies the word of God. Others think, (with whom I rather agree,) that, under the pretext of inquiring into the cause, he would indirectly weaken their confidence in the word. . . . [T]he artifice of Satan is to be noticed, for he wished to

10. Translation by Battles in Calvin, *Institutes of the Christian Religion.*

> inject into the woman a doubt which might induce her to believe *that* not to be the word of God, for which a plausible reason did not manifestly appear.[11]

According to Calvin's reading of the text, therefore, the serpent's opening gambit is to cast doubt on the command's status as the word of God on the grounds that the command on its own has a somewhat absurd ring. This is followed up in Genesis 3:4-5 by a change in strategy, upon which Calvin comments as follows:

> [H]e denies that a fruit which is useful and salutary can be injurious. When he says, "God doth know," he censures God as being moved by jealousy, and as having given the command concerning the tree, for the purpose of keeping man in an inferior rank.[12]

This is at once a more subtle and, as events reveal, a more devastating approach to the words of God. Here, the serpent does not deny that the command is the word of God; rather, he questions the motivation that lies behind the command. This application of a "hermeneutic of suspicion" serves to sever the necessary connection that we have argued above needs to exist between God's capabilities and intentions, and the words he speaks if the basic idea of a trustworthy God is to hold water and if his promise is to be worthy of trust. By severing the words from God's intention, the serpent effectively makes the latter a hidden matter, ripe for cynical speculation, and thereby lays the foundation upon which Eve's disobedience is built. Eve's fall from grace is facilitated by the crisis in her belief in God's trustworthiness caused by the assault of the serpent upon the relation between who God is and the words he speaks.

Both of the serpent's approaches, then, call into doubt the trustworthiness of God, first by the doubting of his word and second by the doubting of the God who speaks the word. In both cases, it is the words spoken that form the focus of the attack; yet it is ultimately the integrity of the one who speaks, God himself, which is undermined. The ontic basis of the relationship with God, that is, who God is and how he has deter-

11. John Calvin, *Genesis*, trans. John King (Edinburgh: Calvin Translation Society, 1847), pp. 147-48.

12. Calvin, *Genesis*, p. 150.

mined to be towards humanity, is undermined by an attack on the noetic basis of the relationship, the words God has spoken to humanity. Eve is persuaded that God is not his words, not who his words indicate that he is. The result: sin.

Moving forward in Genesis, the supreme example of faith in God's word, and thus faith in God, is, of course, Abraham himself, both because of his status as the patriarchal recipient of the promises to the chosen people and because of that most extreme challenges to his faith: the command to sacrifice Isaac.

This incident, however, cannot be treated in isolation from the life of Abraham as a whole and must be understood particularly in terms of the various commands and promises given to Abraham from Genesis 12 onward. When we examine Calvin's treatment of this narrative, we can see a significant development in the way in which God deals with Abraham and in which Abraham responds, a development that is instructive in understanding the relationship between God and his word.

The first encounter of God and Abram of which there is mention is the command in Genesis 12 to leave Haran and go to a land that the Lord will show him. While Calvin assumes that Abraham and Terah had previous knowledge of God,[13] the overriding emphasis in his discussion of this passage is on the unconditioned response of Abram to the command of God.[14] In addition to the command, of course, God also appends a promise because, as Calvin observes, human beings are slow to obey God unless they see that in doing so there is some gracious benefit to themselves and, furthermore, that faith does not ultimately consist in obedience to a command but in trust in a promise.[15] Nevertheless, Calvin goes out of his way to underline the fact that Abram has no earthly, empirical reason at this point for hoping that the promise will be fulfilled, since Sarai was barren. Only the word of God in itself provided grounds for hope; Abram's trust in God's intention and ability to fulfill the promise rested entirely on the rev-

13. Calvin, *Genesis,* p. 342.

14. For example, "For why does God not immediately point out the land, except for the purpose of keeping his servant in suspense, that he may the better try the truth of his attachment to the word of God? As if he would say, 'I command thee to go forth with closed eyes, and forbid thee to inquire whither I am about to lead thee, until, having renounced thy country, thou shalt have given thyself wholly to me'" (Calvin, *Genesis,* p. 344).

15. "For it is certain that faith cannot stand, unless it be founded on the promises of God" (Calvin, *Genesis,* p. 346).

elation of the promise itself. His faith is simply that God is who his words indicate that he is.

God meets with Abram again later in the same chapter (v. 7) and then in Genesis 13:14-17, on both occasions reiterating his promise regarding Abram's descendants and the land. Again, Calvin emphasizes in his comments on these passages that it is simply the word, not outward empirical circumstances, that proved the basis for faith; in other words, Abram's belief that God is who he says he is and is able to deliver what he promises is based entirely upon God's words to him.[16] Nevertheless, we should also perhaps note in passing that God, in his dealings with Abram, demonstrates a gracious condescension to his servant, particularly in adopting a covenant to the relationship that exists between them, whereby God commits himself to blessing those who bless Abram and to cursing those who curse him.[17] By so doing, God underlines the trustworthiness of his promises.

The next significant moment in the narrative from our perspective comes in Genesis 15, where God makes his great covenant promise to Abram, indicating that it is not through Ishmael, the child of Abram's own efforts, that the promise will be fulfilled, but through another child, Isaac, the child of grace. In a very illuminating comment on Genesis 15:7, which is worth quoting in full, Calvin makes the following comments about God's delivery of this promise:

> Since it greatly concerns us to have God as the guide of our whole life, in order that we may know that we have not rashly entered on some doubtful way, therefore the Lord confirms Abram in the course of his vocation, and recalls to his memory the original benefit of his deliverance; as if he had said, "I, after I had stretched out my hand to thee, to lead thee forth from the labyrinth of death, have carried my favour towards thee thus far. Thou, therefore, respond to me in turn, by constantly advancing; and maintain stedfastly thy faith from the beginning even to the end." This indeed is said, not with respect to Abram alone, in order that he, gathering together the promises of God, made to him from the very commencement of his life and faith, should form them into one whole; but that all the pious may learn to regard the beginning of their vocation as flowing perpetually from Abram, their common father; and may

16. Calvin, *Genesis,* pp. 353, 374-75.
17. Calvin, *Genesis,* pp. 347-48.

> thus securely boast with Paul, that they know in whom they have believed, (2 Tim. 2:12) and that God, who in the person of Abram had separated a church unto himself, would be a faithful keeper of the salvation deposited with him. For this very end, the Lord declares himself to have been the deliverer of Abram, appears hence; because he connects the promise which he is now about to give with the prior redemption; as if he were saying, "I do not now first begin to promise thee this land. For it was on this account that I brought thee out of my own country, to constitute thee the lord and heir of this land. Now therefore I covenant with thee in the same form; lest thou shouldst deem thyself to have been deceived, or fed with empty words; and I command thee to be mindful of the first covenant, that the new promise, which after many years I now repeat, may be the more firmly supported."[18]

The passage is extremely important for understanding how Calvin sees the relationship between God and his word. We have observed that Calvin makes no room for ordinary, empirical considerations as providing foundational grounds for believing God's words. Indeed, it would appear that thus far empirical considerations (above all, the age and barrenness of Sarah) militate against such belief. Nevertheless, God is a God of promise, and the crucial element in believing a promise is believing that the promiser can and will deliver on the promise made. In Genesis 15:7, what Calvin sees God doing is reminding Abram of his earlier deliverance and God's redemptive fidelity in the past in order to demonstrate to Abram here and now that his words are neither deceptive nor empty — in other words, to point out to Abraham that he has both the intention and the ability to deliver on his current promise, that God is indeed trustworthy.

Is Calvin here arguing that the biblical text makes room for empirical criteria outside of God's words, God's own speaking, by which the validity of God's words can be established? Not at all. The act to which the verse refers, that of bringing Abram out of Ur of the Chaldees into the land of Canaan, is a redemptive act, part of God's redemptive purpose, as Calvin himself points out, and is thus intimately connected to the promise of redemption that Abram has already believed and that led to the very actions of which God now speaks. The action of deliverance has meaning only within the context of the promise that has been spoken; without the prom-

18. Calvin, *Genesis*, pp. 410-11.

ise, the action is of no real lasting significance at all. God has promised; God has started to deliver on his promises; God has demonstrated to Abram that he is and will be towards Abram that which his words said he would be; and, while Abram believed God from the start, Abram's hand is now strengthened as, at the end of his life, God condescends to point out to Abram just how trustworthy he has proved. What God is doing is simply indicating that his actions in history indicate that he is precisely who the words he has spoken to Abram require that he is. The context, then, is not one where empirical evidence is independent of God's word or words, but one where that evidence is intimately connected to it; indeed, one where God's deeds are really subordinate to, and in a sense arise out of, the words of promise. This is a sound reminder that, while Abram's faith is built solely on the word that God speaks, it is yet no existential "leap" into the dark in the sense that he has no more reason to believe God than to disbelieve God; rather, God's redemptive faithfulness in the past gives Abram every reason to trust God's redemptive faithfulness in the future.

In Calvin's theology, redemptive history has, of course, significance well beyond the person of Abraham, as is clear from a number of comments he makes on the Psalms. One good example is his commentary on Psalm 105, which recounts God's dealings with his people up until the Exodus from Egypt. The whole narrative of events is, as Calvin is careful to point out, addressed "to none but true believers," a statement that confirms what has been said above concerning redemptive history as confirmation of the promise, not as independent grounds for believing the promise.[19] This approach is reinforced by Calvin's comment on the renewal of the covenant with Isaac and Jacob:

> God then deposited his covenant with Abraham, and by solemn oath engaged to be the God of his seed. But to give greater assurance of the truth of his promise, he was graciously pleased to renew it to Isaac and Jacob. The effect of such an extension of it is, that his faithfulness takes deeper hold on the hearts of men; and, besides, his grace, when it is thus testified on frequent recurring occasions, becomes better known and more illustrious among men.[20]

19. John Calvin, *Commentary on the Psalms,* vol. 4, trans. James Anderson (Edinburgh: Calvin Translation Society, 1847), p. 173.

20. Calvin, *Psalms,* 4:178.

The renewal of the covenant does not, therefore, indicate any insufficiency, far less any revocation, of the earlier covenant with Abraham. The act is rather to be interpreted along the lines of God's accommodating himself to human capacity, meeting men and women in their weakness and reinforcing their faith through the reiteration of his promise by acts that confirm that he is the one the promise requires him to be, and that only have meaning when set within the context of that promise. His acts in history and, just as important, the remembrance and rehearsal of those acts, fulfill the function of reminding humanity of the unconditional nature of God's promise — and the fidelity of God to his promise.

These two elements, God's unconditional grace and his covenant fidelity, are constant refrains during his exposition of the rest of the psalm. Commenting on verses 12-15, Calvin points out that references to the Israelites as being few in number yet being protected and preserved by God underscore the fact that "long before the deliverance from Egypt, the covenant was not ineffectual."[21] At the same time, this preservation, which even led God to rebuke kings for their sake (v. 14), was a sure sign that the promise was not given to the Jews on any ground of intrinsic merit.[22] Most significant of all, the departure of Joseph and family from Canaan into Egypt is cited as proof that God is faithful to his promise to bless and preserve Abraham's descendants at a time when "the covenant itself might seem to be void and disannulled."[23] The whole commentary on the psalm continues in this vein, and a similar concern for the reality of God's actions in history as confirmation of the reality of the divine intention behind the covenant is also found throughout Calvin's discussion of the next two psalms.[24]

A very similar point is made by Calvin in *Institutes* 3.20.26, where, in the context of a discussion of the intercession of the saints, he comments as follows on David's declarations in Psalm 31 concerning God's faithfulness and his salvation:

21. Calvin, *Psalms,* 4:180.

22. Calvin, *Psalms,* 4:182.

23. Calvin, *Psalms,* 4:183.

24. Calvin, *Psalms,* 4:205-67. The emphasis in Psalm 106 is on the Israelites' disobedience rather than on God's fidelity, and in 107 on God's divine providence. In both cases, however, the importance of God's actions in history as underscoring who his words of promise have revealed him to be is maintained.

> After praising God for his salvation, he adds that He is trustworthy. For if he were not forever like himself, from his benefits a sufficiently firm reckoning could not be adduced to trust him and call upon him. But when we know that as often as he helps us he gives us an example and proof of his goodness and good faith towards us, we need not fear lest our hope put us to shame or deceive us.[25]

As in the case of Abraham, the context is that of the redemptive promise. David's experience of God's faithfulness cannot be separated from that redemptive promise, and thus the "empirical evidence" of God's trustworthiness that David sees in his salvation is not a separate and independent source of knowledge of God as trustworthy but arises from his prior grasp of the promise by faith. It may strengthen that faith, it may give him cause for rejoicing, but it only exists as a result, and in the context, of the trustworthy promise. Furthermore, as with Abram, this evidence has a future reference: it serves to strengthen David's hope for what is to come.

To return to Abraham and Genesis, it is against the background of events in Genesis 15 that we come to Genesis 22, in many ways the climax of Abraham's relationship with God, where he is commanded by the Lord to sacrifice the very child of promise through whom God had declared that his redemptive purpose would be fulfilled. For Calvin, it is in this peculiar situation that the real tragedy of Abraham's predicament lies:

> God, as if engaging in personal contest with him, requires the death of the boy, to whose person He himself had annexed the hope of eternal salvation. So that this latter command was, in a certain sense, the destruction of faith.[26]

The command of God was "the destruction of faith" at this point precisely because what God was asking of Abraham seemed to call into serious question the nature of God's trustworthiness. The proposed slaying of Isaac, because it seemed incompatible with the previous word of promise, would seem to call into doubt God's intention to deliver on that promise, and thus to throw the whole of his redemptive activity to the wind. Calvin follows this up by highlighting the fact that the text quite clearly refers to

25. Translation by Battles in Calvin, *Institutes of the Christian Religion.*
26. Calvin, *Genesis,* p. 560.

God *speaking* to Abraham, underlining the fact that "God would shake the faith which the holy man had placed in His *word*, by a counter assault of the word itself." If God's trustworthiness depends upon an identity between who God is towards human beings and what he says to them, then Abraham now finds himself in a dilemma, with two apparently contradictory "words" coming from the Lord.

What emerges in Calvin's discussions of this passage, both in the commentary on Genesis and that on Hebrews (11:17-19), is Abraham's absolute commitment to the notion that God is trustworthy and that this trustworthiness, this identity between divine intention and divine promise, has decisive priority when it comes to understanding God's word. In short, it means that the promise will be fulfilled *despite* the apparent contradiction between the two words:

> [A]s before, when he expected seed from his own dead body, he, by hope, rose above what it seemed possible to hope for; so, now, when, in the death of his son, he apprehends the quickening power of God, in such a manner, as to promise himself a blessing out of the ashes of his son, he emerges from the labyrinth of temptation; for, in order that he might obey God, it was necessary that he should tenaciously hold the promise, which, had it failed, faith must have perished. . . . [H]e was unwilling to measure, by his own understanding, the method of fulfilling the promise which he knew depended on the incomprehensible power of God.[27]

A couple things are here worthy of note. First, Calvin clearly sees that Abraham's trust in the promise is ultimately the same as his trust in the promiser: the two simply cannot be separated. It is because Abraham has such confidence that God is the one who can and will deliver on the covenant promise to him that he believes God will deliver him from this situation, whatever outward circumstances or human reason might lead him to expect. Not even the command to sacrifice the son of promise can, there-

27. Calvin, *Genesis*, p. 564; cf. comments on Heb. 11:17-19: "He [Abraham] then did not renounce the promise given to him, but extended its power and its truth beyond the life of his son; for he did not limit God's power to so narrow bounds as to tie it to Isaac when dead, or to extinguish it. Thus, he retained the promise, because he bound not God's power to Isaac's life, but felt persuaded that it would be efficacious in his ashes when dead no less than in him while alive and breathing" (Calvin, *Hebrews*, p. 288).

fore, shake his confidence in the God who is revealed specifically in the words of the covenant promise. Calvin makes substantially the same observation when commenting on the speech of Stephen in Acts 7.[28] We also noted earlier that, in *Institutes* 3.1.6, Calvin emphasizes the importance of a belief in God's trustworthiness that is *logically* (though again we should note, not *chronologically*) prior to an understanding of God's revelation. Without this, one will be blown hither and thither and find no sound basis for one's faith. The case of Abraham and Isaac is the classic example of such basic faith in the essential trustworthiness of God, where the patriarch's faith in God's ultimate trustworthiness allows him to obey God's command.

This leads to the second point: we also see once again Calvin's sensitivity to God's dealings with Abraham: Abraham has been here before, in a manner of speaking, with God speaking of something that seemed nonsensical and futile when he promised the aged patriarch a son;[29] God had in those circumstances already revealed himself within the context of the redemptive promise, and Abraham's trust in this promise indicates his belief that God has both the ability and the intention of delivering on his promise; and it is against this background that Abraham's act of faith at this point must be seen. Again, this is no irrational "leap" of faith: Abraham is simply continuing, albeit under extreme circumstances, the life of faith in God's promise that he has pursued since he first received God's call. His confidence that God is the God who the promise, to be worthy of faith, requires that he is, overrides any despair; and his action, in the context of the redemptive promise that had already been given some time previously, far from being an act of blind, contentless faith, is in fact perfectly reasonable, even if in somewhat extreme circumstances. Only if we discount the connection that Abraham presupposed as existing between God

28. "[W]e must note, that though God did not show Abraham the thing itself as yet, yet did he uphold him by his word. And this is our stay, when God promiseth that that is laid up for us which as yet we possess not. Therefore, when as the thing, that is, the possession of the land, was wanting, Abraham had for his help and stay the promise of God; and being content with the same alone, he desired nothing in the land of Canaan save only an uncertain resting-place wherein he might sojourn" (John Calvin, *Commentary upon the Acts of the Apostles*, vol. 1, trans. Henry Beveridge [Grand Rapids: Eerdmans, 1949], p. 255).

29. In his commentary on Acts, Calvin even goes as far as to say that the promise to Abraham must have appeared little short of a joke; but, because the promise was spoken by God, Abraham yet embraced it by faith (*Acts*, 1:255).

and God's words of promise does his action in Genesis 22 become irrational or absurd.[30] Then Abraham would be putting blind faith in a hidden God; in actual fact, he is putting reasoned faith in a revealed God.

This, of course, resonates with the comment that Calvin made earlier concerning God's reminder to Abraham of how he had demonstrated himself to be faithful in the various redemptive acts by which he had led Abraham over the years. As noted then, these acts do not form independent grounds for trusting God; rather, they are to be understood in the context of God's promise as confirming and strengthening faith in the promise. A father's gifts to his child are not, after all, independent grounds for the child's believing in the father's love; they are simply consequences of the relationship that already exists between father and child, and thus serve as tokens and confirmations of that relationship. Divorcing them from the context of the family would render them meaningless. In the same way, divorcing God's redemptive acts from the context of his promise would evacuate them of significance.[31]

Conclusion

Recent years has witnessed much debate, even within evangelical circles, concerning the usefulness and value of Reformation theology to the world of today's Church. A large part of this discussion has focused on the New Perspective on Paul that has called into question the nature and importance of that most distinctively Protestant doctrine of justification by grace through faith. Whatever the outcome of that particular debate, it would be a shame if discussions about righteousness, covenant, and law served to ob-

30. In his commentary on Hebrews, Calvin underlines the basic continuity that Abraham's faith gives to his entire earthly pilgrimage: "He first teaches us that faith was the cause why he immediately obeyed God when he was commanded to remove from his own country; and then that through the same faith it was that he went on without wavering, according to what he was called to do even to the end" (*Hebrews,* p. 278).

31. See Calvin's comments on Exod. 12:25, where the Israelites are told to celebrate the Passover in the context of telling their children about God's redemption of his people from Egypt: "[T]he proclamation of the blessing is annexed to the sign; because otherwise it would be an empty and unmeaning proceeding. God, therefore, would have the fathers proclaim it unto their children, so that knowledge of their redemption, being handed down by tradition, may flourish in all ages" (*Harmony of the Pentateuch,* vol. 1, trans. Charles William Bingham [Edinburgh: Calvin Translation Society, 1852], p. 223).

scure another important aspect of Reformation theology that most, whatever their views on justification, would recognize as reflecting a central category of biblical theology: that of God as the trustworthy God who promises. The brief discussion above has shown that a Reformer such as Calvin was acutely sensitive to the implications of the promising God for theology and theological epistemology. To argue for a promising God is to argue for a trustworthy God, and to argue for a trustworthy God is to argue for a God whose words and deeds are basically consistent with each other and reveal one who is committed to being a certain kind of God for us.

Rejection of God as trustworthy is always going to be disastrous: in Calvin's comments on Genesis 3, it is this that undermines human obedience and leads to the fall; in his comments on Abraham, it is only through Abraham's absolute commitment to God's trustworthiness that he is able to live the life of remarkable and principled obedience that Genesis describes. For Calvin, then, a firm belief in God's trustworthiness is essential to any correct theology, for only this can supply the foundation for understanding God's revelation and God's redemptive acts, and for certain and assured faith. There are obvious implications here for Scripture in terms of its perspicuity, its interpretation, its doctrinal claims, and its accounts of God's historical acts; and any theology that claims to stand in continuity with that of Calvin and the Reformation, or that wishes to argue for a trustworthy God, must surely take these into account if it is to do justice to concerns about faith, assurance, and the God who gives himself in unconditional promise.

The Diversity and Sufficiency of Scripture

Timothy Ward

It has always been noticed that the Bible includes a wide diversity of material, diverse in both content and literary form. From the earliest times of the Church, Christian believers did not generally consider this diversity to be so extensive as to lead to theological incoherence. In this, according to John Goldingay, Christians were applying to their expanded Scriptures the view held by Jews of the Hebrew Scriptures.[1] Although scriptural diversity occasionally raised problems for some,[2] the general view that the diverse Scriptures represented a theological unity held right up to the Reformation and beyond. For example, Martin Chemnitz, a sixteenth-century Lutheran theologian, concluded from his detailed examination of the four canonical Gospels that they exhibit "a very concordant dissonance" *(concordissima dissonantia)*.[3]

1. "It is historically certain . . . that the Jewish community believed that its Scriptures were theologically coherent, . . . and the first Christians naturally shared such a belief" (John Goldingay, *Theological Diversity and the Authority of the Old Testament* [Grand Rapids: Eerdmans, 1987], pp. 27-28).

2. Bruce Metzger, following Oscar Cullmann, argues that in the early Church the existence of a plurality of authoritative Gospels was seen as a theological problem by those for whom to accept such a plurality was "as good as admitting that none of them is perfect" (Bruce M. Metzger, *The Canon of the New Testament: Its Origin, Development, and Significance* [Oxford: Clarendon, 1987], p. 262).

3. Chemnitz thought that the Holy Spirit had given the Gospels this characteristic "in order to exercise the minds of the faithful in humble and careful investigation of the truth,

The questions of how much "dissonance" Scripture in fact possesses and of how much "dissonance" can be tolerated in a supposedly "concordant" scriptural canon before we must give up and judge it "discordant" are questions that separate orthodox theologians like Chemnitz from later critical biblical scholars and theologians. Thus, in a recent short article on the inspiration of Scripture, Wolfhart Pannenberg argues that the doctrine of the literal inspiration of Scripture, articulated especially by Chemnitz's orthodox Protestant successors in the seventeenth century,

> disintegrated in the course of time, not so much because theologians turned to other norms of truth than Scripture, but primarily because the idea of a doctrinal unity among all the sentences of Scripture without any contradiction among them, an idea that followed from the doctrine of literal inspiration, could not be defended in the long run. It was falsified by observations of scriptural exegesis. This conception of the inspiration of Scripture broke down, then, because it proved to be irreconcilable with the first principle of the Protestant Reformation, the authority of Scripture in judging all the teaching of the church.[4]

The doctrine of the sufficiency of Scripture is as vulnerable to such exegetical observations as the doctrine of the literal inspiration of Scripture. The Reformation doctrine of the sufficiency of Scripture is simply a particular expression of the principle of *sola scriptura:* since Scripture is the ultimate norm for Christian faith and life, the sole *norma normans non normata,* it may not, as the ultimate norm, be supplemented either with extrascriptural material content (Church traditions or personal spiritual experiences) or with equally authoritative extrascriptural sources of interpretation (the teaching office of the Church or individual conviction regarding its correct interpretation). These two aspects of the sufficiency of Scripture may be termed, respectively, material and formal, and it is especially the latter that Pannenberg suggests broke down under the alleged

---

whereby we learn that the four evangelists did not write by mutual agreement but by divine inspiration" (quoted in Robert D. Preus, *The Theology of Post-Reformation Lutheranism: A Study of Theological Prolegomena* [St. Louis and London: Concordia Publishing House, 1970], p. 360).

4. Wolfhart Pannenberg, "On the Inspiration of Scripture," *Theology Today* 54 (1997): 212.

recognition of Scripture's doctrinal tensions, even contradictions. A book so diverse as to contain contradictions cannot display the coherence required of the ultimate norm of Christian theology and practice.

More recent defenders of the doctrine of the literal inspiration of Scripture are vulnerable to the charge that they have not offered a significant response to those who conclude from exegesis that Scripture is too diverse doctrinally to function as the ultimate authority in the Church. This is a significant gap, for there is at least *prima facie* plausibility in the claim that the diversity of denominations and practices to which Protestantism has given rise is a precise enactment of the diversity of the Scriptures that Protestants take as their chief authority. B. B. Warfield is regularly referred to in this regard. One of Warfield's favorite terms to describe the Bible is "oracles of God," and cognate phrases.[5] The regularity with which he uses this term might suggest an insensitivity to and flattening of the complex and diverse nature of Scripture, and a consequent glossing over of the difficulties involved in moving from text to theology. Some of his vocabulary, suggesting a rather static conception of Scripture, does not lessen the anxiety: on one occasion he describes the Scriptures, rather ponderously to contemporary ears, as "a compact mass of words of God,"[6] and at another place he says that the New Testament writers regarded the Old Testament as "nothing other than the crystallized speech of God."[7] Indeed, he describes the "oracular" view of Scripture as conceiving of each book and even each sentence of the Bible "as an unmediated divine word coming directly to the soul."[8]

However, we should not be too hard on Warfield, whose work is not always read today with as much care as it deserves. It is clear that he does not mean in practice what the word "unmediated" in the latter phrase might suggest: he demonstrates a high degree of scholarly philological endeavor (rarely matched in contemporary writing on biblical authority) in determining the precise meaning of biblical words in their textual and cultural context;[9] nor did he believe that correct belief could simply be read straight

5. See Benjamin Breckinridge Warfield, *The Inspiration and Authority of the Bible* (Philadelphia: Presbyterian and Reformed, 1948), passim.

6. Warfield, *Inspiration and Authority*, p. 147.

7. Warfield, *Inspiration and Authority*, p. 406.

8. Warfield, *Inspiration and Authority*, pp. 388-89.

9. See his lengthy and detailed discussion of the meaning of *theopneustos* in ch. 6 of *Inspiration and Authority*, "God-Inspired Scripture."

off the pages of the biblical text.[10] (This is one reason why Warfield cannot properly be called an early representative of modern American fundamentalism.) It seems, in fact, that Warfield's use of "oracular" as a description of the Bible has only one aim: to articulate and protect the claim that Scripture is to be permanently identified with the word of God, and that it is a book of thoroughly divine origin. At one point he says that the traditional doctrine of biblical inspiration views Scripture as "a book which may be frankly appealed to at any point with the assurance that whatever it may be found to say, that is the Word of God." He then adds that the Bible is "an oracular book."[11] It is likely that the latter description is intended as no more than a summary of the immediately preceding statement. As far as the *content* of his argument is concerned, then, Warfield's use of the language of "oracle" probably adds nothing substantive to his fundamental claim that "what Scripture says, God says," and that with no other instance of human linguistic activity than Scripture may this identification be made.

The simple answer to the question of why Warfield chooses to describe his view of the Bible in terms of "oracles" is that it is a term that the New Testament uses for the Old Testament (or possibly for just the Torah, or the Decalogue): for example, in Romans 3:2.[12] However, in his chapter on "The Oracles of God" it becomes evident that a significant influence on Warfield's choice of terminology in this case is Philo, for whom, says Warfield, every passage of Scripture is a *logion,* and whose most common term for the Bible as a whole is probably *hoi chresmoi.*[13] Douglas Farrow rightly criticizes Warfield for being "paralyzed by Philo," pointing out that the New Testament's uses of *ta logia tou theou* provide no warrant for "any leveling of biblical passages to a 'compact mass of words' like some gigantic and tedious pagan χρησμός."[14]

In general terms, it may be said that Warfield lacks, simply by virtue of

10. Warfield wished to distinguish his exegesis from proof texting, claiming to have learned from the mistakes of "the older dogmaticians," who, he says, relied too much on isolated proof-texts. Quoting Schleiermacher with approval, he says he wishes to learn from "the whole body of modern scholarship" to seek "a form of Scripture proof on a larger scale than can be got from single texts" (Warfield, *Inspiration and Authority,* p. 198).

11. Warfield, *Inspiration and Authority,* p. 106.

12. Warfield, *Inspiration and Authority,* p. 148.

13. Warfield, *Inspiration and Authority,* pp. 384-87.

14. Douglas Farrow, *The Word of Truth and Disputes about Words* (Winona Lake, Ind.: Carpenter, 1987), p. 104.

his particular historical location, a set of conceptualities that would allow him to articulate a sophisticated approach to the genre, literary characteristics, and communicative purpose of the whole biblical text being studied. Such conceptualities would allow a more nuanced description of how the various statements and literary units in the Bible function in relation to one another than the model suggested by the description of the Bible as "a compact mass of words of God." Such a description should also aim to be more nuanced than those offered by much critical biblical scholarship, which, as will be discussed briefly below, has often worked with a very narrow conception of what qualifies as doctrinal unity.

Since Warfield's day much work has been done in literary studies on the subject of how different texts relate to one another, usually under the heading of "intertextuality." This is not of course an entirely new interest in literary theory, but in the last thirty years the term "intertextuality" has become prominent and has itself acquired a diversity of meaning, covering both old and new ways of reading texts together. In what follows I will look first at some uses of "intertextuality" in recent literary theory and at some appropriations of these literary theories by biblical scholars. I shall then examine some linguistic concepts developed in the middle part of the twentieth century by the Russian philosopher and literary theorist Mikhail Bakhtin, whose work lies behind much contemporary interest in intertextuality, and argue for the fruitfulness of adopting these concepts in theological accounts of the Bible, especially in light of work done on the function of biblical language and literature by the philosopher Paul Ricoeur.

Of course, this will not provide a category of "unity in diversity" that will be able to account for all the contradictions in biblical doctrine that critical exegesis has alleged; evangelical believers will always need to respond to some of this with biblical exegesis of their own. Instead the intention is to introduce concepts of literary relationships between texts, and of literary meaning and reference, under which it might be possible to conceive a broader conception of theological unity than has often been allowed in the case of the Bible, and to reflect on how a consequent recognition of the Bible's diverse coherence may affect Christian theology. In conclusion, a description of the sufficiency of Scripture, understood as exhibiting something like Chemnitz's "concordant dissonance," will be outlined.

Intertextuality in Literary Theory and Biblical Studies

In general literary theory, "intertextuality" has come to cover a diverse group of theories and practices, a situation that occasionally leads to seemingly fruitless arguments about who has the best claim on the term as a description of her particular position. Borrowing terms from the theorist Heinrich Plett, two different approaches to "intertextuality" will be described here: "progressive intertextualists" give the term a postmodern or deconstructive slant; "traditional intertextualists" use the concept to rediscover the wealth of quotations and allusions in literary works.[15]

"Progressive Intertextuality"

The term "intertextuality" was introduced around thirty years ago by the theorist Julia Kristeva, particularly in two essays produced in 1966-67: "The Bounded Text" and "Word, Dialogue, and Novel."[16] (The latter essay, especially, helped to introduce the work of Mikhail Bakhtin to a Western audience.) Its original meaning was what Plett terms "progressive" — that is, with a deconstructive slant. Attributing the initial insight to Bakhtin, Kristeva asserts: "any text is constructed as a mosaic of quotations; any text is the absorption and transformation of another. The notion of *intertextuality* replaces that of intersubjectivity."[17] From this perspective, according to Kristeva, the text is "a permutation of texts, an intertextuality: in the space of a given text, several utterances, taken from other texts, intersect and neutralize one another."[18] It is not just that a text is influenced by earlier texts that leave their mark on it; it is actually defined in terms of them: texts never escape intertextuality. Kristeva's move beyond both Bakhtin and structuralism is evident here in the emphasis on the mutual neutralizing in a text of the many previous texts ("intertexts") of which it is composed, and in the displacement of the field of active human subjec-

15. Heinrich F. Plett, "Intertextualities," in *Intertextuality,* ed. Heinrich F. Plett, Research in Text Theory 15 (Berlin and New York: Walter de Gruyter, 1991), pp. 3-29.

16. They appear in English in Julia Kristeva, *Desire in Language: A Semiotic Approach to Literature and Art,* ed. Leon S. Roudiez (New York: Columbia University Press, 1980), pp. 36-63 and 64-91, respectively.

17. Kristeva, *Desire in Language,* p. 66.

18. Kristeva, *Desire in Language,* p. 36.

tivity by a realm of intertextuality.[19] It is for Kristeva's poststructuralist, deconstructive trajectory that many have wished to preserve the term "intertextuality."

However, the term has also been adopted by writers working on theories of influence (Plett's "traditionalists"), who retain a concept of "intersubjectivity," tracing how particular texts, authors, and traditions influence subsequent writing. In the 1970s, Kristeva objected to this broadening of the term, referring to its new use "in the banal sense of 'study of sources'"; she proposed a new term for her original concept, which she now described in clearly deconstructive terms: "we prefer the term transposition. . . . If one grants that every signifying practice is a field of transpositions of various signifying systems (an intertextuality) one then understands that its 'place' of enunciation and its denoted 'object' are never single, complete, and identical to themselves, but always plural, shattered, capable of being tabulated."[20]

What Kristeva particularly takes from Bakhtin's work is the insight that the utterance of any speaker or writer is always a borrowing of previous utterances, genres, and styles. Thus Bakhtin: "Language is not a neutral medium that passes freely and easily into the private property of the speaker's intentions; it is populated — overpopulated — with the intentions of others."[21] Kristeva casts this point in semiotic terms, describing the historical formation of the "specific signifying system" of the novel, for example, as "a result of a redistribution of several different sign systems: carnival, courtly poetry, scholastic discourse."[22] Thus, by "intertextuality," and subsequently "transposition," Kristeva has in mind much more than relations between written texts; she is thinking of highly complex relations within a universe of sign systems.

Along with Kristeva, Roland Barthes is the outstanding example of a

19. Toril Moi says that "Word, Dialogue, and Novel" is "in many ways a divided text, uneasily poised on an unstable borderline between traditional 'high' structuralism . . . and a remarkably early form of 'post-structuralism'" (*The Kristeva Reader,* ed. Toril Moi [Oxford: Basil Blackwell, 1986], p. 34).

20. Julia Kristeva, *Revolution in Poetic Language,* trans. Margaret Waller (New York: Columbia University Press, 1984 [1974]), p. 60.

21. M. M. Bakhtin, "Discourse in the Novel," in M. M. Bakhtin, *The Dialogic Imagination,* ed. Michael Holquist, trans. Caryl Emerson and Michael Holquist (Austin, Tex.: University of Texas Press, 1981), p. 294.

22. Kristeva, *Revolution,* p. 59.

literary critic who has taken intertextuality in a poststructuralist direction, applying it to literary texts and linking it with his notion of "the death of the author." He argues that all writers are caught between, on the one hand, the push towards freedom and creativity, committing themselves and showing themselves clearly as individuals by the choice "of tone, of ethos" in their writing,[23] and, on the other, the power exerted by the fact that we only ever use secondhand language, whose earlier usages echo in our own. "[W]riting still remains full of the recollection of previous usage, for language is never innocent: words have a second-order memory which mysteriously persists in the midst of new meanings."[24] The act of writing has powerful effects on history, although its duration as a free act is only momentary: "Writing as Freedom is therefore a mere moment. But this moment is one of the most explicit in History." As soon as the "moment" is past, the literary tradition in which one is writing starts to raise its own voice over that of the late-come writer. Beyond the "moment," all our language is so shop soiled that we can never truly make it our own:

> True, I can today select such and such a mode of writing, and in so doing assert my freedom, aspire to the freshness of novelty or to a tradition; but it is impossible to develop it within duration without gradually becoming a prisoner of someone else's words and even of my own. A stubborn after-image, which comes from all the previous modes of writing and even from the past of my own, drowns the sound of my present words.[25]

However, it is hard to understand this as a coherent claim. Barthes does not say how the previous words and "modes of writing" ever gained

23. Roland Barthes, *Writing Degree Zero,* trans. Annette Lavers and Colin Smith (New York: Hill & Wang, 1967), p. 13.

24. Barthes, *Writing Degree Zero,* p. 16. As is common in poststructuralist writing, the term "writing" is a complex one in Barthes's work. By it he means primarily, like Derrida, neither the act of putting pen to paper (or finger to keyboard) in order to produce words, nor the words so produced. Unlike Derrida, he uses it to refer to the relation between intention and language. In her introduction to his *Writing Degree Zero,* Susan Sontag suggests that, rather than "writing," "[a] more helpful translation of what Barthes means by *écriture* — the ensemble of features of a literary work such as tone, ethos, rhythm of delivery, naturalness of expression, atmosphere of happiness or malaise — might be 'personal utterance.' . . . In contrast to a language and a style *écriture* is the writer's zone of freedom, 'form considered as human intention'" (Barthes, *Writing Degree Zero,* pp. xiii-xiv).

25. Barthes, *Writing Degree Zero,* p. 17.

sufficient force over time ("within duration") to drown out the sound of his own present words. An infinite regress is established: how do the previous words manage still to sound above the din of what was said before them? Barthes is caught between Romantic desires for a moment of the creation of an absolutely free language and deconstructive despair over the possibility of the durability of the distinctiveness of any authorial voice. He thus establishes a false dichotomy, presenting us with a momentary authorial "meaningful gesture . . . [that] reaches the deep layers of History," and then with a posthistory of the created text that sees the authorial voice drowned out in the cacophony of "all the previous modes of writing."

A number of writers have applied a deconstructive model of intertextuality to the Bible. The most notable example is probably Stephen Moore, who blurs the Bible together with an extraordinary variety of texts.[26] The editors of a volume of the journal *Semeia* devoted to the topic reject the use of the term "intertextuality" "as a restrictive tool for nailing down authorial intent and literary influence"; they have in mind such "traditional intertextualist" biblical scholars as Richard Hays, whose work will be discussed below. "Thinly veiled in such efforts," they argue, "are conservative ideological and theological interests in maintaining the primacy of certain (usually Christian) texts over against secondary (usually Jewish) precursors."[27]

26. See, e.g., his reading of the Gospels of Mark and Luke inspired by James Joyce, in Stephen D. Moore, *Mark and Luke in Poststructuralist Perspectives: Jesus Begins to Write* (New Haven and London: Yale University Press, 1992), and his reading of the Bible's anthropomorphisms together with Jewish mystical texts and contemporary body-building literature, in *God's Gym: Divine Male Bodies of the Bible* (New York and London: Routledge, 1996).

27. George Aichele and Gary A. Phillips, "Introduction: Exegesis, Eisegesis, Intergesis," *Semeia* 69/70 (1995): 7-8. See also, from a similar collection of essays on intertextuality and the Old Testament: "discovering intertextual connections is a reader-oriented enterprise. While some texts direct our attention to other texts through explicit allusion, more often it is the reader who perceives textual relations" (Danna Nolan Fewell, "Introduction: Writing, Reading, and Relating," in *Reading Between Texts: Intertextuality and the Hebrew Bible,* ed. Danna Nolan Fewell [Louisville, Ky.: Westminster/John Knox, 1992], pp. 17-18). In the same volume, Timothy K. Beal concludes: "Every text — as an intersection of other textual surfaces — suggests an indeterminate *surplus* of meaningful possibilities. Interpretation is always a *production* of meaning from that surplus" (Timothy K. Beal, "Ideology and Intertextuality: Surplus of Meaning and Controlling the Means of Production," in *Reading Between Texts,* p. 31).

"Traditional Intertextuality"

A significant counterexample to Barthes's false dichotomy between the absolute power and absolute freedom of a writer can be found in the work of Richard Hays on Paul's use of the Old Testament. Taking his cue from the work of the literary critic John Hollander on the trope of metalepsis ("allusive echo"),[28] Hays asserts that Paul "repeatedly situates his discourse within the symbolic field created by a single great precursor text: Israel's Scripture."[29] He sets this claim in explicit contrast to liberal Protestantism, especially as represented by Adolf von Harnack and Rudolf Bultmann. In Bultmann's view, the Old Testament provides no serious constitutive elements in Paul's theology; he simply occasionally expressed the kerygma through mythological language and symbols.[30] The bulk of Hays's book is taken up with substantiating his own counterclaim in great and subtle exegetical detail. Using Ferdinand de Saussure's terminology, he describes Paul's relationship to the Old Testament in a way that flatly contradicts Barthes's confident assertion of his own inability to be heard above the babble of previous modes of speech. Hays writes, for example, of Romans:

> It would be inadequate to say that Scripture was *langue* and Paul's discourse *parole,* as though Scripture were merely a pool of lexemes from which Paul draws; rather, Scripture's poetry and narratives materially govern his confession. Scripture's *parole,* already spoken, rebounds and is heard once again in Paul's discourse. Consequently, Paul's sentences carry the weight of meanings acquired through earlier narrative and liturgical utterance. This allusive evocation of earlier declarations of God's faithfulness to Israel covertly undergirds the burden of Paul's overt argument.[31]

Moreover, most of Paul's quotations from the Old Testament "require the reader to engage in serious sustained deliberation about the relation between Scripture's *mundus significans* and the new situation Paul is addressing."[32] Paul simultaneously locates his discourse within the world-

28. Richard Hays, *Echoes of Scripture in the Letters of Paul* (New Haven and London: Yale University Press, 1989), p. 20.

29. Hays, *Echoes of Scripture,* p. 15.

30. Hays, *Echoes of Scripture,* pp. 7-8.

31. Hays, *Echoes of Scripture,* p. 70.

32. Hays, *Echoes of Scripture,* p. 175.

view of the Old Testament (he is fundamentally un-Marcionite) and proclaims the new message of the gospel of Jesus Christ; indeed, the latter is only possible by virtue of the former.

Thus, against Barthes's portrayal of human agency in authorship, Hays mounts a convincing argument that Paul's discourse both develops "within duration" (in his own lifetime and beyond) and is enormously in debt to previous modes of writing (the Old Testament) without becoming captive to those previous modes. The Old Testament does indeed provide a "stubborn after-image" in Paul's texts — but this fact does not drown out Paul's own voice; it is rather a necessary condition of his saying what he wanted to say. Subsequent readers of Paul can properly hear the distinctive contours of his texts in their own right only if they hear them in relation to the previous modes of writing that he indwells. Whereas Barthes sees authors moving only between absolute freedom and absolute slavery, Paul, according to Hays, develops the particular creativity and even freedom of his discourse precisely by virtue of his captivity to earlier texts. Barthes and Hays seem to be working with very different underlying notions of the nature of human freedom.

Hays's work concentrates on intertextual biblical relationships at the level of citation and allusion and suggests that they are complex. Paul creates his own discourse only by virtue of his indwelling of Old Testament discourse; he moves beyond the Old Testament without silencing it. How might such textual interrelationships, which are in effect mutually supplementing relations between biblical texts, themes, and genres, be described hermeneutically? A key term here, I suggest, is "polyphony." Under the concepts of "heteroglossia" and "speech genres," Mikhail Bakhtin offers a philosophical description of language that, I will argue, may support a "polyphonic" account of the intertextual interaction between the diverse canonical texts.

Polyphonic Scriptures

A Philosophical Resource: Mikhail Bakhtin's Concepts of "Heteroglossia" and "Speech Genres"

Bakhtin is deeply opposed to any attempt to treat language in any scientific way as a system of signifying words and phrases. The basic unit of language — what he calls "the real unit of speech communication" — is for him not the word or sentence but rather what he calls an "utterance." A sentence is a string of words that could be used for a variety of utterances; an utterance is always language *in use.* For example, the string of words "There's a bull in that field" is a sentence; however, when actually used for a communicative purpose — to inform, to warn, to threaten, or whatever — the sentence becomes an utterance.[33]

Furthermore, Bakhtin argues, despite attempts to regularize grammars and linguistic usage, for example, into "standard" and "nonstandard," every utterance is inhabited by a variety of *genres,* that is, of modes of speaking. This is the case because "[e]ach separate utterance is individual, of course, but each sphere in which language is used develops its own *relatively stable types* of these utterances. These we may call *speech genres.*" There is an "extreme *heterogeneity* of speech genres (oral and written) . . . from the proverb to the multivolume novel."[34] Two commentators on Bakhtin summarize the point well: for him, language is always language*s.*[35] It is this characteristic of language that Bakhtin refers to as *heteroglossia.* This word is a translation of the Russian word that Bakhtin seems to have invented for his concept; I will generally prefer the more common English word "polyphony" because it has been used, as we will see, by a number of writers on the Bible who have a basically Bakhtinian view of biblical language.[36]

33. Bakhtin's philosophy of language thus shares much in common with the speech-act theory of language developed by the philosophers J. L. Austin, John Searle, and others, which has been applied to the Bible fruitfully by Anthony Thiselton, *New Horizons in Hermeneutics* (London: HarperCollins, 1992), and Kevin Vanhoozer, "God's Mighty Speech-Acts: The Doctrine of Scripture Today," in *A Pathway into the Holy Scripture,* ed. Philip E. Satterthwaite and David F. Wright (Grand Rapids: Eerdmans, 1994), pp. 143-81; *Is There a Meaning in This Text? The Bible, the Reader and the Morality of Literary Knowledge* (Leicester: Apollos, 1998). Bakhtin's concept of "utterance" is very close to what speech-act theorists mean by their basic concept of an "illocutionary act," namely, the action one performs in uttering a word or sentence: promising, warning, asserting, naming, etc.

34. M. M. Bakhtin, "The Problem of Speech Genres," in M. M. Bakhtin, *Speech Genres and Other Late Essays,* trans. Vern W. McGee, ed. Caryl Emerson and Michael Holquist, University of Texas Press Slavic Series 8 (Austin, Tex.: University of Texas Press, 1986), pp. 60-61.

35. Gary Saul Morson and Caryl Emerson, *Mikhail Bakhtin: Creation of a Prosaics* (Stanford, Calif.: Stanford University Press, 1990), p. 140.

36. Bakhtin has a separate concept, which he in fact terms "polyphony," which does not concern us here. It applies to a fictional novel if the author genuinely allows his fictional

An example of what Bakhtin means can be found in the sophistication with which native speakers of a language can identify certain social and personal characteristics by the distinctive turns of phrase that different kinds of people habitually use. A great deal of character comedy works by exaggerating these speech genres; also, speakers of a foreign language, even if highly competent in pronunciation, grammar, and vocabulary, can still sound stilted and comical because they are often unable to recognize and use appropriate speech genres.

Bakhtin also has a fundamentally *dialogical* view of language. To be a listener or reader is for him not simply to be a passive receptor of someone else's meaning: "all real and integral understanding is actively responsive, and constitutes nothing other than the initial preparatory stage of a response. . . . Any utterance has, so to speak, an absolute beginning and an absolute end: its beginning is preceded by the utterances of others, and its end is followed by the responsive utterances of others."[37] This means that the speech genres that arise out of different spheres of language use in the world reflect different ways in which people habitually respond to the world, and especially to one another. These different responses represent different viewpoints and angles from which the world may be viewed, and different meaning- and value-related stances that may be taken towards the world. We therefore come to take specific and different positions with regard to the world by means of the multiple heteroglossia of language — that is, by ourselves inhabiting these inherited linguistic viewpoints on and stances towards the world:

> All languages of heteroglossia, whatever the principle underlying them and making them unique, are specific points of view on the world, forms for conceptualizing the world in words, specific world views, each characterized by its own objects, meanings and values. As such they may be juxtaposed to one another, mutually supplement one another, contradict one another and be interrelated dialogically.[38]

---

characters to speak for themselves. Bakhtin thought that only Dostoevsky succeeded in creating polyphonic novels (see Mikhail Bakhtin, *Problems of Dostoevsky's Poetics,* ed. and trans. Caryl Emerson, Theory and History of Literature 8 [Manchester: Manchester University Press, 1984], pp. 3-7).

37. Bakhtin, "Problem of Speech Genres," pp. 69, 71.

38. Bakhtin, "Discourse in the Novel," pp. 291-92.

Kevin Vanhoozer, developing the insights of speech-act theorists, says of *literary* genres exactly what Bakhtin says of heteroglossic speech genres: "genres are literary practices that enable complex ways of engaging reality and of interacting with others." He also suggests that there are generic illocutions that supervene on individual sentences: for example, following Susan Lanser's work on narrative, "the novel's basic illocutionary activity is ideological instruction."[39]

Bakhtin's basic observation about language is therefore strikingly similar to Barthes's: human speech is not some linguistic *creatio ex nihilo.* We cannot avoid using secondhand forms of language. However, from the same observation he draws precisely the opposite conclusion to that of Barthes. For Bakhtin, a complex speech genre, such as a literary genre, composed out of simpler speech genres, is sufficient to bear a mark of the author's individuality, distinguishing his utterance from that of other works: "The speaker's will is manifested primarily in the choice of a particular speech genre."[40] Words exist for speakers in three different aspects, he asserts: as a neutral word, belonging to no one (as in *langue*); as another's word; and as my word.[41] Of these, Barthes allows only the first two aspects to persist. Bakhtin agrees that human linguistic creativity is not easy — we do not always mark our speech with our own individuality: "many words stubbornly resist, others sound alien, sound foreign in the mouths of the one who appropriated them and now speaks them." However, unlike Barthes, he does not think it impossible to make something of one's own out of what has been used by others: "The word in language is half someone else's. It becomes 'one's own' only when the speaker populates it with his own intention, his own accent, when he appropriates the word, adapting it to his own semantic and expressive intention."[42] Ultimately, Bakhtin thinks, if we each had to originate our own speech genres in order to speak, communication would be impossible.[43] Barthes establishes as a necessary condition for "free speech" that the human speaker

39. Vanhoozer, *Is There a Meaning?* pp. 338, 341.

40. Bakhtin, "Problem of Speech Genres," pp. 75-78 (original italics removed).

41. Bakhtin, "Problem of Speech Genres," p. 88. "Speech genres" therefore functions as a third term between Saussure's *langue* and *parole,* offering a more sophisticated account of the forms that language takes in actual use.

42. Bakhtin, "Discourse in the Novel," pp. 293-94.

43. Bakhtin, "Problem of Speech Genres," p. 79.

be like God; Bakhtin thinks that, to speak for herself, a human person does not have to be the Creator.[44]

Heteroglossia, then, is a fruitful standpoint on language from which to consider the work of Richard Hays, outlined above. Hays's exegetical conclusions on the relationship between the Pauline epistles and the Old Testament can be expressed in Bakhtinian theoretical terms: Paul makes the languages of the Old Testament his "own" by successfully "populating" them with and adapting them for his own intention; yet in this act of "appropriation" the languages of the Old Testament are not silenced — that is not at all Paul's intention. Of course, it is intended here to portray these inner-biblical textual relationships as always "mutually supplementing" and never contradictory, as Bakhtin characterizes some relationships between "the languages of heteroglossia." Whether this is in fact the case with the Bible can only be established in the discussion between theology and biblical exegesis.

Accounts of the Biblical Canon As Polyphonic

Karl Barth asserts that "theology confronts in Holy Scriptures an extremely polyphonic, not a monotonous, testimony to the word and work of God." The Scriptures have this character because of "the objective multiplicity and inner contrasts sustained within the motion of the history of the covenant which they recount and affirm."[45] This kind of description of

44. Bakhtin probably had his own particular view of how his ethical and philosophical agendas were related to theology. This summary has been suggested of Bakhtin's attitude to Christian theology: "To participate directly in the 'world symposium,' God allowed Himself to be incarnated and tested. . . . Christ 'lived into' the world and proved himself to be the perfect dialogue partner, addressing people with 'dialogic intuition' that never finalized them" (Morson and Emerson, *Mikhail Bakhtin,* p. 267). Bakhtin's ultimate image of dialogic faith is *conversation* with Christ: "The word as something personal. Christ as Truth. I put the question to him." Morson and Emerson suppose that Bakhtin's conversation with Christ would be interminable and absorbing disagreement (Morson and Emerson, *Mikhail Bakhtin,* p. 62, quoting Bakhtin). In that case, what the book of Revelation says of heaven — "When the Lamb opened the seventh seal, there was silence in heaven for about half an hour" (Rev. 8:1) — is more like Bakhtin's notion of hell; similarly Matthew's claim, presented at the end of his Gospel, of the authoritative position held by the resurrected Christ.

45. Karl Barth, *Evangelical Theology: An Introduction,* trans. Grover Foley (London: Weidenfeld & Nicolson, 1963), p. 33.

the canon of Scripture has been developed by Paul Ricoeur in two thematically overlapping essays. Before I discuss Ricoeur, reference will be made to a work by Mark Wallace that, at the end of a comparison of Barth and Ricoeur, offers a reflection on biblical polyphony that, while very like Ricoeur's, is different in one significant respect.

Wallace argues: "If and when revelation has occurred within the Christian environment, this disclosure should be read through the polyphonic play of meaning within the Bible, a play that should not be stopped by an isolation of one trajectory of meaning within Scripture as 'the' biblical message."[46] He adds: "all discourse about God, including that of the Bible, both is and is not adequate to that about which it speaks."[47] Thus, the biblical texts are to be held in determinate relations to one another, in that dynamic polyphonic play occurs within the Bible, not running over the limits of the canon. It is in this dynamic set of relationships, not in the reduction of the themes of the Bible to a single theme, or in the reduction of the diversity of biblical genres to one mode of expression, that the Bible's discourse becomes in some way adequate to that about which it speaks.

However, Wallace provides in addition a significant role for the reader in establishing the nature of the interrelationships between different biblical trajectories. The kind of hermeneutics he advocates "will focus on the give-and-take between text and audience; it will maintain that Scripture is more like a lively and open-ended game between its world and the world of the reader than it is a closed book whose meaning is exhausted by the standard theological lexicon." He provides a practical example of what he means. We note, he says, that at times God is described in the Bible as a mighty warrior — " [y]et this martial and patriarchal imagery is questionable in a time when many of us have been victimized by sacralized violence." However, the Bible also depicts God as a mother brooding over her young and as the liberator of the poor, and it is these images that we should now privilege.[48]

It seems here that, despite his stated intention, Wallace has stopped the play of intercanonical ways of naming God somewhat, isolating, if not one trajectory of meaning in Scripture, then at least a group of trajectories that

46. Mark I. Wallace, *The Second Naiveté: Barth, Ricoeur and the New Yale Theology,* Studies in American Biblical Hermeneutics 6 (Macon, Ga.: Mercer University Press, 1990), pp. 117-18 (original italics removed).

47. Wallace, *The Second Naiveté,* p. 121.

48. Wallace, *The Second Naiveté,* p. 119.

seem to him relatively easy to reconcile with one another — and this for modern socio- and gender-political reasons. However, it is questionable whether the biblical texts that contain this martial imagery can be so easily exculpated. It surely cannot be the case that "sacralized violence" is only a modern phenomenon, that no one fell victim to it in the ancient world, in the period when these texts were written. If such imagery is questionable now, why not then? This is particularly curious, since Wallace also laments the present theological scene, in which, he says, the void left by the removal of the assumption that God has revealed himself has been filled with "a dizzying array of various genitive theologies (such as liberation theology or feminist theology)."[49] In fact, many liberation theologians do precisely what Wallace does — relegating the authoritative significance of certain biblical "names" of God, and promoting others, such as "liberator of the poor," in the light of modern concerns, as expressive of "the" message of the Bible. Wallace delimits the breadth of biblical polyphony by means of precisely the same criteria whose implementation has led directly to the present splintered theological scene beyond which he wishes to move.

Like Wallace, Ricoeur argues that the individual biblical texts should be understood as each separately saying something determinate of God, who, while escaping each separate attempt to refer to him, is nevertheless successfully referred to by the Bible's collective diversity — that is (we may say), "canonically." Speaking of the different ways in which the Bible "names" God, Ricoeur says:

> The referent "God" is thus intended by the convergence of all these partial discourses. It expresses the circulation of meaning among all the forms of discourse wherein God is named. . . . The referent "God" is not just the index of the mutual belonging together *(appartenance)* of the originary forms of the discourse of faith. It is their common goal, which escapes each of them.[50]

Ricoeur takes the individual texts and genres of the Bible to be real, albeit partial, acts of discourse. Where texts meet or intersect they refer to something beyond themselves — to a real extratextual and "extrareaderly" God. Unlike Kristeva, Ricoeur does not think that intertextuality swallows

49. Wallace, *The Second Naiveté,* pp. 113-14.

50. Paul Ricoeur, "Naming God," *Union Seminary Quarterly Review* 34 (1979): 222.

up texts. Francis Watson outlines a conception of the mode of biblical reference very similar to Ricoeur's which he calls "intratextual realism," and which "would understand the biblical text as referring beyond itself to extra-textual theological reality, while at the same time regarding that reality as accessible to us only in textual form, in principle and not only in practice."[51] Ricoeur would add that our access to theological reality is necessarily polyphonic.

In a related article Ricoeur applies this concept to revelation. His aim, he says, is "to carry the notion of revelation back to its most originary level, the one, which for the sake of brevity, I call the discourse of faith or the confession of faith." His subsequent discussion of various biblical genres shows that the latter terms refer primarily to the Bible. In Bible reading, rather than "transforming these different forms of discourse into propositions, we encounter a concept of revelation that is pluralistic, polysemic, and at most analogical in form."[52] This is where he wants theology to start. We should not begin with some philosophical notion that "God exists"; rather, if we succeed, as we should, in avoiding turning the Bible into mere assertion and proposition, "we arrive at a polysemic and polyphonic concept of revelation."[53] This model asserts the irreducibility of biblical polyphony, and, unlike that of Wallace, provides no extrabiblical criteria by which to deemphasize certain biblical names for God.

The practical significance of this aspect of Ricoeur's account can be shown by Bruce Metzger's comment on recent attempts, especially in continental Europe, to discern "a canon within the canon." He judges that such attempts, along with such historical positions as Luther's qualms over the epistle of James, always succumb to arbitrariness because they fail to

51. Francis Watson, *Text, Church and World: Biblical Interpretation in Theological Perspective* (Edinburgh: T. & T. Clark, 1994), pp. 224-25.

52. Paul Ricoeur, "Toward a Hermeneutic of the Idea of Revelation," in Paul Ricoeur, *Essays on Biblical Interpretation,* ed. Lewis S. Mudge (London: SPCK, 1981), pp. 74-75.

53. Ricoeur, "Toward a Hermeneutic," pp. 90-92. For the significance to theology in general of Ricoeur's proper recognition of the polyphonic nature of revelation, see David Tracy's summary of the recent history of the doctrine of revelation, in which he has Ricoeur specifically in mind: "The need for second-order, conceptual discourse for a doctrine of revelation was studied with care and precision. The contours of the actual first-order religious discourse of the Scriptures (prophetic, narrative, poetic, wisdom, proverbial, parabolic, letters, hymnic) were, with a few notable exceptions, left largely unthematized until the last fifteen years" (David Tracy, *On Naming the Present: God, Hermeneutics, and Church* [London: SCM, 1994], pp. 109-10).

envisage situations in which the books proposed as marginal could become of vital significance for the Church: "New Testament scholars have the responsibility as servants of the Church to investigate, understand, and elucidate, for the development of the Christian life of believers, the full meaning of every book within the canon and not only of those which may be most popular in certain circles and at certain times. Only in such a way will the Church be able to hear the Word of God in all of its breadth and depth."[54]

Ricoeur regards "poetic discourse," by which he means a diversity of literary genres, as fundamentally performing something more than an act of reference: "My deepest conviction is that poetic language alone restores us to that participation-in or belonging-to an order of things which precedes our capacity to oppose ourselves to things taken as objects opposed to a subject."[55] He adds that biblical poetic language is unique in that the name of the unnameable God is the vanishing point of all the Bible's partial discourses about God.[56] One may ask, however, whether the divine referent of human biblical language is unique in this way. Not even a human person is fully captured by a single discourse; as referents of the discourse of others and of ourselves about ourselves, we too escape each of them, but may be known and referred to, by ourselves and others, partially but nevertheless adequately and truly, as the common goal that escapes each of the discourses itself. As God presents himself to us in the world, the biblical canon, in its polyphonic intercanonical poetic functions, allows us to name him in the same way. Kevin Vanhoozer argues thus:

> In an important sense, we can say what lies beyond our words. While we may not have nouns that "name" God, speaking is more than a mere matter of "labelling" the world. . . . Where individual words are unable to articulate the majesty and glory of God, sentences succeed in so doing. I do not wish to be misunderstood. I am not suggesting that sentences describe the divine reality without remainder, but rather that some sentences themselves contain a "surplus of meaning" (Ricoeur) which is richer than any literal paraphrase.[57]

54. Metzger, *The Canon of the New Testament,* p. 282.
55. Ricoeur, "Toward a Hermeneutic," p. 101.
56. Ricoeur, "Toward a Hermeneutic," p. 104.
57. Vanhoozer, "God's Mighty Speech-Acts," p. 172 n. 92.

What Vanhoozer describes as a "surplus of meaning" at the level of the sentence may be called, also following Ricoeur, the polyphonic circulation of meaning, exceeding the capacity of any one of the individual discourses, at the level of the biblical canon as a whole.

Canonical Polyphony and Biblical Authority

The literary critic Walter Reed, reflecting on his own readings of a number of biblical narratives performed in the light of Bakhtin's philosophy, judges that the diversity of the biblical canon is "always an embarrassment to the theologian, even the 'biblical' theologian."[58] However, given Bakhtin's arguments about the sheer complexity and irreducible polyphonic nature of even the simplest utterance, it is possible to account for a greater degree of canonical coherence-in-diversity than Reed supposes before the "biblical theologian" need blush in the face of the biblical texts. Both biblical literary genres and thematic statements derived from the content of the Bible are points of view on reality. The themes of justification, adoption, and reconciliation, for example, are each partially and truthfully expressive of the reality of God's act of salvation as it is depicted in the Bible. Moreover, when language is used to give expression to each of these themes, it can only be done in a variety of linguistic genres — in the case of the Bible, literary genres. Each of these genres takes a different viewpoint, a different stance or angle, on the theme: as a narrative that demonstrates the reality of God's act of (for example) adoption of a people in history; as a prophecy that speaks direct encouragement regarding the future for those who have been adopted; as a psalm that provides a model of praise to God for his act of adoption; as a set of laws that prescribe how the adopted should live; and so on.

As far as biblical interpretation is concerned, a model of "traditional intertextuality," in the sense given by Plett, may be proposed, according to which the interpreter is aware of the extent to which canonical texts, in the wealth of their mutual quotations, and especially of their literary and thematic allusions to each other, refer in polyphonic ways to divine revelation. Since "canon" implies a clearly delimited set of texts, this intertextuality

58. Walter L. Reed, *Dialogues of the Word: The Bible as Literature According to Bakhtin* (New York and London: Oxford University Press, 1993), p. 170.

may also be called an "intratextuality"; it is Scripture that interprets Scripture. This is Ricoeur's basic hermeneutical view of the Bible and may be regarded as a "polyphonic" explication of Watson's notion of "intratextual realism": we necessarily have access to reality via linguistic genres, that is, via specific points of view on the world — in the case of the Bible, via a variety of mutually supplementing literary genres.

To determine how far the diversity of the Bible's content can stretch before its polyphonic unity breaks — that is, before it becomes unworkable as the supreme authority in the Church — is of course an enormous task. However, as a preliminary to such work, it can be argued, on the basis of such observations as Ricoeur's, supplemented by a Bakhtinian philosophy of language, that it can stretch further — indeed, must stretch further — than is often supposed. The diverse nature of the referents of Scripture — God, humankind, the world, God's action in Christ, protology and eschatology, the history of redemption — seems to require, as regards both theme and genre, a wide range of "partial discourses" and a high degree of heteroglossic languages (complex "speech genres") in the canon if the texts are to render the referents to readers at all adequately.[59] If a unique hypostatic union of human and divine natures really did take place in the person of Jesus of Nazareth as the culmination of a process of divine action in history, anything less diverse than the canon of Scripture we have might be thought too simplistic to speak of such a reality.[60] John Goldingay writes, in a work that shares a similar view of the Bible's theological diversity: "Recognizing the complexity of reality itself, we attempt the task of comprehending as fully as we can that complex reality as a whole, in the light of the witness the OT has given to various aspects of it in unsystematic ways."[61] What confronts us in the Bible is what David Tracy has called "the extraordinary complexity of a full scriptural understanding of the many faces of

59. See Michael Fox's comment that in biblical interpretation "[m]uch of what is called indeterminacy is actually effective mimesis of a determinate but complex reality" (quoted in Vanhoozer, *Is There a Meaning,* p. 302).

60. In speaking of "the canon of Scripture *we* have," no distinction between different Christian versions of the biblical canon, such as the different lists of Roman Catholic and Protestant canons, and the different forms of Hebrew and Greek canons, is necessarily made here. As regards diversity at the theoretical level of the present discussion, they are similar enough to one another to be described under the same categories. The choice of a particular list and form of the canon is made on other theological and historical grounds.

61. Goldingay, *Theological Diversity,* p. 184.

God disclosed in the many scriptural genres to name God."[62] If the canonical texts of Scripture ultimately sing in unison about the whole of the divine redemption of humankind in Jesus Christ, that is only by virtue of their singing polyphonically, in unsystematic, mutually supplementing ways.[63] Biblical polyphony neither reduces into monotony nor expands into cacophony, just as Paul's discourse neither collapses into nor contradicts the Old Testament in its simultaneous indwelling of it and moving beyond it.

The Polyphony and Sufficiency of Scripture

Some particular examples may be offered of how this concept of biblical polyphony might both address some of the exegetical evidence offered in support of the critical claim that the Scriptures are a disunited cacophony, and help in the continual renewal of the use of the Bible in evangelical life and theology.

R. W. L. Moberly has argued that much critical biblical scholarship has too hastily treated biblical polyphony as evidence of conflicting theological trends in the Bible, which it then ascribed to evidence of the texts' prehistory. He suggests that the existence in close proximity in the Bible of a narrative of Yahweh speaking to Moses face to face and a denial from Yahweh that Moses can see his face (Exod. 33:11, 20) is not incoherent but is "a typical theological paradox straining to express the possibilities and limitations in man's approach to God." Further, he rejects Gerhard von Rad's argument that the tent and the ark in the book of Exodus represent the quite different theologies of visitation and presence, on the basis of which von Rad decides that Exod. 29:45 is a disharmonious vestige of an earlier tradition. Moberly suggests that these two themes are in fact an Old

62. Tracy, *On Naming the Present,* p. 33.

63. "Polyphony" is preferred, in order to catch the unsystematic character of Scripture, over "symphony," which Origen uses to describe the relationship between the Old and New Testaments (referred to in J. N. D. Kelly, *Early Christian Doctrines* 5th ed. rev. [London: A. & C. Black, 1977], p. 69). "Unsystematic" here has both a historical and a theological sense. The theological sense is developed in the following section. Metzger explains the historical sense: "The homogeneity of the canon is not jeopardized even in the face of tensions that exist within the New Testament. These tensions, however, must not be exaggerated into contradictions as a result of giving inadequate consideration to the divergent situations within the early Church to which the writers addressed themselves" (Metzger, *The Canon of the New Testament,* pp. 280-81).

Testament version of the theological paradox of immanence and transcendence. In other words, von Rad's treatment of Exodus is based on an ungrounded assumption of what does and does not count as theological inconsistency.[64] Another writer has argued that, in the context of the faith of Israel, the notion of canon requires variety; Old Testament writers seem to have avoided dissolving tensions within and between texts.[65]

How might a different theological assumption — one that allows for a much greater degree of polyphonic consistency than von Rad could tolerate — be grounded? The fundamental Christian doctrine of the Trinity may be helpful here. With reference to the Trinity, John Milbank has argued, in another context, that "Christianity . . . recognizes no original violence. It construes the infinite not as chaos, but as a harmonic peace which is yet beyond the circumscribing power of totalizing reason. Peace no longer depends upon the reduction to the self-identical, but is the *sociality* of harmonious difference."[66] Milbank is talking here of the nature of God; perhaps we may regard Scripture, the semantic mediation of this divine triune nature, as commensurately characterized by a "sociality" of literary and conceptual harmonious difference. To be up to the task of naming a triune God, Scripture must reflect him in at least this ontological respect: it must say genuinely different things in different places, which faith receives as harmonious. If it is appropriate to take this as the theological background against which all faithful biblical reading is ultimately performed, then Walter Brueggemann, in his recent large work of Old Testament theology, is wrong to judge that " [i]nterpretation, in the end, cannot overcome the *irascibly* pluralistic character of the [biblical] text,"[67] for he fails to take account of a basic Christian belief about the peaceable nature of the divine reality communicated in the texts.

In light of a claim that the Christian Scriptures are irreducibly poly-

64. R. W. L. Moberly, *At the Mountain of God: Story and Theology in Exodus 32–34,* Journal for the Study of the Old Testament Supplement Series (Sheffield: JSOT Press, 1983), pp. 33-34.

65. Mark E. Biddle, *Polyphony and Symphony in Prophetic Literature: Rereading Jeremiah 7–20,* Studies in Old Testament Interpretation 2 (Macon, Ga.: Mercer University Press, 1996), p. 119.

66. John Milbank, *Theology and Social Theory: Beyond Secular Reason* (Oxford: Basil Blackwell, 1990), p. 5.

67. Walter Brueggemann, *Theology of the Old Testament: Testimony, Dispute, Advocacy* (Minneapolis: Fortress, 1997), p. 64 (italic added).

phonic, the question arises of the sense in which the Bible may be said to offer an all-encompassing story — a meta-narrative. Mark Coleridge offers a distinction here. The notion of the Bible as "one *kind* of meta-narrative" has gone, he argues:

> Any totalising meta-narrative, any master-narrative which seeks or claims to be univocal, has had its day; and this is true of the Bible insofar as it seeks or claims to be a totalising or univocal master-narrative. But this allows, perhaps demands, the discovery of the Bible as *a new kind of meta-narrative* — a meta-narrative not univocal but polyphonic in Mikhail Bakhtin's sense, not monologic but dialogic. . . . many stories comprise *the* story.[68]

Brueggemann has developed this suggestion. He argues that the Old Testament expresses both a constant (covenantal) and a dynamic (historical) theological witness, and that behind this problem lies the character of God, "who also refuses tameness and systematization."[69] In tension with this, it might be added that God also promises to be constantly faithful to his uttered promises. Brueggemann suggests that "Old Testament theology" is something of an oxymoron in that "theology" has long been taken to stress the "constant" pole:[70] "Conventional systematic theology cannot tolerate the unsettled polyphonic character of the text."[71]

The latter statement is certainly correct if by it Brueggemann means that every systematic theology, in that it is inevitably limited with regard to the polyphony of Scripture, functions to silence the scriptural voices to which it fails to give adequate expression. A small example may be given. In current evangelical writing on the atonement (at least in the British circles I know best), whether theological, exegetical, homiletical, or devotional, there is a relative neglect of the theme of the union of believers with Christ and a relative overemphasis on penal substitution.[72] This is under-

68. Mark Coleridge, "Life in the Crypt or Why Bother with Biblical Studies?" *Biblical Interpretation* 2 (1994): 147-48.

69. Brueggemann, *Theology of the Old Testament,* pp. 39-42.

70. Brueggemann, *Theology of the Old Testament,* p. 40.

71. Brueggemann, *Theology of the Old Testament,* p. 106.

72. For a similar observation in an American context, see James Montgomery Boice, *Foundations of the Christian Faith* (Downers Grove, Ill. and Leicester: Inter-Varsity Press, 1986), p. 389.

standable because the latter doctrine has been widely attacked and has needed concerted defense that asserts its vital place in Christian soteriology. However, this apologetic focus has sometimes been transformed into a systematic and homiletical organizational center and has skewed contemporary evangelical theology, blinding it to the historical significance of the doctrine of the mystical union in orthodox Protestant theology, both Reformed and Lutheran.[73] J. I. Packer, in an excellent defense of penal substitution, has noted that for Luther and his successors penal substitution was one of four "moments" in what Luther called "the wonderful exchange," which begins with the incarnation of the Son of God and ends with the glorification of believers. Insisting on the centrality of penal substitution, Packer argues that the ontological union of Christ and believers provides a particular viewpoint on the event of Christ's substitutionary work on the cross, from the perspective of which it can be seen to *include* believers, "in a manner transcending bounds of time and space"; however, he argues in addition that, for Protestant orthodoxy, penal substitution was itself (rightly) grounded in the ontological union.[74]

Similar arguments may also be made with regard to other relational biblical images of salvation, such as adoption and reconciliation. The current emergence of community and relationality as significant themes across a range of disciplines, including many branches of philosophy and theology, may help evangelical theology to recover the significance of these biblical images of the event and fruits of the cross.

My argument is certainly not that the defense of penal substitution should be abandoned or even downgraded in importance. It is, rather, that it should be clearly contextualized theologically by being related more organically, in evangelical thinking, preaching, and personal piety, to the diversity of images by which the Bible speaks polyphonically of the mystery of salvation in Christ. Packer argues that a "one-track-minded" exposition of penal substitution, though common, is unhelpful, and that different models of the event of the cross sometimes treated as contradictory — for example, victory over hostile spiritual forces and satisfaction for sin — are

73. For assertions of the centrality of union with Christ from within twentieth-century conservative Reformed theology, see John Murray, *Redemption — Accomplished and Applied* (Edinburgh: Banner of Truth Trust, 1955), p. 170; L. Berkhof, *Systematic Theology* (Grand Rapids: Eerdmans; London: Banner of Truth Trust, 1939, 1941), pp. 447-53.

74. J. I. Packer, "What Did the Cross Achieve? The Logic of Penal Substitution," *Tyndale Bulletin* 25 (1974): 31-33.

in fact complementary.[75] In other words, account must be taken of the mutually supplementing polyphony of the biblical models without necessarily trying to locate any one model as logically central. It is impossible for us fully and definitively to systematize the diversity of biblical images, both legal and relational, of salvation in Christ; the unsystematic form of the scriptural mediation of God's salvific act is sufficient to warn us not to set such a goal for ourselves. To neglect any one image because one happens to find it in some way inappropriate or offensive, as liberal theology has largely done with penal substitution, or to subsume it into another image defined as 'logically' central, as some evangelical theology has done with the theme of union with Christ, is to lose the dynamic tension between the different standpoints — to narrow the kaleidoscopic vision — that the Bible gives on the same ultimately mysterious event of salvation.

Thus, it is not correct to argue that systematic theology is *inherently* unable to tolerate biblical polyphony; decisive here is not the nature of the systematic enterprise itself but the epistemological mood in which it is conducted. (This is perhaps what Brueggemann alludes to when he refers to "conventional" systematic theology.) A systematic theology that makes no ultimate normative claim for its particular form and content thereby acknowledges its own provisional character and its inability to reflect the polyphony of Scripture in full. Theologians should not be attempting to write the theology that puts an end to the writing of theology by somehow saying everything, but they nevertheless rightly attempt to give a certain kind of expression to the meta-narrative that is partially but adequately grasped in our limited comprehension of Scripture's polyphonic account of God's single act of salvation in Christ.[76] Of course, it is impossible in practice to hold the diversity of Scripture's themes and generic voices in one's mind all at once and to put them into practice in one's life all at the same time. This, though, does not make systematic theology a fruitless exercise, just as it does not render futile the attempt to live a coherent Christian life. Rather, it should make us humble and hopeful, not despairing, in both our Christian living and in our more formal doing of theology. In re-

75. Packer, "What Did the Cross Achieve?" pp. 21-26.

76. The point is informed by what Vanhoozer calls "The Christian morality of literary knowledge": "the claim that there is knowledge is not the same as the claim that one possesses it or that the possession of such knowledge allows one to impose one's opinions on others. There is always something more that can be said in an argument" (Vanhoozer, *Is There a Meaning,* p. 302).

ferring by our language in part to God and in embodying in our lives in part the life of Christ, we nevertheless speak truly of God and are truly the body of Christ, as we look for our full redemption, as Paul knew very well (1 Cor. 13:12).[77]

As regards the sufficiency of Scripture in Christian life and theology, in light of the above discussions of the diversity of Scripture, I propose a principle of *canonically limited polyphony,* which would establish three necessary conditions, collectively forming a sufficient condition, for the "naming" of the personal God of revelation. God must be named polyphonically. To name him in only one way would be to view and know his reality in only one dimension. God must also be named by a limited polyphony. To name him in limitless ways is not to name him at all, and to seek to delimit the polyphony by any other criterion than by the canon of Scripture is to risk naming a God after our own image. The formal aspect of the sufficiency of Scripture, then, the rule of Scripture as its own interpreter, is best viewed as a vital doctrinal statement of the necessary and sufficient conditions for the "naming" of God. Since it is sufficient in this way and for this purpose, Scripture is insufficient to provide warrant for dogmatism about knowledge. Since no one may ever grasp the full polyphonic self-revelation of God at one time, no one ever succeeds in fully nailing God down. (Only idols are susceptible to nailing down; they even require it, sometimes.[78]) The polyphonic sufficiency of Scripture therefore both authorizes and chastens any theological endeavor and any Christian believing and practice.

God gives himself to us in Scripture, truly and in part, in testimony that he gave himself on the cross for our present and future redemption, truly and completely. It is as such that God gives himself to us as a God to be trusted. Christian faith, if it is rightly expressed as trust in God's supreme self-revelation in Christ, as that revelation is now sufficiently mediated to us by the polyphonic Scriptures, is therefore appropriately thought of as an eschatological hope.

77. I have claimed several times that human knowledge, though partial, may be adequate. See, further, Vanhoozer's recent rich theological account of "a hermeneutics of humility and conviction," on which I draw here (Vanhoozer, *Is There a Meaning,* pp. 455-68).

78. Isa. 41:7.

Towards Trust

Stephen Williams

A Matter of Taste

How has modernity upset the classical way of the viewing the interrelationship of the doctrines of God and Scripture?

Definitions and interpretations of modernity abound. Discussion of it today is especially relevant for those who believe that postmodernity is mounted on modernity, or that postmodernity is a form of late modernity. For present purposes, we are understanding modernity as a project that has attempted to subject the great bulk of the Western intellectual and religious tradition to the canons of scientific reason. Such reason is to be interpreted quite broadly and applied to social as well as natural science, morality, and cosmology alike. Postmodernity (a term retained in the company of "modernity" though there is a good case for preferring "postmodernism" here) denies that these canons possess criteria and declares that difference is destructive of norms. Modernity and postmodernity seem to be connected thus: modernity essentially locates authority in the human self, and postmodernity radicalizes that. The significance of locating authority in the self is based on the relation of modernity to the theistic or Christian form of thought that has dominated the West for so long. On the one hand, in a theistic scheme of things, the self is subject to an authority that is other than itself. On the other hand, modernity broadly speaking ascribes authority to reason, which is located within.

It is easy to describe the contrast wrongly, for, clearly, in the theistic tradition, reason has been involved in the judgment that authority ought to be ascribed to that which is external to itself. Furthermore, in the modern project, clearly many of its representatives have held that reason must be determined in its findings by reality external to itself. Yet, to pick up the vocabulary of trust, on the former view of things, what is regarded as ultimately trustworthy is that which is external to reason; on the latter, reason itself. That may be badly put, but nothing in this chapter hangs on the best characterization of these things. As far as postmodernity goes, its view of reason and of selfhood is stated in a way contrary to modernity. Yet it is by concentrating deconstructive power in the place where modernity concentrated constructive power — in the self, in reason — that postmodernity executes its project. Its fundamentally negative relation to a theistic — or a Christian — scheme of things appears to be parasitic on what modernity did to authority, and, arguably, one can go further and claim for it a strong family resemblance.[1] There is no commitment here to an optimal characterization of postmodernity either: we are merely broaching the question of authority to provide a broad context for discussion.

As we move away from modernity, the question of what constitutes the classical view of the relationship between God and Scripture arises as a matter of dispute both within and without those circles that discuss the pedigree and merits of belief in biblical inerrancy. That dispute is not our concern. So, whether or not the following is adequate as a historical statement, it is adequate for our present purposes: Scripture has been traditionally conceived as uniquely God's word both in form and in content. It has unique textual authority as the inspired record of divine speech and self-communication.[2] It conveys unique religious truth that ought to be promulgated and believed everywhere, for it is about salvation. God, triune and incarnate, creator and redeemer, is presented to us in the Bible, and that is because he has revealed himself as such.

The tale of the developing modern challenge to this view of God and Scripture, whose impetus became increasingly evident from the second half of the seventeenth century, has been told often enough. There was the scientific revolution, which not only turned up data that challenged received interpretations of the Bible but furnished a paradigm for knowl-

1. Despite the drawbacks involved in this characterization, Christianity is understood here as a form of theism.

2. The phrasing is not meant to preclude the conviction that it is itself inspired speech.

edge that was demonstrable and secure, public, testable, and true. There was the application of historical criticism to the Bible, which not only challenged the veracity of its accounts but encouraged a cultural relativism, a conviction that definitive religious truth can not be expressed in a particular space and time. There was the project of modern philosophy, which not only established a critico-skeptical starting point for its enterprise but arrived, with Kant, at a critical rejection of traditional claims to knowledge. Of course there is much more to the tale, such as the evolution of moral sensibility and, behind it all — if not grounding it all — the new ways of conceiving society and social existence that were stimulated by the depressing religious conflicts that went on for more than a century after the Reformation.

Those of us who want to defend in our day the classical way of viewing God and Scripture may understandably derive the agenda from the facts set out above. We may seek to relate religion and science aright, rebut received skepticisms in historical criticism, surmount the epistemological obstacles placed by Kant, and so forth. Yet even if such an enterprise is to be respected, welcomed, or pursued, it is one thing to deny that modernity should be allowed to consider itself victorious on these fronts and to give reason for that; it is another to hold that these are the things we should attend to in the first instance as we set about something like a restoration of the belief that Scripture is a trustworthy revelation of a trustworthy God. The reason for so suggesting is given in a telling aphorism of Nietzsche. Writing in *The Gay Science* over a century ago, Nietzsche said: "What is now decisive against Christianity is our taste, no longer our reasons."[3] This lays fair claim to being a rubric under which the entire project of rehabilitating a traditional Christianity should be considered, and it is steering much of the discussion in this essay.[4]

This is not quite to go along with the contrast as Nietzsche states it. If the idea is that there has been a historical shift from rational to quasi-aesthetic or perhaps emotional objections to Christianity, this needs to be carefully tested. In *The Sources of the Self*, Charles Taylor distinguished different strands of thought about the self that run through modernity. One,

3. Friedrich Nietzsche, *The Gay Science* (New York: Vintage, 1974), sec. 132.

4. Some of us who identify ourselves or who are identified as standing within that tradition will balk at the use of the word "traditional" because it smacks of an innately conservative outlook on the world.

associated with and inaugurated by Descartes, is disengaged, viewing the self in its scientifically objectifiable nature. However, before Descartes came on the scene, there was Michel de Montaigne.

Montaigne is at the point of origin of another kind of modern individualism, that of self-discovery, which differs from the Cartesian both in aim and in method. Its aim is to identify the individual in his or her unrepeatable difference, where Cartesianism gives us a science of the subject in its general essence; and it proceeds by a critique of first-person self-interpretation rather than by proofs of impersonal reasoning.[5]

One may indeed wonder whether the contrast with Descartes is quite right.[6] Yet when one meets the phrase "unrepeatable difference"; when one considers the trajectory Taylor depicts from Montaigne to Goethe via Rousseau; and when one realizes that Montaigne was much admired by Nietzsche, who was not extravagant in his admiration, one is encouraged to seek out sources of modernity that are other than what we find in science, historical criticism, and post-Cartesian philosophy in the classical lineage through Locke and Kant. It remains possible, of course, that Montaigne or like epigones can not be accounted for except in terms of earlier developments in science or epistemology that are subsequently developed in their fashion by Descartes, Locke, and Kant. However, we need to call Pascal as witness at this point. As he saw it, when Montaigne failed to plumb religious depths, it was less on account of sincere failure than of inadequate receptivity. The result was: "He inspires indifference regarding salvation: 'without fear or repentance.'"[7] Specifically, the question of some sort of taste is close to the surface in Varro's words, which Montaigne cites: "Since man only wants to find such truth as sets him free, it can be thought expedient for him to be deceived."[8]

5. Charles Taylor, *The Sources of the Self: The Making of Modern Identity* (Cambridge: Cambridge University Press, 1989), pp. 181-82.

6. Descartes is constantly telling us that his discoveries are his own, of him and for him. This is not to be read uncritically, yet it is to be noted that he keeps up his insistence on this point even in the less celebrated works, like *The Search for Truth;* see, e.g., Eudoxus in *Philosophical Writings* (Cambridge: Cambridge University Press, 1984), 2:419.

7. Blaise Pascal, *Pensées* (London: Penguin, 1966), p. 680. See Stephen N. Williams, *Revelation and Reconciliation: A Window on Modernity* (Cambridge: Cambridge University Press, 1995), pp. 20ff.

8. Michel de Montaigne, *Apology for Raymond Sebond* (London: Penguin, 1987), p. 109. The themes of why people want the truth and the function of illusion are important to Nietzsche too. Admittedly, we are proceeding at this point without analyzing the notion of "taste."

The reference to freedom brings us to what appears to be at or close to the heart of the distaste for Christianity that many have experienced since and before Nietzsche. Hegel famously concluded that history should be read as the development of the idea of freedom, a pronouncement that rings true for many both historically and experientially.[9] It seems plausible to think of the Reformation giving freedom from the tyranny of papacy; the Enlightenment, freedom from the tyranny of the Bible; and postmodernity, freedom from the tyranny of reason. We could also, of course, and perhaps should first, chart the course of political freedoms from monarchies to assorted democracies and republics. The ideal of and bid for freedom appear to underlie explicitly or implicitly much of the general strife that marks the perturbations of contemporary culture. This has largely powered the rejection of the God of Scripture and the Scriptures of the Church. Taking his leave of God in 1980, Don Cupitt rehearsed the problems with arguments for the existence of God and the still greater problems with the coherent intelligibility of theistic discourse, but he awarded the palm in the business of leaving God to our consciousness, on which morality depends and which is now riveted to autonomy.

> Today everyone wishes to be his own master and captain of his own soul, and that splendid idea determines how we think of ourselves and what we hope for. We are irreversibly committed to it because in these matters there is no going back. Once one has fully understood that it is possible to be the captain of one's own soul, then the idea is established in one and has thereafter an unshakeable authority.[10]

The fact that the first words have for so long sounded trite is no reflection of Cupitt's work; it just shows how used we are to that kind of perception. These words are cited not just as exemplary but because the claim of "irreversibility" constitutes a strong challenge to those who dispute this

9. Not that one experiences the history of the world, but Hegel's words undoubtedly express the impressions and experiences of many. The point will be taken dialectically, though, if "dialectic" is not too callous a word to use to allude to the horrendous facts of tyranny, oppression, and fascistic authoritarianism that many find linked to the Western experiment with freedom.

10. Don Cupitt, *Taking Leave of God* (London: SCM, 1980), p. x. For morality depending on consciousness, see p. 144; for the possession of autonomous consciousness, see pp. 12-14.

kind of autonomy. How, for a great number of people, can the God of Scripture be anything except repellent, because he is an Other who creates, judges, and gives a law that cuts against or slaughters self-definition, autonomy, and value creation? If we insist in response that God is love, he is still Other, still lawgiver and so forth, on a theistic scheme of things.[11] This state of affairs suggests that, in approaching today the claim that Scripture is a trustworthy disclosure of a trustworthy God, one wants to displace the ingrained conviction that the idea of such a deity is obnoxious and to remove the psychological and emotional barriers to hearing the biblical message. The task is difficult. Opposition to this God is very strong; not only is the modern consciousness estranged from Christian belief, but ways of going about the whole business of cognition seem incommensurably diverse.[12] Further, some will say, why try to woo moderns anyway? Why demand an accounting of Christianity on non-Christian terms?

A systematic answer to these questions would be a distraction here. We have to reckon with the commendation of Christianity to many constituencies. Faced with genuine brokenness, the oppression of sin, and deep hurt, the Christian today does not necessarily need to justify Scripture in light of modernity, for the love of Jesus Christ, and hence his reality, should be commended through the ministry of the body of believers that constitute the Christian Church. Though the hurt may not realize it, the experience of love received evokes trust. Indeed, this essay could have taken the line that it is by practice, and not by argument, that one reestablishes the trustworthiness of God and Scripture. The line could be advanced on account of (a) the strong element of intrinsic correctness in this claim, (b) the role of religious feuding in turning post-Reformation Europe away from Christianity, and (c) the interest that attaches to Bonhoeffer's "religionless Christianity" in light of our use of Bonhoeffer later in this essay.[13] Again, faced

11. Just how little distance that may get the traditionalist is indicated by, e.g., the work of Julia Kristeva; see Graham Ward, ed., *The Postmodern God: A Theological Reader* (Oxford: Blackwell, 1997), ch. 10.

12. "[J]ust what religious unbelief is among the educated today is . . . difficult to say. Exactly what the breakdown of concepts has to do with it is a very complicated matter." So Paul Holmer, *A Grammar of Faith* (New York: Harper & Row, 1978), p. 125. This seems applicable to the less educated too.

13. This is not to say that the explicit and growing rejection of Christianity in Europe after the turbulent period of Reformation owed nothing to any preceding causes in the Middle Ages.

with impenitent lawbreakers of the moral order, the Christian may have no occasion to argue much about the trustworthiness of Scripture since its message might be regarded with utter indifference by those concerned. The intellectual makers of modernity and postmodernity may themselves harbor such indifference or contempt or hostility. In that case, Pascal understood much better than Schleiermacher what one is up against here.[14] Yet there is no room for arrogance in the churches, for our own tarnishing of our message should be judged with greater severity than we judge the indifferent, the contemptuous, and the hostile outside the churches.

This chapter assumes the relevance of its reflections but proceeds without much discrimination in such matters of constituency, although the question of addressees will return to us in some form when we come to Bonhoeffer, the *eminence grise* behind this essay. Before that, we must ask about "the other."

What About the Other?

Christians, taught to twin the commandments to love God and neighbor, are bound to ask themselves the following question: If God's otherness is an imposition on freedom, is the otherness of my neighbor so as well? The cases are different, we may initially think, because the neighbor is not a creator or a lawgiver. Yet does not the neighbor make demands?

One of the most noteworthy attempts in twentieth-century thought to establish the fact, nature, and transcendent implications of this kind of demand is that of Emmanuel Levinas. We draw attention here to just two points. First, Levinas insists that confrontation with the concrete other is immediately ethical. I gaze at the unprotected face of the other, and the moral imperative not to kill is written upon it.[15] Indeed, very strongly: "The fear for the death of the other is certainly at the basis of the responsibility for him."[16] Second, Levinas saw in the face of the other mastery

14. The contrast is between Pascal's perception of the blockage to the gospel caused by human pride and Schleiermacher's *Speeches on Religion to Its Cultured Despisers* right at the close of the eighteenth century, where he is, we may say, broadly appealing to "taste."

15. Levinas gives a very short but quite powerful resume of some of this in his "Signature," published in *Difficult Freedom: Essays on Judaism* (London: Athlone, 1990).

16. Emmanuel Levinas, *Ethics and Infinity* (Pittsburgh: Duquesne University Press, 1985), p. 119.

rather than equality, my responsibility more than the other's rights. In his later writings, we apparently find "the increasingly important role played by passivity in the constitution of ethical subjectivity. The material instant lies at the base, as it were, of the superlative passivity, the extremity of inwardness, demanded of a subject in response to the extremity of the transcendence of the other person."[17] Ethical obligation is not just given with intersubjectivity; it is given as asymmetrical in the phenomenon of encounter with the face of the other. Against, then, an individualistic celebration of freedom, we learn that "responsibility for another comes from what is prior to my freedom."[18] Against the belief that there are moral obligations to the other based on the principle of equality, we learn that servanthood takes precedence.[19]

Those who are persuaded that Levinas is right on these points will naturally find that the scandal of God as an oppressive other is mitigated if not removed. Of course, we need both to sort out some phenomenological philosophical arguments at this point and to figure out the relation of Levinas's notion of the transcendent to the view of God implicitly present in this essay. Whatever the results of an examination, Levinas's thought is striking alike in its conclusions and its formulations. It suggests that the one who finds God oppressive has found the neighbor oppressive. Karl Barth was arguing along quite similar lines in his discussion of "Man in His Determination As the Covenant-Partner of God," which contained exposition of Nietzsche as the man who is without his fellow man, humanity lacking co-humanity, thus attaining inhumanity.[20] When Barth speaks of Jesus as the "divine Other, Neighbour, Companion and Brother," the notions of "Other" and "Neighbour" are fruitfully brought together.[21] Even if the notion of God as a loving "Other" is oppressive for moderns, the shabby collision between my vaunted freedom and divine imposing reality seems largely generated by the picture of God as just a transcendent lawgiver. Yet Jesus, as man, is my neighbor in history; and Jesus, as my neigh-

17. Richard A. Cohen, *Elevations: The Height of the Good in Rosenzweig and Levinas* (Chicago and London: University of Chicago Press, 1994), pp. 138-39.

18. "God and Philosophy," in Ward, *The Postmodern God*, p. 65.

19. If we were to linger with a response to Nietzsche at this point, we would profitably bring Rosenzweig into the discussion too; see Cohen, *Elevations*, ch. 3.

20. Karl Barth, *Church Dogmatics* III/2 (Edinburgh: T. & T. Clark, 1960). Pp. 231ff. are on Nietzsche.

21. Barth, *Church Dogmatics* III/2, p. 135.

bor, speaks of the good and the evil, the right and the wrong, the true and the false. His authority to do so is derived from God, and in the doctrine of the incarnation we affirm the identity of Christ with God so that the divine lawgiver is as much the suffering servant as the transcendent Creator.

Surely the morally serious are all morally obligated to heed the Scriptures of the Christian tradition and, we might want to add, of other religious traditions. My obligation to my neighbor ("obligation" is not just cold, stark duty here) is set before me as a phenomenon in terms of the three senses of touch, sight, and hearing. These respectively summon us to friendship, compassion, and attention.[22] Perhaps one can mount an elaborate case for the claim that I ought to attend to deceased humans as part of my service to living ones; the dead can receive neither friendship nor compassion, but we can attend to them and give them a hearing. Certainly attention to real, live neighbors in the context of friendship and compassion constitutes a training in appropriate attention to any who once came among us in the name of truth and love.[23] So we to turn to the biblical portrayal of Jesus Christ.

According to Bonhoeffer

"When we think of the humanity of Jesus," says Karl Barth, "humanity is to be described unequivocally as fellow-humanity."[24]

> There is not in Him a kind of deep, inner, secret recess in which He is alone in Himself or with God, existing in stoical calm or mystic rapture apart from His fellows, untouched by their state or fate. He has no such place of rest. He is immediately and directly affected by the existence of His fellows. His relationship to His neighbours and sympathy with them are original and proper to Him and therefore belong to His innermost being.

22. A phenomenological elaboration of this must be omitted here. It is not essential to the argument.

23. As Barth put it: ". . . We cannot be reminded too often that this man once dwelt in the midst of humanity" (*Church Dogmatics* III/2, p. 160).

24. Barth, *Church Dogmatics* III/2, p. 208. The following quotations come from pp. 210-22.

"What emerges" in the New Testament "is a supreme I wholly determined by and to the Thou." This way of putting it has deep roots in Barth's doctrine of God, and we shall not ferret these out.[25] On the face of it, this orientation of Jesus towards his fellow humans, as Barth presents it to us here, invites us to consider the attractiveness of the God of the Bible, who is identical with Jesus, the "man for others." This last was Bonhoeffer's phrase. Yet when we turn to Bonhoeffer I think that we find a significant contrast.[26] "Jesus is there only for others," said Bonhoeffer, and the connection between this and transcendence invites comparison with Levinas's connections between intersubjectivity and transcendence.[27] Actually, however, if we go to the mature, sustained reflections put together under *Ethics*, we confront a slightly different portrayal.[28]

Comparison with Barth gives us a felicitous point of entry into this. Barth says of Jesus Christ: "His being as a man is the whole of His action, suffering and achievement. His being as a man is His work. In this His work He has a human nature. . . ."[29] If the interpretation of Bonhoeffer is controversial, the interpretation of Barth makes equal, if different kinds of, demands. I shall not worry about the precise contextualization of these words, nor their unimpeachably accurate interpretation, nor, *a fortiori*, any systematic and fair comparison between Barth and Bonhoeffer. We just take the words, for what they do is to point up a difference from what Bonhoeffer does in the *Ethics*. Strikingly enough, Bonhoeffer, theologian of co-humanity, the man for others and the suffering God, introduces Je-

25. For example, "But it is not the case that as this free Subject — for His is the divine freedom — He might have been something very different from the Neighbour and Saviour of His fellows. . . . He is originally and properly the Word of God to men, and therefore His orientation to others and reciprocal relationship with them are not accidental, external or subsequent, but primary, internal and necessary" (Barth, *Church Dogmatics* III/2, p. 210).

26. When the phrase appeared in his *Letters and Papers from Prison* (London: SCM, 1971), this was "in fact a new christological title for Bonhoeffer" (Eberhard Bethge, "Bonhoeffer's Christology and His 'Religionless Christianity,'" *Union Seminary Quarterly Review* 23.1 [1967]: 75).

27. See Bonhoeffer, *Letters and Papers*, p. 381. This was one of the sentiments taken up in the "death-of-God" attempts in the sixties to present a radical Christianity with the aid of Bonhoeffer.

28. D. Bonhoeffer, *Ethics* (New York: Macmillan, 1965). No attempt will be made here to inquire into the fabric and internal consistency of Bonhoeffer's thought overall. This is quite a demanding area.

29. Barth, *Church Dogmatics* III/2, p. 59.

sus to us in his individuality. Precisely so does Bonhoeffer make an impression, and precisely so, as we shall now see, does he engage with the modern quest for freedom.[30]

In this work, Bonhoeffer attempted to situate the notion of freedom. Characteristically, Christianity and Christian ethics have been understood in the dualistic terms of right and wrong, good and evil. Nietzsche, although Bonhoeffer does not allude to this here, is no doubt representative of many in reacting to the Sermon on the Mount less as a noble humanitarian ideal than a self-division of man, and in attempting to get an existential purchase on life "beyond good and evil."[31] Bonhoeffer's crashing entry into his exposition of ethics is a declaration that Christian ethics is not about the knowledge of good and evil. Such knowledge is a sign of disunion, an estrangement of humanity from its origin, a function of the Fall. We were not created to know good and evil. We were created to know God, God alone, God our good. Christian ethics celebrates the recovery of unity here, the unity of man with the word and will of God. On account of such unity, "the life and activity of man," as portrayed in New Testament ethics, "is not at all problematic or tormented or dark: it is self-evident, joyful, sure and clear."[32] The "world of recovered unity" in which man finds his liberation by being joined with his creator, God, is given its crowning revelation in Jesus Christ:

> The freedom of Jesus is not the arbitrary choice of one amongst innumerable possibilities; it consists on the contrary precisely in the complete simplicity of His action, which is never confronted by a plurality of possibilities, conflicts or alternatives, but always by one thing. This one thing Jesus calls the will of God. He says that to do this will is His meat. This will of God is His life. He lives and acts not by the knowledge of good and evil but by the will of God. There is only one will of God. In it the origin is recovered; in it there is established the freedom and the simplicity of all action.[33]

30. By "individuality" is meant "without reference to co-humanity." One has to be very watchful, of course, when building any argument on the basis of the ordering of the *Ethics* because Bonhoeffer did not complete it as an ordered whole, and various editorial arrangements have been offered over the years.

31. Friedrich Nietzsche, *Human, All Too Human* (Cambridge: Cambridge University Press, 1986), sec. 137, p. 74.

32. Bonhoeffer, *Ethics*, p. 26.

33. Bonhoeffer, *Ethics*, p. 30.

Before we go on to say why this should ring a chord, we must face the obvious objection that this is idealistic rhetoric and untrue either to the human condition, in which we struggle to know and do the good, or to Jesus Christ, tempted as we are, if yet without sin. Bonhoeffer does not deny the struggle involved. On the contrary.[34] Then how is he coherent? As in other literature, including *The Cost of Discipleship*, Bonhoeffer is not inclined to make many concessions in this work to any clamor for prosaic elaboration, but study of his thought confirms the judgment that he is not playing dialectical games and is charting deep waters. We have to inquire *what* is right. We have constantly to pray for strength to *do* the right. A Christian life does not get off the ground until it is determined to know only good, only God. It does not aspire to being poised between knowledges. Returned to its origin, it is concerned only with that. In action, it moves secure in the knowledge that life is held within the judgment and mercy of God, which is grounded in the reconciliation achieved through Jesus Christ. The movement of thought and appropriation of gospel truth is this: integration, which spells simplicity; freedom, which is unity with the word and will of God; and action, which is the Christian alternative to Pharisaic spirituality centered on judgment.[35]

What is the importance of this exposition; is it supposed to strike chords? It lies in the straight line of integrated action that Bonhoeffer draws. On the one hand, a craven apologetic tries to persuade the world that God loves it and entreats it to give God a bit of a chance and not to regard him as oppressive. Bonhoeffer will not spend time on persuasion but on exposition, nor on entreaty but on action. On the other hand, a hectoring declaration tries to assault the world with the pronouncement of unassailable truth and awesome judgment. Bonhoeffer proclaims the unity of God and the world in Jesus Christ and believes judgment is meted out in the achievement of reconciliation.[36] Human liberty in unity

34. "Thus the Bible speaks of an entirely proper and necessary questioning with regard to the will of God and of an equally proper and necessary examination of oneself, without thereby coming into contradiction with the fact that those for whom the knowledge of good and evil is nullified are no longer confronted with a choice between many different possibilities . . ." (Bonhoeffer, *Ethics*, p. 37). One should note the context of this point and the theological elaboration that immediately follows on from the portion where the quotation has been broken off.

35. This is a very telling discussion (Bonhoeffer, *Ethics*, pp. 26-37).

36. Bonhoeffer's understanding of reconciliation lies outside the scope of the present

with and discipleship to Christ is so radical that in knowing all things in Christ it is possessed of humanly highest liberty, for it finds itself in its marrow and in its totality reconciled to God and to self. That entails some kind of reconciliation to world and neighbor too, but that bestows on us a project into which we are liberated, for reconciliation with God through Christ is so complete that there is no room to pass judgment on others — the reconciled person is riveted to action. Bonhoeffer may be in quite serious breach of Luther's theology at times, but the comparable note of reconciliation and triumphant freedom in Luther's Reformation classic, *The Freedom of the Christian,* seems often ignored. Justified by faith and so united with Christ, humans can turn their attention to the service of neighbor.

Nor is reconciled humanity sailing high, six thousand feet above man and time.[37] It is immersed in life's activities, decisions, and sufferings. It is humanity, not divinity. What Bonhoeffer said about suffering and being-for-others has rightly been highlighted, but one cannot help but notice the contrast with, for example, Barth here. For Bonhoeffer, Jesus is the free man, one with God. In freedom, perfectly integrated, he is led into suffering. So are we. It seems not to be true that "His being as a man is His work" (Barth), or that it is so for us. We are established as persons; then we have our work to do. If this is not quite right as a comprehensive interpretation of Bonhoeffer, I believe that it nevertheless captures what is expressed in *Ethics,* and that has an important implication as we think of Scripture today. The individual and the other are given their weight. In such a context, the suffering God ("only a suffering God can help") is no concession to a world that has decided that God had better renounce omnipotence to be credible.[38] Jesus is God incarnate and risen, not just crucified, and the eschaton will establish the perfection of the kingdom of God.

The idea of God that emerges on Bonhoeffer's account makes talk of the oppressiveness of this Other pitifully feeble. Bonhoeffer's account is not crafted to attract. Faced with the reality that meets us in the Gospel

---

discussion. In light of my generally partial (favorable) use of Bonhoeffer in this essay, it is worth adding that not recording criticisms is not the same as not having them.

37. In contrast to Nietzsche at Lake Silvaplana (*Ecce Homo* [London: Penguin, 1979], p. 99).

38. Jürgen Moltmann greatly admires Bonhoeffer, but he seems closer to making concessions to the "world" at this point than is Bonhoeffer. See particularly, of course, Jürgen Moltmann, *The Crucified God* (London: SCM, 1974).

and biblical accounts, one can but present it, not bend it.[39] Yet are these accounts trustworthy? Bonhoeffer, at least, thought so and, having grasped the message and understood its truth, aspired to let it possess his person in freedom.[40] The case for or against the trustworthiness of the accounts still gets rehearsed a lot, and sophisticated options on what is meant by trustworthiness have long abounded. As was said near the start of this essay, such issues — like those surrounding the "third quest" for the historical Jesus — can profitably be gone over, but it is good to sketch in faint pencil the lines of a view of God and of Jesus Christ that comes to light in the allegedly oppressive Scriptures of the Christian Church. Whether people can believe that the Gospels portray an idea but not a life; whether they can believe that this life was integrated by an idea but not a reality; whether, then, moderns can find a better way of life in a surer freedom than is afforded by belief in the historical Jesus — all that is left aside here. Let us keep pondering the portrayal and accept life's tasks without frivolity. Only thus can we expect to see what there is to be seen of God through Scripture, to appreciate the God of Scripture.

Our Time

We are implicitly appealing to those with ears to hear. Two interrelated themes in Bonhoeffer's work meet us here. One is Christ and the good. The other is the times in which we live. Georg Huntemann, writing ten years ago, said of Bonhoeffer that "he is a theologian of an era that has not yet begun in theology or the church. Above all, he is a challenger of modernism."[41] We shall not focus here on what exactly prompted this reaction to Bonhoeffer, though our trajectories may be compatible.[42]

39. Heinrich Ott wrote an account of Bonhoeffer's theological legacy aptly entitled *Reality and Faith* (London: Lutterworth, 1971), and Andre Dumas published an account of Bonhoeffer titled *Dietrich Bonhoeffer: Theologian of Reality* (New York: Macmillan, 1971).

40. Dietrich Bonhoeffer, *Christology* (London: Collins, 1960), pp. 71-77.

41. Georg Huntemann, *Dietrich Bonhoeffer: An Evangelical Reassessment* (Grand Rapids: Baker, 1993), p. 12. It is appropriate in our volume to cite words that follow: ". . . Bonhoeffer will be their [the evangelicals'] church father in the future — or else evangelicals will have no future" (p. 12).

42. Huntemann said that the aim of his book was "to show that Bonhoeffer was a Christ-mystic," and a "religionless" one at that (*Dietrich Bonhoeffer*, p. 12). His is a contro-

Bonhoeffer experienced in his time what he saw as

> the void made god. No one knows its goal or its measure. Its dominion is absolute. It is a creative void, which blows its anti-god's breath into the nostrils of all that is established and awakens it to a false semblance of new life while sucking out from it its proper essence, until at last it falls in ruin as a lifeless husk and is cast away. The void engulfs life, history, family, nation, language, faith. The list can be prolonged indefinitely, for the void spares nothing.[43]

What was happening and had happened in Germany was portentous for European civilization. Yet what gave Europe its unity? Historically, Jesus Christ. And he is the destiny of Europe and of the world.

> In the face of the Antichrist only one thing has force and permanence, and that is Christ Himself. Only he who shares in Him has the power to withstand and to overcome. He is the centre and the strength of the Bible, of the Church, and of theology, but also of humanity, of reason, of justice and of culture. Everything must return to Him; it is only under His protection that it can live. There seems to be a general unconscious knowledge which, in the hour of ultimate peril, leads everything which desires not to fall victim to the Antichrist to take refuge with Christ.[44]

Bonhoeffer was persuaded that all that is good has reference to Jesus Christ. "He that is not against us is for us" (Mark 9:40) was one of his texts. He found from the harrowing experience of the Hitler years and his own political involvement that people seriously concerned for humanity, truth, and justice cannot take Christ lightly. In fact, he believed, they live under his protection. The doctrine of the participation in Christ of all that is good and all who are good is derived not from a cosmology or soteriology

---

versial account but certainly sobering in its relating of contemporary Western life to the fateful history of Germany in the time of Bonhoeffer. It deserves to be read alongside dire warnings about the future of what happened in Germany from very different sources, such as Allan Bloom, "The German Connection," in Allan Bloom, *The Closing of the American Mind* (New York: Simon & Schuster, 1987); and Elton Trueblood, *The Predicament of Modern Man* (New York: Harper&Row, 1944).

43. Bonhoeffer, *Ethics*, p. 106.

44. Bonhoeffer, *Ethics*, p. 56.

but from lived experience, especially of suffering. That is why the Christological question must be: "Who is Christ for us today?"[45] In Bonhoeffer's day "[i]t is not Christ who must justify Himself before the world by the acknowledgement of the values of justice, truth and freedom, but it is these values which have come to need justification, and their justification can only be Jesus Christ."[46] This is no standard apologetic attempt to relate Christianity to shared moral convictions. There is no moral argument offered for the existence of God or some parallel one for the truth of the Scriptures. It is the actual adherence to what is good and right and true that will draw people to Jesus Christ. The Reformation related Christ to sinners. We must relate Christ to good people.[47] Bonhoeffer means that we must not try to find a gap for God in life by manipulative and predatory talk of death, guilt, anxiety, and fear — the genius of too much cheap Lutheranism. We must take seriously worldly people with serious concerns, demonstrated by responsible actions. Here belong discussion of religionless Christianity and the world come of age.

The matter in question demands some sifting and goes too deep and far for us here. Yet at the least we are invited to distinguish carefully between an appeal to the trustworthiness of God and Scripture directed to the conscientious unbeliever and one directed to the indulgently indifferent. Our present discussion has been somewhat oriented to freedom, but however compellingly and imperatively Bonhoeffer describes freedom, of course it will not be universally attractive. Pascal, for example, was on to a different audience, and his famous wager was evidence of this.[48] The force of his argument does not lie in its surface logic but in forcing the issue of the logic of commitment: one cannot choose but to be committed; life is commitment; even if I change commitments on the hour and suspend be-

45. Addressed in Bonhoeffer, *Christology.*

46. Bonhoeffer, *Ethics,* p. 59. Bonhoeffer also refers to those who are not for Christ being against him.

47. Of course, there is a lot going on here, and there is a fair amount of discussion in the *Ethics* (pp. 188ff.). Here we are into the whole business of "religionless Christianity" or "non-religious interpretation" (see Bethge, "Bonhoeffer's Christology," p. 61). It must be approached with sympathetic and critical caution, the theme being picked up from before the famous letter of April 30, 1944 (Bonhoeffer, *Letters and Papers,* p. 278).

48. Pascal argued in terms geared to the gambling fraternity. The outcome is this: in the event of uncertainty, one should opt for Christianity, for if one is right one gains all, and if one is wrong one loses nothing, whereas if one lives atheistically, if one is right one gains nothing, and if one is wrong one loses all. See *Pensées,* pp. 149ff.

liefs perpetually, life and decision goes on, with a past that cannot be undone and a present that cannot be shrugged off. Pascal too reminds us that a clear revelation is not to be expected from God.

> . . . Because so many men had shown themselves unworthy of his clemency . . . he wished to deprive them of the good they did not desire. It was therefore not right that he should appear in a manner manifestly divine and absolutely capable of convincing all men, but neither was it right that his coming should be so hidden that he could not be recognised by those who sincerely sought him. . . . There is enough light for those who desire only to see, and enough darkness for those of a contrary disposition.[49]

Bonhoeffer is not thinking along these lines at all but is trying to set forth Jesus Christ to the indirect effect that it is a commendation of God, Christ, and Scripture, to all with ears to hear.

In words quoted above, Bonhoeffer spoke of an "unconscious knowledge" of the deep reality of Christ. Here, even if we agree that he read the German situation aright, we may lament what the passing half century has done to unconscious knowledge. Bonhoeffer may still instruct us in relation to those who are serious, few though they may be. Can anyone seriously concerned for humanity, truth, and justice have a sustained and informed exposure to the Christ of the Gospels and find him anything but true, and so anything but a rock of justice? Will he not, by virtue of all that, be as distant as can be from some false pretension to deity? Will aspirants to a true humanity really believe that Jesus never existed as portrayed and that he invoked an imagined deity? Yes, of course, it is possible, and one must beware of rhetorical romanticizing. Yet everything has its context, and one wonders whether the sense of socio-moral collapse under the shadow of evil in the West today will persuade many that as civilization cuts loose from its Christian moorings a radical choice must be made to quit disappearing moral middle ground and be committed to Jesus Christ or face the void. In our context, I believe that Bonhoeffer helps us to secure ourselves on the trustworthy foundation of the God of the Bible and the Bible of the Church, or he aids the serious seeker.

49. Pascal, *Pensées,* pp. 79-80.

Conclusion

"The air that we breathe is so polluted by mistrust that it almost chokes us."[50] Where can you learn trust — a lesson that is not useless but positively destructive if nobody is trustworthy? "Trust will always be one of the greatest, rarest, and happiest blessings of our life in community. . . ."[51] There is a deep futility — perhaps that is too strong, perhaps it is too weak — in the attempt to persuade anyone of the trustworthiness of Scripture and the God of Scripture where the reality of the *ecclesia* gives no support for such ideas. In the third millennium, the doctrines of God and of Scripture will flourish only as we understand and "practice" church and kingdom. They will only be well commended by argument if they are first commended by existence.

50. Bonhoeffer, *Letters and Papers,* p. 11.

51. Bonhoeffer, *Letters and Papers,* p. 12, although the quotation proceeds: ". . . though it can emerge only on the dark background of a necessary mistrust."

The Perfect Trustworthiness of God

Paul Helm

In this chapter I aim to do two things: first, to say as clearly as I can what is meant by the Christian claim that God is trustworthy and to defend that meaning by some arguments; second, to apply this idea, which I take to be a fundamental Christian idea, to our approach to the study of Holy Scripture.

The Trustworthiness of God

Let us begin some distance away from the idea of divine trustworthiness. If we say that God is infinitely good, or powerful, or that he is timeless and spaceless in his being, then we are asserting matters that are all essential to God. God could not be God and fail to be any of these things. They are part of his nature, just as being capable of being conscious is part of our nature as human beings, though in God's case his infinite goodness, or his omnipotence, is part of his individual essence. They are not part of some general nature that God might share with others, but they are part of what makes God the individual thing that he is, just as having certain parents is part of what makes one the individual conscious thing that he or she is.

In saying that these attributes are part of God's essential nature, I am not claiming that the meaning of such terms is always clear or uncontroversial. Take, for example, the meaning of omnipotence: "having unlimited or very great power, force or influence" (*Shorter Oxford Dictionary*). This may, at first glance, seem clear enough. If God is omnipotent, then he (and he alone) has such unlimited or very great power. Yet (as is well known) matters become more difficult when we inquire more precisely into the meaning of omnipotence. What exactly are the limits that omnipotence does not have, and what are the very great powers that an omnipotent being possesses? For example, is the omnipotence of God "limited" by the laws of logic, or by the character of moral principles or laws, or even by the nature of God himself? Can God make it, by an act of his power, that 2 + 2 = 5, or that adultery is morally permissible? Two people may each agree that God alone is omnipotent, but they may disagree on the connotation of the term. Thus, while Thomas Aquinas believed that the power of God was subject to the laws of logic, René Descartes thought otherwise. So there is philosophical disagreement among major philosophers about the connotation of "omnipotence" as this applies to God.

Similarly with omniscience. Omniscience might be defined as the knowledge of all truths, but of course such omniscience is limited by what it is possible for God to know. Some have argued that it is not possible for God to know the future since there is no future to know (though God could, presumably, have beliefs about the future), and that it is not possible for him to know what it is like to be a bat, or to know what a red surface looks like.

So, there is scope for disagreement about the precise connotation of "omnipotence" or "omniscience." However, it seems a reasonable principle, in reflecting upon the concept of God in philosophical fashion, that *the connotation of such "omni" terms as omnipotence and omniscience when applied to God should be as wide as possible.* Thus the term "omnipotent" is more appropriately applied to God when it connotes power over more types of actions and events than when it connotes power over fewer types of actions and events. Further, the term is more appropriately applied to God when it connotes power over more tokens of each type of action over which power is exercised, than power over fewer such tokens. Similar connotations regarding the scope of omniscience also apply. After all, the rationale for employing such "omni" terms in the first place is to convey the idea of maximality, and so not to limit their application unnecessarily; otherwise, such terms when applied to God come to possess only rhetorical or hyperbolic value.

So I am claiming that wherever possible one should interpret such terms as "omniscience" and "omnipotence" when applied to God, and indeed all of God's essential attributes, as generously as possible, pushing the scope of their connotation as far as one can, unless there are overriding reasons not to do so. It seems clear that there is such an overriding reason in the case of the laws of logic, for such laws mark the bounds of the possible. One simply misunderstands the scope of divine power rather than pays respect to it if one says that God can do the logically impossible, though it is very difficult to argue for this position decisively, and obviously Descartes would not agree. Matters are less clear in the case of God's power over moral principles, as the popularity of the divine command theory of ethics shows. There is controversy over whether one can integrate the idea of divine command ethics with our intuitions about the necessity or overridingness of certain moral principles. Parallel problems arise over whether God has power over the past.

Despite all these difficulties, to say that God is infinitely good, or omnipotent, is therefore to say something essential about God. It is not just that God happens to be infinitely good, or omnipotent, and could conceivably not be. He could not be God without being omnipotent. To embed these powers in the very nature or essence of God is part of what it means to think of God as the most perfect being, and such claims are fully supported by statements of Scripture, as we shall see. Not only are such properties or predicates or attributes of God necessary to him, but they do not need anything other than the existence of God himself in order for them to be true. Even if nothing else existed other than God, he would still be infinitely good, and omnipotent, and so on down the list of all of God's attributes.

With respect to the trustworthiness of God matters are somewhat similar, but also somewhat different. They are somewhat similar in that the trustworthiness of God is also an essential part of his nature because it is entailed by such features of his nature as his knowledge, power, and goodness, which are also essential parts of his nature. Whatever is entailed by what is essential must itself be essential. God could not but be trustworthy. (We'll come back to this.) Yet trustworthiness is somewhat different from the other attributes that we have been discussing in that it is a relational power or property of God. That is, just as God could not be the creator without there being a creation (though he necessarily has the power to become the creator), so God could not be trustworthy if there was not something or someone to be trustworthy to (though no doubt he would have the disposition to be trustworthy, a disposition entailed by the essential properties of omniscience, omnipotence, and goodness). Trustworthiness is a relational expression, and usually, if not always, it expresses a relation between persons. Sometimes that relation involves nonhuman animals, but here we are concerned with its use in God-man relations.

There is also an important element of reflexivity to trustworthiness; that is, trustworthiness has to do with a relation between what the one who is trustworthy has said or done and some other individual, some other person to whom what is said or done was initially addressed. So trustworthiness involves an initial action, and then a further act or action that is the act or action of being faithful or trustful to what one has said or done.

I hinted earlier that divine trustworthiness presupposes certain nonrelational powers or properties. What are these? I suggest three, though there are perhaps more. First (though in no special order of significance) is power, and particularly power over the future, our future, the future of those to whom the word or warrant or covenant of God has come, that to which (we are supposing) he is faithful. God cannot be faithful if he cannot bring about his own actions in the future and insure in some way that he can suitably cope with the actions of other agents than himself in order to bring about the fulfillment of his word or promise. This power has therefore to be very great power; it has to be omnipotence generously defined.

Second, besides power, great power, there has to be knowledge, very great knowledge, in particular knowledge of the future, including the actions of agents other than himself. If God's promises are concerned with territory in which nondivine agents act, then God, to be faithful, will have to know what these actions are and take the necessary steps to cope with them. (Perhaps what I have just written is too deistic a way of thinking about God's relation to his created universe, but this is deliberate, in order to avoid getting into the perfectly legitimate but thorny questions of the relation between the divine decree and human actions.)

Third, besides power and knowledge there has to be goodness, including the element of veracity. Power and knowledge could, by themselves, be used in the interest of untrustworthiness; they could be used malevolently, so as to sow distrust. To be faithful to promises of goodness, of blessing, the giver of those promises also has to be good. (Trustworthiness, as such, does not imply goodness but merely consistency; nevertheless in its usual usages it has connotations of beneficence.) Putting it crudely, God has to want that his promises or covenant be fulfilled, and mere knowledge and power by themselves do not insure such wantings. Furthermore, his wanting has to be an efficacious wanting, wanting that is not subject to weakness of will or to frustration of any kind, wanting that carries through to the accomplishment of what is wanted.

All these requirements do not entail strict immutability in the divine character; they do not entail that God cannot change in any single respect, but they do entail the immutability of whatever it is that God promises (I take this up again below).

The general point that I want to insist upon here — however we may fill in the details — is that in order for the trustworthiness to be of the sort that is divine, the divine properties or attributes that are necessary conditions for it, and given a divine promise, sufficient conditions for trustworthiness, must be fully *modal* properties or attributes or accurate and consistent expressions of such. That is to say, the knowledge or power or goodness that God has essentially is knowledge that he could in no circumstances lack. The two points being made here are different, and their difference is worth stressing. It is one thing to have knowledge or power essentially. The knowledge or power that God has is not knowledge or power that he just happens to have; it is knowledge or power that he could not fail to have. This is so too with goodness or veracity. Yet in addition, the knowledge or power or goodness that God essentially has is omniscience and omnipotence and perfect goodness. He is not more powerful or knowing or good at one time than another, and there is no possibility of his being less than omniscient and omnipotent.

It is sometimes said that all that is needed for divine trustworthiness or faithfulness is for God to resolve, or to have resolved, by an act of his will, to be trustworthy. Yet this is incorrect, in my view, for if this is all that God has to do in order to be trustworthy — merely to resolve to be so — then he could resolve to be trustworthy and yet fail to carry out his resolution. He could fail to carry out his resolution because, though he was very powerful or very knowledgeable, he suffered from a lack of resolve and failed for rather the same reasons that we sometimes fail to carry out our resolutions. However, if God is essentially all powerful, all knowing, and all good, he cannot suffer from any impediments like weakness of will. To put these points in the language of current metaphysics, for divine trustworthiness to be truly such there must be no possible world in which, having promised to do a thing, he is unable to keep his promise. In order for this to be the case those properties that are necessary conditions of divine trustworthiness must also be properties that God has in every possible world in which he exists. Even if, like Luther in this world, he can do no other, just as there are for Luther other worlds in which he could have done other, so also for God there may be, if his power, knowledge, and beneficence are not truly modal in character. There are possible worlds in which his resolve gives out, and perhaps one of these possible worlds is this one, the actual world.

The reason for all this is obvious. If there are possible worlds in which God, having made a promise or established a covenant, does not carry out his word faithfully, then for all we know to the contrary this world, the actual world, may be that possible world, or, if there are several such worlds, one of them. Even if God is trustworthy today, he may not be trustworthy tomorrow. Even if we suppose that there is good inductive evidence that in this world God has, as a matter of fact, kept every promise that he has made, nevertheless, if he is not essentially trustworthy, then for all we know to the contrary his power may give out, or his knowledge fail, or his goodness falter, or all three may fail, just when we need him most.

This tells us something about the nature of faith, I think, the human faith that engages with the trustworthiness of God. Faith involves both belief and desire. Evidence for the perfect faithfulness of God always, and necessarily, fails to guarantee that faithfulness. The evidence on which our faith is based may be very great, but it is partial nevertheless. So in trusting in the perfect faithfulness of God, while faith is not exactly a leap in the dark, we can say that in true faith the desire for God outreaches the evidence on which the belief component of faith is based. Only in the consummation of all things, when faith becomes sight, will evidence catch up with desire.

So biblical religion, at the heart of which is trust in the trustworthiness of God, requires a metaphysical understanding of the nature of God even though, of course, it has to be said that such an understanding — our understanding — is ever only partial. A corollary of this is that if our conception of God is too anthropomorphic, then it will not sustain our religion, for trust in the trustworthiness of God, in intent and aspiration, is unreserved trust. Of course in practice trust is not unreserved in this way, for it is mixed up with doubt, unbelief, misinformation, and much else. Yet in the aspiration of the Christian believer it is so, and such aspirations can only be met by a trustworthiness of God that is necessary trustworthiness, part of his nature, true of him in every possible world in which he exists.

If A is less than completely trustworthy but still very trustworthy, then if A asserts p, then probably p will occur; if he promises p, then probably p will occur. Such probabilities are insufficient to meet the full aspirations of a truly Christian religion.

By now some will be itching for some biblical support for what I have been claiming, for, after all, I have said that I am talking about the idea of the trustworthiness of God as far as Christianity is concerned.

When the writer to the Hebrews (6:13-20) wished to reassure his readers who had fled for refuge to lay hold on the hope set before them, when he endeavored to give them strong consolation, he referred them to the immutability of God, and particularly to the immutability of his promise, and to the oath that confirmed that promise. These, he says, are two immutable things. It is impossible for God to lie — and I take it that the impossibility here must be the modal sense of impossible — and it is impossible for God to break his oath. Of course when God confirmed his promise with an oath, it did not add to his immutability any more than when a mutable being adds an oath to a promise it diminishes his mutability. Rather, the added oath *displays* the immutability; this is an immutability that God wanted Abraham to know about and be sure of. The immutability of the promise is not, as our English idiom might suggest, merely that the fact of the promise being made is immutable, but that its content, what is promised, is so. Only then can the immutability of the promise give strong consolation in the face of loss or adversity of the kind that the Hebrew Christians were experiencing. That God had resolved not to lie, but nevertheless might break his resolve through some internal weakness, or be forced to break it by some other agency, would not have provided for Abraham or for the Hebrew Christian an adequate basis for their strong consolation; nor would it, I suggest, for us.

A similar case is Titus 1:2, according to which God, who cannot lie, promised eternal life before the world began. Such a verse as this, incidentally, shows the difficulty of giving a satisfactory account of divine omnipotence. If God is omnipotent, can he do everything? Well, yes and no. He can do everything that is consistent with the other perfections of his nature besides his perfect power, and one of those perfections, as we have seen, is his goodness. So God cannot lie; not in the sense in which George Washington could not tell a lie, but in the sense that truthfulness, veracity, is part of his essential nature. George Washington was resolved not to lie, but his resolve might have given out. God's inability to lie is deeper than that, part of his essential nature without which he would not be God.

We can see from such passages as these that there is a sense in which the character of God is imputed or transferred to his word. If God is trustworthy in the sense indicated, then whatever is identified as his word — his speech — is also trustworthy. This principle of transference applies *par excellence* to the Incarnate Word, but it counts with equal validity to anything else that is identified as the word of God, to the words of prophets and apostles, for example. He is faithful who promised (Heb. 10:23; 11:11). The testimony of the Lord is sure (Ps. 19:7). If nothing counts as the speech of God, then the point is purely a theoretical one. However, if something — anything — counts as the speech of God, then that speech is as trustworthy as God himself is. So, in the idea of the perfect trustworthiness of God metaphysical and epistemological considerations come together; our epistemological confidence must be built upon a metaphysical foundation of sufficient strength to bear it, and I have argued that this must be a modally necessary foundation.

I wish now to consider certain objections to my general claim that the trustworthiness of God must have a truly modal or metaphysical necessity to support it. Otherwise, we cannot have any confidence that the divine trustworthiness will hold out, and, in particular, we cannot have confidence that the Bible, taken to be God's revelation, is itself trustworthy, a word sufficiently strong to bear the weight of our faith, with all its concerns and fears.

One objection is this: that we cannot trust a revelation as being completely trustworthy unless one first knows that God is trustworthy, and that one can only know this independently of the revelation by some piece of natural theology. So, the issue only arises, or only may arise, the issue of the trustworthiness of God and Scripture, if we have an *a priori* understanding of divine trustworthiness. To this there are at least three replies: first, could any form of natural theology deliver a God who is trustworthy in the sense required? If the objection is intended to require that we first establish the existence of a perfectly trustworthy God by independent reasoning, then it is hard to see how this can be accomplished; how, that is, it is possible to argue as a piece of natural theology that there exists an omniscient, omnipotent, all good God. Certainly such an endeavor would go way beyond the project of natural theology adopted by, say, Thomas Aquinas, who was content to have proved *that* God exists without having attempted to prove anything about *what* God is. So there is no chance of our first establishing the trustworthiness of God and then showing that the Scriptures are an expression of this trustworthiness. If we are required to do that, then we can't. This is not to reject all natural theology but to recognize its limitations.

In any case, there are serious difficulties with the idea of establishing the reasonableness of any religious belief that is noncircular. According to William Alston our epistemic practices are self-supporting.[1] It is plausible to suppose that we cannot know anything about God in a noncircular way, that our epistemic practices are self-supporting. Suppose we derive our idea of the perfect faithfulness of God from a combination of intuition and Scripture testimony, and even correct our intuitions by Scripture, what I'm claiming is that such perfect trustworthiness has a particular metaphysical character and structure, that the idea of trustworthiness is fundamental to the Christian faith, and that perfect trustworthiness transmits itself to whatever is the word of whoever is trustworthy.

Second, let us suppose that a person is convinced of the existence of God. How does he gain the further conviction that God is perfectly trustworthy? Perhaps from more than one source. Perhaps partly from reflection upon what it means to be the most perfect being, one who is truly worshipful. If God is the most perfect being, then how could he fail to be perfectly trustworthy? And partly from the actual revelation of God in the Bible that he is perfectly trustworthy.

A third reply is that, in the particular dialectical context that we are assuming, one may reasonably take it for granted that, by whatever means, the connection between a trustworthy God and the claim that the Bible is his revelation is already made. This underlines the fact that the main argument of the paper is ad hominem in character; it is addressed primarily to fellow Christians for whom the perfect faithfulness of God is a credal commitment.

So, in discussing the idea of the perfect trustworthiness of God and its connection with his word I am less concerned here with where, ultimately, we obtain the idea that God is trustworthy than with the fact that as Christians we possess it and confess it. The thought that God might be less than utterly trustworthy is surely abhorrent to us. Further, this is an intrinsic aspect to the Christian religion because at the heart of biblical religion is the

1. William Alston, *Perceiving God: The Epistemology of Religious Experience* (Ithaca, N.Y.: Cornell University Press, 1991), ch. 3 and in summary form in "On Knowing That We Know: The Application to Religious Knowledge," in *Christian Perspectives on Religious Knowledge*, ed. C. S. Evans and M. Westphal (Grand Rapids: Eerdmans, 1993).

divine promise or covenant. If that promise or covenant were to waver, or to be thought to waver, then biblical religion becomes something else. God's covenantal character may and must be applied to our understanding and approach to the Scripture because we take Scripture to be the word of this God. Amplifying this, we can say that the Christian gospel would be unintelligible — a different thing, a different message — if it did not have the perfect trustworthiness of God at its heart.

Further, and most tellingly, the trustworthiness of God would be an idle concept if there was no appropriate epistemological vehicle for that trustworthiness. Though, as we have seen, there are purely dispositional senses of the idea of trustworthiness, and a person may be trustworthy, or potentially trustworthy, without that trustworthiness ever being in exercise, nevertheless we are concerned with the trustworthiness of God, or with its absence, as it relates to us, in its occurrent, not its dispositional, sense — not with an unexercised disposition, but with the character of God, if you will pardon the expression, at full stretch. The notion is, as I stressed at the beginning, a relational one. One may be trustworthy, worthy of trust, in a void, but one cannot actually be trusted unless there is believed to be something to be trusted for, and, in the case of God, unless there is something for God to be trusted for.

Furthermore, a trustworthy God who desired to be trusted would surely not leave an untrustworthy account of himself. Note what this is saying and what it is not saying. I am not for one moment saying that God could not leave an unclear, or puzzling, or surprising account of himself, or more exactly an account that had puzzling or surprising or unclear aspects; but he could not provide an account that, when properly understood, led us astray about himself, or about his intentions, and that resulted in our being let down.

Therefore, any treatment of or attitude to Scripture (or to whatever else is taken to be the vehicle of divine revelation) that undermines confidence in its character as trustworthy is inadequate or ultimately destructive of the Christian faith. We cannot reject the trustworthiness of Scripture (or whatever else is the vehicle) without undermining any coherent basis for knowing that God is trustworthy. We might affirm God's trustworthiness *a priori,* but the idea would not, in such circumstances, be operational because it would not have an appropriate vehicle. What use is the idea of the perfect trustworthiness of God if God cannot, in fact, be trusted?

There may be further objections to what is being argued, as follows:

It may be said that any reasonable idea of divine revelation requires us to recognize the fact of epistemic distance. Epistemic distance is appealed to by contemporary philosophers of religion, such as John Hick and Richard Swinburne, in order to provide a rationale for the fact that the evidence for the existence and character of God is not clearer than it is. On this view, there are purposive elements of ambiguity, elements placed there by God himself, it is said, in order that in coming to learn the truth about God we might exercise our responsibility in so doing; nothing is obvious, and divinely provided clues to what is true have to be followed up. There are undoubtedly, as a matter of fact, elements of epistemic distance in the divine revelation, for example, explicitly in Jesus' teaching by parables. Yet the fact that the rationale for this is to enable us to exercise personal responsibility in the exercise of our cognitive powers seems doubtful. It is also not clear that we are in a condition of what we might call intrinsic epistemic distance; it is more likely that the many occasions of the experience of such epistemic distance are due to the effects of sin upon our evidence-gaining and evidence-interpreting powers rather than an epistemic distance no matter what. After all, the heavens declare the glory of God, and there does not seem to be much epistemic distance about that. Nevertheless the point about epistemic distance underlines the fact that there is a gap between what might be called the intrinsic character of Scripture as God's trustworthy word, perspicuous and sufficient, and the actual conditions necessary and sufficient for sinful men and women to exercise trust in it.

So whatever the correct account of the phenomenon of epistemic distance, and of its theological rationale, may be, it seems obvious that it is perfectly compatible with utter divine trustworthiness. Take an example: if I play "I Spy" and you have to guess what I spy, it does not follow that when you say that you think that what I spy is something beginning with "t," a tree, then I'm not to be trusted when I say "Yes, it is" or "No, it is not." More generally, a trustworthy God may have reasons, obvious reasons or less obvious ones, or ones that are not obvious at all, for making us sweat to discover the details of his revelation; it does not follow from this that when we have discovered those details we are not in possession of something that is worthy of our utter trust. Nor is it obvious that what is obtained without sweat is more likely to be true, and therefore more likely to be trustworthy, than what is obtained with sweat.

This last remark may lead to a more general way of putting the objection, as follows. If we have to search for the meaning of God's revelation, or for the meaning of aspects of his revelation, if his revelation is not obvious, how can we ever be sure that we have got it? There are two replies to this. First, there *are* elements of obviousness about God's revelation, despite all that has just been said about epistemic distance (the analogy of faith). "Obvious" is perhaps the wrong word here; they are certainly not obvious if it is the case that for something to be obvious to A it has to be obvious to everyone. Rather, there are elements of God's revelation that are so central, and accepted, that they are constitutive of the Christian life and the life and identity of the Church. Perhaps these are obviously true to some people, or obviously true to anyone who is in a certain kind of mental set. Were they not as they are, the Christian life would be something entirely different, and the Church would also be.

Second, these central elements, together with the more peripheral, are to exercise a regulative control over our thinking in the way that the idea of a perfectly straight line exercises a regulative control over the life of an engineer, or the idea of perfect justice exercises such an influence over the intentions of drafters of legislation and the rulings of judges. (One hopes!) To the objection that no existing bridge has perfectly straight lines or that no existing legislation is perfectly just, the proper retort is to say that we have ideas of a straight line and of perfect justice, and we are striving to attain these ideals in what we do. Likewise with the perfect trustworthiness of the word of God. In fact, this idea has two regulative aspects: there is a primarily cognitive regulative aspect — we are striving always to attain more completely an understanding of the revelation of God in Scripture — and there is a primarily regulative and volitional aspect — we are striving always to respond more adequately to the understanding of God in Scripture that we have already gained.

In our endeavor to interpret the Scriptures there is always a danger of what might be called scriptural rationalism, just as there is a danger of what might be called scriptural skepticism. Perhaps the trustworthiness of God takes unexpected forms; as Christians we believe that it has taken unexpected forms, for however it is possible to explain, say, the incarnation, to explain its appropriateness and even its necessity, *post eventum*, there is no taking away its surprising, not to say its offensive, character. Our understanding of what it means for the Scriptures to be trustworthy must allow for all this.

Recognition of the phenomena of surprise, and of contingency, and of what we earlier called epistemic distance might make us swing in the other direction, in the direction of skepticism about Scripture. If it is possible to be mistaken about some scriptural interpretation, how can we ever be sure about that interpretation? Yet this, as I have said, is to discount the plainness of much of the faithful God's revelation, and of the fact that it is constitutive of the life of the Christian and the life of the Church, and that it is the word of a trustworthy God.

Some Consequences

A God who is limited in knowledge (especially knowledge of our futures) and limited in power (power to bring about in the future what he will) would not be completely trustworthy. Even when we had completely fulfilled our epistemic obligations (supposing that we could) with regard to some putative revelation of such a God, we could not be sure that what God said in Scripture that he would be, or that he would do, he would in fact be or do, for his power and his knowledge and his will might not be sufficient to enable him to be as he said he would be, or to do what he said he would do. More pointedly still, a God whose knowledge of the future and his power to bring about the future is limited, limited by human perverseness or human freedom, say, or by some other factors at present unknown to us, could not be the primary author of a trustworthy vehicle of his will. The connection between trustworthy God and trustworthy revelation will be severed.

This fact, and the radical consequences it has for the nature of Scripture, seems to be a little-noticed consequence of the so-called "open theology," as propounded by Clark Pinnock, William Hasker, and others, which is currently attracting attention. Such a conception of God is regarded as attractive for a number of reasons: for example, it is said to safeguard the character of what the openness theologians take to be a truly person-to-person relationship with God, and to do justice to the narrative passages of Holy Scripture; it is said to offer a de-Hellenized theology, and to enable us to construct a theology on thoroughly trinitarian principles; and no doubt there are other reasons.

If the upshot of such theological work is a God who is limited in power and knowledge because of his need to interact with human beings who possess free will, and if he can never ensure the outcome of any such relationship (just as one human being can never noncoercively ensure the outcome of a relationship with another human being), then the whole basis of scriptural authority dissolves.

What do I mean? As the matter has been usually understood in the Christian Church, the Scriptures are the product of both the divine inspiration of God and the human authorship of men such as Isaiah and Peter. Holy men spoke as they were moved. The result — so the Christian Church has always believed — was as God intended it to be. Yet suppose that the relationship between the Lord and Isaiah was as the open theologians claim. Suppose that God's relationship to Isaiah was closer to a relationship of one human being to another than to a relationship of any other kind. Suppose that in God's striving to communicate his mind to Isaiah, while at the same time respecting Isaiah's autonomy, Isaiah, due to exercising his share of human willfulness and misapprehension due to his sin, causes God to experience surprise, anguish, and a sense of failure. In these circumstances God cannot be sure that what he intended Isaiah to say Isaiah will say, for Isaiah may freely choose to spurn or modify God's speech to him, as a person might spurn or modify the speech of another person to him. Of course, having failed to persuade Isaiah to speak as God intended, God might try again, and again. Perhaps, by an incredible fluke, God's intentions were faithfully carried out the first time by all parties; perhaps, by a series of incredible flukes, Isaiah and Jeremiah and Paul and Peter and all the other human authors of Scripture spoke just as God intended them to speak even though there was a real chance that they got it wrong.

But perhaps not. The point is, this is highly unlikely given the understanding of divine knowledge and power that is being employed by the openness theologians, and we never can know. Perhaps there have been numerous attempts by God to make known his will, though there is no empirical evidence for this. There is also no evidence of many versions of, say, the First Letter to the Corinthians that were discarded until the one that we have in our canonical Scriptures was penned by Paul. What is true of the original inspiration of Scripture is also true of their providential preservation. Perhaps by a series of flukes the original autographs were penned exactly as God intended. Yet how can we be sure that they were kept intact down through the years?

Earlier I have stressed that responsible Christian interpretation of Scripture, hermeneutics, exegesis, or whatever can only be carried on against a background in which the Scriptures themselves, understood as the revelation of an utterly faithful God, exercise a regulative influence. Whatever the difficulties and intricacies of exegesis, and however often our initial expectations may be overturned by our second and subsequent thoughts as interpreters, we can be confident that behind these efforts stands the authentic word of a faithful God. Yet we can now see, I hope, that if we believe the Scriptures to have been written in a universe in which a God such as is envisaged by the "Openness of God" theologians exists, then they cannot exercise any such regulative influence; any such influence will be immeasurably weakened. Scripture will take on the character of a merely human document.

Similar consequences will follow if we believe that the canonical Scriptures are a mixture of the faithfully divine and the faithlessly or less faithfully human. Suppose that we receive information from two different sources about some matter that cannot be checked empirically, that we have reason to believe (it does not matter what the reason is) that one of these sources is utterly reliable and that the other is unreliable, and that we have no means of interrogating these sources to attempt to find out which is which; then it follows that we are in an epistemically inferior position to the position in which we know that both sources are reliable, or in which we know which is and which isn't. In fact, not only are we in an epistemically inferior position in such a situation, we are completely stymied.

Conclusion

In this article I have attempted to do two things. In the first place I have tried to persuade you that there is an intrinsic connection between the sort of religion Christianity is, in intent and in its best expression, and what might very baldly be called the metaphysics of theism. If the Christian religion has the resources to enable men and women to trust God-in-Christ through all the vicissitudes of this life, and for eternity, as Christians believe that it has, then these resources must include an understanding of the character of God that is fully modal, in the sense explained.

In the second place I have attempted (in a very sketchy way, I realize) to apply this basic claim to our interpretation of Scripture, both to our recognition of Scripture as God's word and to the detailed work of interpretation, giving due recognition to the regulative function of Scripture, a function that it can properly perform only if it is taken to be the word of a God who is necessarily all powerful, all knowing, and all good. This is starkly seen, I argued, if we contrast this position with that of the openness of God theologians who, because they had bidden farewell to the utter trustworthiness of God, will, if they are consistent, find it impossible to take the Bible to be the word of God unreservedly.

A Realist Conception of Revelation

Sebastian Rehnman

Introduction

Suppose the existence of an omnipotent, omniscient, and perfectly good Creator, who performs restoration of a morally depraved humanity through an appointed person; what would it take for him to reveal himself in a trustworthy manner?[1] Christian theists believe that, for the glory of God and the salvation of humanity, God has worked through creation, fall into sin, and redemption through Jesus Christ, and that this work was accompanied by a revelatory process culminating in the Redeemer. One such theist wrote: "In the past God spoke to our forefathers through the prophets at many times and in various ways, but in these last days he has spoken to us by his Son, whom he appointed heir of all things, and through whom he made the universe" (Heb. 1:1-2, NIV).

In this paper I would like to consider whether someone omnipotent, omniscient, and perfectly good could reveal himself redemptively in a cognitively accessible way to human beings in history. I take it that the traditional Christian understanding of revelation (contrary to some radical forms from the eighteenth century onward) is that God can and did reveal himself in time and space, and that it is typical of mainstream Christianity

1. All pronominal references to God in this article conform to the practice of the theistic traditions without thereby necessarily conveying any commitment to any controversial theory or attitude that might be associated with that style.

to believe that that revelation was cognitively accessible to the recipients. In other words, what the early creeds describe are reliable and trustworthy summaries of divine revelation. Behind this view is the belief that without certain actions of God some things (about him and about redemption) would have remained unknown.

I call this a realist conception of revelation according to which statements of revelation that appear to be factual are indeed so and are as such assessable as true or false depending on whether such a revelation took place. Revelation, according to this view, is what it is (constitutively) independently of human beliefs, theories, conceptual schemes, and so forth. The reception of revelation no doubt involves human concepts, but the former cannot be reduced to or is not dissolved by the latter because, according to the realist, human cognition is capable of grasping revelations as they are in themselves, and so on this view we have the immediate human experience of the original recipients and possibly a later verbal or textual transmission of revelation. At the same time the Christian tradition affirms the difference between divine transcendence and absoluteness, on the one hand, and accessibility to humanity, on the other, so that God is said to adjust himself *(accommodatio Dei)* in revelation to the disparate intellectual, cultural, and social levels of humanity at different times in history. On the divine side, then, God accommodates himself in revelation to the beliefs, theories, and conceptual schemes of the recipients, but on the human side revelation is not constituted by the conceptualizing activity.[2] (Most Christians have supplemented this doctrine of revelation with some idea of divine preservation or inspiration of that revelation to other generations, but I will not go into this. Nor will I take into account whether God continues to reveal himself redemptively.)

I will not argue that there was such a redemptive revelation in time and space, sufficiently cognitively accessible to the needs of humanity, but that such a concept is coherent. I will do this in opposition to what is perhaps the majority report in current theology. There is a fundamental divide on this issue (as on so many others) with the Enlightenment and Kant. Theologians inhabiting the earth before Kant and non-Kantians ever

2. I have explored John Calvin's doctrine of divine accommodation from the point of view of contemporary philosophy of revelation and language in "*Accommodatio Dei revelationis:* Om en Gud som talar barnsligt," in *Med smak av nåd: Hur skall tron utformas och gestaltas idag?* ed. Tomas Nygren, Sebastian Rehnman, and Lars Olov Eriksson (Örebro: Libris, 2000).

since claim that humans can have immediate access to reality, whether it is that of nature or that of divine revelation. Kantians claim that there is no such immediate access but that we can only have human thoughts about reality. Contrary to the realist view of revelation, and predominant among twentieth-century theologians, seems to be the view that if there is a God and if this God does reveal himself, then that revelation is inaccessible to humans since their epistemic activities are only about intuitions and concepts. I will call this a Kantian conception of revelation, not because it is Kant's moral (re)interpretation of religion (for it is not) but because it is eventually an original application of his metaphysics to divine revelation. This is probably due to the stronger influence of *Prolegomena zur einer jeden künftigen Metaphysik, die als Wissenschaft wird auftreten können* (1783) than that of *Religion innerhalb der Grenzen der blossen Vernunft* (1793).

In dealing with these issues I will attempt to spell out the different conceptions of (purported) divine revelation neutrally, as I believe propositional and conceptual exploration is independent of commitment and adherence to any notion of revelation. I will first set out the Kantian conception of revelation and discuss its tenability. Then I present the traditional Christian and realist view of revelation and argue for its coherence.

The Kantian Impasse

Important influences on twentieth-century theologians are continental, and from them spring the predominant view of revelation. The German-language tradition of academic theology is to some minds the most sustained and intense engagement with modernity and its reductionist foundationalism, historicism, and naturalist explanations of religion. The modern movement can ultimately be traced back to Kant, who argued for the limits of human reason and the subjective input into knowledge, and who disallowed natural theology and revelation. This tendency received further impetus from Hegel, Schleiermacher, and Nietzsche, and so today the idea is prominent in continental epistemology that the human mind constructs knowledge. "Whilst many British and American theologians would hesitate to adopt the same philosophical and theological perspective, nevertheless the *mood* of uncertainty to which late nineteenth-century Neo-Kantianism gives rise in theology has spread far beyond Germany."[3] If by "hesitation to adopt" we understand conscious and explicit adherence to Kantian metaphysics, I think Thiselton is right: contemporary theologians worldwide are usually sympathetic to this continental epistemology although with different degrees of penetration.

Let us turn to Karl Barth, for he was without doubt one of the most impressive and commending theologians of the twentieth century, and the wealthy material of his writings has been explored by many contemporary theologians. In the words of Eberhard Jüngel, Kant "made a strong impression" on Barth.[4] The adverse influence of idealism on Barth has been noticed at least since the time of Dietrich Bonhoeffer, and careful research has been published, for example, by Simon Fischer, Bruce McCormack, and Joseph McLelland on his Kantianism.[5] Barth was first steeped in Marburg Neo-Kantianism, a form of idealism, but moved (when he broke with his teacher Wilhelm Herrmann) towards a more properly Kantian position. Barth then changed from a metaphysically irrealist position to a metaphysically realist view of God but retained an irrealist or epistemic conception of truth. McCormack succinctly states Barth's view: "The 'given' (or what we customarily think of as the 'real') is the product of the knowing activity of the human subject."[6] When we turn from this general philosophical position and look at Barth's idea of divine revelation, it appears that the denial of the possibility of theoretical knowledge of things that transcend the phenomenal world has been applied to the doctrine of revelation so that revelation cannot be a part of time-space reality and hence cannot be accessible to humans. According to Barth we may not describe

3. A. C. Thiselton, "Truth," in *The New International Dictionary of New Testament Theology,* ed. C. Brown (Carlisle: Paternoster, 1976), pp. 899-900.

4. Eberhard Jüngel, *Karl Barth: A Theological Legacy,* trans. Garrett E. Paul (Philadelphia: Westminster, 1986), pp. 24, 28.

5. See, e.g., Simon Fischer, *Revelatory Positivism? Barth's Earliest Theology and the Marburg School* (Oxford: Oxford University Press, 1988); Bruce L. McCormack, *Karl Barth's Critically Realistic Dialectical Theology: Its Genesis and Development 1909-1936* (Oxford: Clarendon, 1995); and, on Kantianism, Joseph C. McLelland, "Philosophy and Theology — A Family Affair (Karl and Heinrich Barth)," in *Footnotes to a Theology: The Karl Barth Colloquium,* ed. H. M. Rumscheidt (Waterloo, Ont.: The Corporation for the Publication of Academic Studies in Religion in Canada, 1974).

6. McCormack, *Karl Barth's Critically Realistic Dialectical Theology,* pp. 66-67; cf. pp. 464-66.

> any of the events of revelation attested in the Bible as *historisch;* i.e., as apprehensible [*wahrnehmbar*] by a neutral observer or as apprehended [*wahrgenommen*] by such an observer. What a neutral observer could or may apprehend of these events was the form of revelation [*Gestalt der Offenbarung*] which he did not and could not understand as such. It was an event that took place in the human sphere with all the possibilities of interpretation corresponding to this sphere. In no case was it revelation as such.[7]

Revelation is, according to Barth, of the order of *Geschichte,* that is, definitive, incomparable, and unrepeatable events with no human court of reference. Human accounts of that which is *geschichtlich* may contain mythical elements (although Barth is opposed to Bultmann's largely mythical conception of the Bible); the narrative type to which the human descriptions of revelation belongs is *Saga.*[8] God's being revealed *(Offenbarseins Gottes)* does not mean that humans are able to grasp God, but that they are able to follow and respond to him.[9] The dichotomy between *Geschichte* and *Historie* appears to be an accommodation to the noumenal and phenomenal realms, respectively. Barth is struggling within the framework of nineteenth-century German theology, and his major problem is God's relation to the world and the epistemological difficulty for a Kantian to affirm the independent existence of divine and created reality.[10]

Barth has been extremely influential, but he was probably more self-conscious of what he was asserting than are sometimes his followers. Another theologian who follows Kant is Gordon Kaufman, who in *God the Problem* argues that God is epistemically inaccessible and cannot be literally characterized by the word "God."[11] Somewhere behind the human conceptualities there is perhaps some *Incognito.* An even more radical view

7. Barth, *Church Dogmatics,* 1:1.325; *Kirchliche Dogmatik,* 1:1.343.

8. Barth, *Church Dogmatics,* 1:1.329.

9. Barth, *Church Dogmatics,* 1:1.330; *Kirchliche Dogmatik,* 1:1.348.

10. It would seem that this polarization of revelation and history grew out of Martin Kähler's bifurcation between the Christ of faith and the Jesus of history, and Gotthold Lessing's famous ditch.

11. Gordon Kaufman, *God the Problem* (Cambridge, Mass.: Harvard University Press, 1972), pp. 85-86, 95. Cf. Gordon Kaufman, "Rationality of Religious Belief," in *The Rationality of Religious Belief: Essays in Honour of Basil Mitchell,* ed. William J. Abraham and Stephen W. Holtzer (Oxford: Clarendon, 1987).

could be found in authors such as Richard Niebuhr, John Hick, and Don Cupitt, but I believe that the above suffice for illustration.

What can be said about this conception of revelation? Here we need to get into technicalities. As I understand it, it is based on certain philosophical assumptions that, as far as I am aware of, are seldom made explicit and are rarely argued for. Still, "one of the most important presuppositional differences concerns the relation between 'reality' and 'interpretation,' and the way in which different views of this relation affect attitudes to revelation."[12] We need to look into the theory. For the Kantian there arises a problem with regard to thought and talk about God because of the postulated boundaries or limits *(Grenzen)* of the human mind. Knowledge arises from experience and understanding, where the former mental faculty represents reality by means of intuitions and the latter by means of concepts. Knowledge is yielded then, according to Kant, by intuitions and concepts in conjunction and is limited to these types of mental representation. In other words, the sensory data of the external world get structured and organized by way of notions innate to the human mind. So what we call an object of knowledge is not, according to antirealists, an external and mind-independent thing but the product of our noetical applications on the sensory data — reality itself is inaccessible to us. This in turn, of course, involves several assumptions about the nature of the human mind.

However, one might well, in the first instance, reject the Kantian assumption that the intuitional content of our mental life consists entirely of mental representations produced in us by reality. We do not have compelling arguments against analyzing perception of an object as awareness of the object perceived. This has been argued for convincingly to my mind in the commonsense tradition since the days of Aristotle, where it is claimed that humans manage to think and talk about things as they really are because there are relations that tie the cognitive to the mind and language-independent reality so that the human cognitive processes attune humans epistemically to reality. Through experience one perceives external objects and comes to have various justified beliefs about them. (What an external object presents itself as may, of course, differ from what that object actually is.) In addition, mental representationalism raises serious difficulties. Antirealists think that reality is inaccessible to us because our thought

12. Erik Fudge, "Can Doctrinal Statements Be Objective?" in *Objective Knowledge: A Christian Perspective,* ed. P. Helm (Leicester: Inter-Varsity, 1987), p. 121.

about reality is always mediated by the conceptual structures in terms of which we represent it, and because concepts are by their very nature alienating. Yet if there are problems with characterizing the world as it really is, then similar difficulties must obtain with inquiring into our conceptual scheme, for we need to apply concepts in characterizing the nature and structure of the conceptual system, and the activity of conceptual representation, according to the Kantian, necessarily hinders apprehension of the object.

Second, granted that we interpret our experience conceptually, it does not follow that the objects of our awareness are mental states. "From the fact that we use a concept to pick out cabbages as vegetables, it does not follow that cabbages are, have, or use concepts or judgments."[13] It would rather seem that the objects are already structured, so that when we perceive an object, we have an awareness of that object. Hence, to possess the concept p truthfully is to grasp under what conditions p is satisfied. Concepts are not therefore barriers but links between mind and reality.

I do not see any reason to accept Kantianism. The content of our mental life does not appear to consist entirely of mental representations produced in us by reality, for perception of an object may well be formulated as an immediate awareness of the object perceived. Although we use concepts in singling out objects, this does not take away the fact that we may be in tune with reality. When this is applied to revelation, the idea of a limit is irrelevant:

> We no longer have to suppose that the applicability of our concepts is confined to our intuitions. So one way we might get God in mind is by the use of definite descriptions. . . . And secondly, it may be that some human beings have had God in mind as that of which they were aware. For a possibility that we now have to take seriously is that human beings sometimes have awareness of God.[14]

So, characterizing revelation as it really is likely involves problems, but a theory about conceptual schemes concerning that revelation does not al-

13. William P. Alston, *Perceiving God: The Epistemology of Religious Experience* (Ithaca and London: Cornell University Press, 1991), p. 41.

14. Nicholas Wolterstorff, "Is It Possible and Desirable for Theologians to Recover from Kant?" *Modern Theology* 14 (1998): 18.

leviate the difficulties; rather, similar problems obtain with inquiring into the conceptual scheme. Characterization of the real is difficult and humans may fail, but that does not mean that it is impossible. Granted that humans interpret an alleged revelation conceptually, it does not follow that the object of that awareness is a mental state. Humans manage to think and talk about the things of God as they really are because there are relations that tie the cognitive to the mind and language-independent reality. Concepts are the vehicles for grasping or the ways of gaining access to the revelation to which they apply.

A Realist Conception of Revelation

Let us then turn to the realist conception of revelation and ask whether it is coherent. A recapitulation of the realist account of divine revelation may be helpful. According to this view statements of or about a (purported) revelation that appear to be factual are indeed so and are as such assessable as true or false depending on whether such a revelation obtained. Divine revelation is what it is independently of human beliefs, theories, conceptual schemes, and so forth, although God may accommodate himself to the social and cultural presuppositions of the recipients. So I take it that the traditional Christian understanding of revelation is that God can and did reveal himself in time and space, and that it is typical of mainstream Christianity to believe that that revelation was cognitively accessible to the recipients.

It is important that we begin with a consideration of the import of "revelation" and "reveal" if we are to understand what a (purported) divine revelation means. We must ask ourselves whether the idea of revelation in the realist account is coherent. Fortunately the use of the idea in everyday language and in the Christian tradition has received careful attention from scholars.[15] The term is not uniquely religious but is per-

15. For example, Paul Avis, ed., *Divine Revelation* (London: Darton, Longman & Todd, 1997); C. Brown, "Revelation," in *The New International Dictionary of New Testament Theology*, ed. C. Brown (Carlisle: Paternoster, 1976); Paul Helm, "Revealed Propositions and Timeless Truths," *Religious Studies* 8 (1972): 127-36; idem, *Divine Revelation: The Basic Issues* (London: Marshall, Morgan & Scott, 1982); George I. Mavrodes, *Revelation in Religious Belief* (Philadelphia: Temple University Press, 1988); Richard Swinburne, "Revelation," in *Our Knowledge of God*, ed. K. J. Clark (Dordrecht: Kluwer, 1992); Richard Swinburne, *Reve-*

fectly idiomatic in other contexts as well. Here lies a semantic advantage as well as the danger of equivocation. With this in mind, let us turn to the idea of revelation.

There is a linkage of revelation with learning and knowledge that makes it clear that it is basically a cognitive concept. Idiomatically revelation involves making the unknown known (or knowable), unveiling the veiled, dispelling ignorance, or exposing the obscured. We can contrast revelation with discovery. In discovery the personal or intelligent agency of the subject is necessary for knowledge to result, but in revelation someone or something else is necessary or has logical priority. Something can be discovered by natural and normal human cognitive procedures, but that which is revealed was inaccessible to those procedures. Hence the unknown that was made known in the revealing was inaccessible until it was revealed and could not therefore have been discovered.

That revelation is a cognitive concept can be illustrated with some everyday uses:

(1) Donald's trousers were rucked up, revealing an inch of hairy white legs.
(2) The book revealed what sort of person J. S. Bach was.

and the New Testament samples:

(3) "This, the first of his miraculous signs, Jesus performed at Cana in Galilee. He thus revealed his glory, and his disciples put their faith in him." (John 2:11)
(4) "God has revealed it [the message about Christ] to us by his Spirit." (1 Cor. 2:10)

From these sentences, moreover, it is clear that the verb "to reveal" does denote more than assertoric speech-acts. It is true that (2) and (4) involve discourse or divulgence, but in (1) and (3) "reveal" has the sense of manifest, display, exhibit, or show.

From this it is also possible to discern a significant distinction on the

---

lation: From Metaphor to Analogy (Oxford: Clarendon, 1992); and Nicholas Wolterstorff, *Divine Discourse: Philosophical Reflections on the Claim That God Speaks* (Cambridge: Cambridge University Press, 1995).

side of the revealer. In (1) Donald did not form or act out of the intention to disclose his seldom suntanned legs and was (likely) rather embarrassed by the event. The unintentional sense of revelation seems thus to be connected to a manifestational mode. Manifestational revelation can, however, be intentional, as (3) shows, and many everyday experiences are imaginable in which a person manifests something intentionally. Furthermore, the communicational mode of revelation is always intentional. It is the intention of the revealer to manifest or communicate something to the recipient(s). In (2) the author wants to convey something about J. S. Bach in the same way that Paul sought to convince the Corinthians of his apostleship by means of his discourse (4).

Look at the examples again. I believe these sentences exemplify the most predominant modes of revelation in everyday language and in the biblical literature, namely, those of manifestation and communication. I will attempt a brief consideration of these revelatory modes.

Manifestational revelation is always mediated by natural signs and involves the terminology of perception. From indicators or evidences one can infer the reality revealed. In (1) hairy white legs were revealed. In the religious sense of this mode there is an encounter with the divine or supernatural agency in which some facts are made available for apprehension and where the manifestation takes place independently of something spoken. Note (4) where the disciples learned Jesus' glory from his miracle of turning water into wine. One could think of other such beliefs referring to God's being or action, such as forgiving, loving, comforting, and guiding.

More specifically, some of the supposed experiences of God by the biblical prophets and apostles resulted in perceptual reports, and these can be accounted for by the perceptual model of William Alston.[16] According to his theory, for S to perceive X is just for X to present itself to S in a certain manner, independently of S's concepts and judgments. Alston sees no reason to limit the possibilities of experiential givenness to powers of the five human senses, and hence perception cannot be restricted to its sensory form. Sense perception is, however, the most common form, so we will have to generalize from that one in order to arrive at a wider idea of perception. Central to perception, then, is the unanalyzable phenomenon of presentation, awareness, or givenness that does not essentially involve conceptualization, belief, and judgment. (Conceptual capacity and tendency may in-

16. Alston, *Perceiving God.*

fluence the *way* an object appears, but not *what* object appears.) Now, if God is perceivable (in the wider presentational sense), can human beings sometimes have genuine perceptions of God? Isaiah's inaugural vision and Paul's Arabian experience, say, are perceptual descriptions of revelatory events where God appears to the recipient of revelation as exalted and merciful. If we take their accounts for granted, it is clear that they conform to our idea of perception. Of course, God is so different from all other things that concepts from more familiar objects had to be used comparatively or by analogy with a univocal core. Yet in this, divine appearances are not different from sensory appearances, for it would seem that all complex patterns of perception are specified by the more familiar cognitive makeup. So, the idea of direct and genuine perceptions of God seems coherent.

There is, however, a nonmanifestational or communicational mode of revelation. Communicational revelation is, according to Nicholas Wolterstorff, the most common basis for religious belief formation among theists. "Most of their convictions about God are not formed in them by experiences of God, nor by abstract reasoning, but by explication of sacred scripture and meditation on the results thereof."[17] Here propositions and illocutionary acts are central. In this mode of revelation propositions are always maintained, and when these propositions are uttered in sentences, this counts or can count as discoursing. The reason is, according to Wolterstorff, that by performing an action one acquires a public standing that is normatively ascribed and is defined in part by a complex of mutual *(prima facie)* obligations. Likewise, the utterance of a sentence normally counts and ought to be counted by the speaker and the audience as a performance of some speech action. Discoursing is then the acquisition of a normative standing in the public domain by the performance of an action that is itself publicly perceptible.[18] One could then think of the biographer of Bach who through some findings reveals, say, something about the composer's first-known work, *Capriccio.* By means of some proposition we believe new things about the eighteenth-century composer. Similarly, if and when God asserts, commands, promises, or asks, humans get to know God and/or his will.

If we look further at nonmanifestational or communicational revelation, assertions appear to be more central than commands and promises.

17. Wolterstorff, *Divine Discourse,* p. 14.

18. Wolterstorff, *Divine Discourse,* pp. 82-85, 197.

Acts of asserting reveal something by the assertion itself, whereas acts of promising and commanding reveal something or other about the agent. Moreover, the aim of promises and commands is to assure commitments toward us and to require things of us, whereas assertions propose to inform us of things unknown.[19]

Now, there are many ways of speaking. There is not only the discourser's own output but what Wolterstorff calls "double agency discourse," that is to say, when one person says something with words that he himself has not uttered or inscribed.[20] In such a discourse it is possible to distinguish between the degree and mode of superintendence in producing the discourse, on the one hand, and variations in the mode of authorization so that the utterance or text is counted as performing some illocutionary act, on the other. It is also possible to distinguish between saying something by authoring a text and saying something by presenting a text (one's own or someone else's) to someone.

This directs us to "deputized discourse," that is, speaking in the name of someone else. Deputized speech is generally "appropriated discourse," which may or may not be supervised.

> In addition, there may be various things said or suggested in the appropriated discourse of which the appropriator doesn't want to say even some equivalent. He wants to embrace the main point but not all the incidentals. Thus to get from the propositional content of the appropriated discourse to that of the appropriating discourse requires subtlety and sensitivity of interpretation. In appropriating, we refashion, not always, but often.[21]

So propositional revelation through linguistic acts may take place through the attribution of speech to a speaker. Illocutionary acts can be performed by bringing about the sounds or letters of some natural language or by appropriating the performance of someone else's doing that. The claim that God performs illocutionary actions seems coherent with this account of communicational revelation, where divine speech may well be understood as appropriated or deputized discourse.

19. Wolterstorff, *Divine Discourse*, p. 35.

20. Wolterstorff, *Divine Discourse*, pp. 39-42, 55.

21. Wolterstorff, *Divine Discourse*, p. 53.

In this connection Swinburne's account of the relation between presupposition (publicly agreed criteria of meaning that are taken for granted) and proposition is also relevant.[22] Communication is easier and becomes more concise if use is made of shared cultural and social assumptions, or at least of those of the audience. Assumptions or presuppositions that are used in describing objects or properties are contingent on that which is asserted, for the primary purpose of declarative sentences is to convey information, and the truth or falsity of the presuppositions are irrelevant to the truth-value of that which is asserted, as the proposition is what the discourser, by public criteria, is seeking to add to the existing beliefs of the recipients. So, when a proposition is expressed in the form of certain presuppositions (as opposed to asserting the truth of those presuppositions), the truth-value of the proposition ought to be judged independently of the truth-value of the presuppositions of the utterance. In order to separate proposition from presupposition the common social and cultural beliefs of the speaker and the hearers must be identified and set aside, while simultaneously leaving intact what the original context would naturally suppose to be the main message. Furthermore, the presuppositions of a culture have a more general influence on the truth-values of its words and sentences by demarcating the area within which they have clear meaning and by defining which situations are possible. Yet when there is no public agreement about what constitutes the truth conditions for a word or a sentence, a certain vagueness will occur in some contexts. This will depend, moreover, on the relation between context and standard of accuracy, for statements are normally uttered to convey information in certain particular contexts that have their own standard of the kind of accuracy required. To convey accurate information the format needs to be sufficiently accurate to satisfy the truth-conditions of the relevant context.[23]

Let us bring all these several aspects of the concept of revelation together by means of summarization, and let us see how the realist view of revelation in mainstream Christianity fits these findings. Following George Mavrodes, the central use of the concept captures the following idea: "(S) *m*

22. Swinburne, *Revelation,* pp. 28-38.

23. Note the similarities with the alternative account in Helm, *Divine Revelation,* pp. 113, 49-51, and his *Eternal God: A Study of God without Time* (Oxford: Oxford University Press, 1988), pp. 2-11, according to which the revelation recorded in Scripture is theoretically underdetermined.

reveals *a* to *n* by means of (through, etc.) *k*."[24] We have seen that revelation is a cognitive concept and that the most predominant modes of revelation are those of manifestation and communication. According to the classical Christian understanding of revelation God intentionally disclosed himself in appearances and utterances with the primary scope of making known a salvation that was not discoverable by natural and normal human cognitive procedures. At many times and in various ways the divine Discourser acted by means of human discoursers, appropriating and accommodating himself to their presuppositions, semantic areas, and standards of accuracy. Looking at Mavrodes' schema, for a genuine revelation to take place there must be instantiations for its variables. The God of Christian theism is an appropriate individual constant for *m* since it is believed that he can reveal something. If we continue with (a), at the least the content of a purported revelation could be God appearing and/or a proposition that he exists. More specifically perhaps, "He appeared in a body, was vindicated by the Spirit, was seen by angels, was preached among the nations, was believed on in the world, was taken up in glory" (1 Tim. 3:16). Humans are, moreover, the recipients of revelation according to traditional forms of Christianity and can replace *n*.[25] The variable *k* would seem to be satisfied either by some manifestation or some communication.[26]

24. Mavrodes, *Revelation in Religious Belief,* p. 89.

25. There are several accounts for how a recipient of revelation may have been justified in believing that he or she had received a revelation (Alston, *Perceiving God,* pp. 96-99; Mavrodes, *Revelation in Religious Belief,* pp. 104-9; Wolterstorff, *Divine Discourse,* pp. 273-80).

26. Traditionally I think Christians have sought to hold these modes of revelation together. I have not dealt with the relation of the manifestational and communicational modes of revelation to each other above, but it seems sufficiently obvious that they do not exclude each other but can rather be combined. It is generally agreed among scholars that in the biblical writings divine revelation often consists of acts *and* higher-level descriptions, of manifestations and propositions. For example, when Moses led the people out of Egypt, God made known the meaning of that event by means of utterances; or, when Christ healed the paralytic, he explained that this implied that he had authority to forgive sins. This pattern of revelation involving both natural signs and assertions about those signs we find throughout the canon. The biblical authors regarded their descriptions of the events as authoritative as the events themselves and as indissolubly linked together (see further James Barr, "The Interpretation of Scripture II: Revelation through History in the Old Testament and in Modern Theology," *Interpretation* 17 [1963]: 193-205; James D. G. Dunn, "Biblical Concepts of Divine Revelation," in *Divine Revelation,* ed. P. Avis [London: Darton, Longman and Todd, 1997]; Langdon Gilkey, "Ontology, Cosmology, and the Travail of Biblical Language," *Journal of Religion* 41 [1961]: 194-205).

As far as I am able to discern, there is nothing up until this point that is incoherent with the realist view of revelation. What remain are the issues whether the God of Christian theism can produce some revelation and, if so, whether such a revelation can be reliably accessible to humans.

Is it possible for God to reveal himself by way of manifestation and communication? Can God causally bring about the generating actions necessary for appearing and speaking? If we suppose an all-knowing, all-mighty, and all-good Creator (and that seems rational following the moderate and sophisticated natural theology of, for example, Alvin Plantinga[27] and Richard Swinburne[28]), it would seem plausible also to suppose that an agent of that sort would be able to produce some revelation to human beings. If the God of classical theism exists, God causally contributes to the occurrence of everything in the world (at least as passive cause), and, according to the concept of *continuata creatio,* the act by which God brought everything into existence out of nothing also provides for their preservation. So, with respect to divine presentations and illocutionary acts it follows *a fortiori* that God can satisfy the causal condition by intentionally appearing or speaking to human beings through, for example, visual, tactile, and aural experiences, as being and/or saying so-and-so. If God exists, occurrences of revelation are possible, or it is even probable that he would intervene in human history to reveal things to humans. Minimally a God involved in redemptive history would be able to work effectively on finite mind and matter, be able to act and communicate in time and space through humans. The possibility of divine action in space and time is then entailed by the theistic notion of God and hence is metaphysically uncontroversial within theism. The divine appearance and discourse purported by classical Christian theism requires direct intervention by God in human history, and I cannot see that contemporary theologians and scientists provide us with any good reason for thinking that such intervention did not occur.[29] Kantians are usually not metaphysical irrealists about God,

27. Alvin Plantinga, *The Nature of Necessity* (Oxford: Clarendon, 1974), pp. 196-221.

28. Richard Swinburne, *The Existence of God,* rev. ed. (Oxford: Clarendon, 1991).

29. On the possibility of divine action in the world, see, e.g., William P. Alston, *Divine Nature and Human Language: Essays in Philosophical Theology* (Ithaca, N.Y. and London: Cornell University Press, 1989), pp. 39-63, 81-102, 197-222; idem, "How to Think about Divine Action," in *Divine Action,* ed. B. Hebblethwaite and E. Henderson (Edinburgh: T. & T. Clark, 1990); idem, "Divine Action: Shadow or Substance?" in *The God Who Acts: Philosophical and Theological Explorations,* ed. T. Tracy (University Park, Penn.: Pennsylvania State

but I do not think that they consistently maintain this *a priori* argument from the metaphysics of God for divine revelation. Theism would seem to entail the possibility of divine revelation in a realist sense.

Yet what would a trustworthy revelation be, or what does it mean to set forth divine revelation in a reliable or trustworthy way? It would seem that a trustworthy person or thing deserves faith or confidence because of loyalty, strength, veracity, and so forth in relevant circumstances. The *New Shorter Oxford English Dictionary* contains

(5) "Could Hannah be trusted not to spill the beans?"

as an illustrative quotation for the term "trust" as faith or confidence in the ability of someone or something to do or be. According to Apostolic Christianity:

(6) "Here is a trustworthy saying that deserves full acceptance: Christ Jesus came into the world to save sinners." (1 Tim. 1:15)

There is throughout the language of the Christian canon a close association of trustworthy and true, involving factuality, faithfulness, and completeness.[30] The content of (6) that has passed from mouth to mouth deserves confidence because of its veracity. There is here both a belief in the truth of the statement and a reliance on Christ as Savior, and this quotation seems to fit the general character of faith in God as involving a combination of propositional belief and a personal attitude of trust. Up until this day, says Keith Ward, the Christian trusts that "God is truly disclosed in the events which the Church proclaims as revelatory of God." This trust is based on, for example, the historical credibility of the Scriptures, religious experiences, and moral transformation.[31]

University Press, 1994); Helm, *Eternal God,* pp. 67-72; and Wolterstorff, *Divine Discourse,* pp. 114-29.

30. Alfred Jepsen, "*'āman,*" in *Theological Dictionary of the Old Testament,* vol. 1, ed. G. J. Botterweck and H. Ringgren (Grand Rapids: Eerdmans, 1977); Roger Nicole, "The Biblical Concept of Truth," in *Scripture and Truth,* ed. D. A. Carson and J. D. Woodbridge (Leicester: Inter-Varsity, 1983); G. Quell, G. Kittel, and R. Bultmann, "*alētheia,*" in *Theological Dictionary of the New Testament,* vol. 1, ed. G. Kittel (Grand Rapids: Eerdmans, 1964); and Thiselton, "Truth."

31. Keith Ward, *Religion and Revelation: A Theology of Revelation in the World's Religions* (Oxford: Clarendon, 1994), pp. 242, 246.

However, that God's revelation is deemed trustworthy is ultimately rooted in the belief that its set of propositions contains trustworthy truths about humanity's relation to God and primarily truths about God. Belief in revelation is traditionally called "faith" due to the incompleteness of the human epistemic situation, and, although the propositional content refers to issues of ultimate concern, the message of redemption is evidentially substandard. Here belief in God's essential faithfulness becomes important, for central to the Christian canon is the concept of covenant: the good news is that God has covenanted or promised salvation. Yet the epistemic incompleteness and difficulties in understanding or interpreting could make trust in the salvific promise unsettled and turn the Christian religion into nothing. So, the faithfulness of God in keeping promises comes in and undergirds the belief that he would not and could not reveal himself in an untrustworthy manner. God's essential trustworthiness and the consistency of his words and deeds with his character outruns the evidence; the belief in the faithful God outruns the belief that God has promised salvation. Whether someone is worthy of trust depends on one's knowledge of his or her future commitment of behavior. Faith in God would seem to involve a combination of propositional beliefs in his strength, veracity, and benevolence and an attitude of trust rooted in those beliefs. God's being trustworthy is therefore a good and valuable thing in itself, for it gives us confidence to commit us to his revelation and trust in it although the evidence is substandard. The epistemic incompleteness of belief in divine revelation is then alleviated by the trustworthiness of God.

This situation seems to explain why talk about revelation involves or implies truth. Some claims of revelation may, of course, be false, but ordinarily the vocabulary used in this connection entails truth. Mavrodes points out that when we do not assent to a certain state of affairs, we are unwilling to use the concept of revelation.[32] The sentence

(7) Copernicus revealed that there are thirty-four orbits.

is not idiomatic. We would normally say that he *claimed* or *argued* for this false belief, but not that he revealed it. In St. Paul's theological reflection this close association of revelation and truth is found in God's presence: "The wrath of God is being revealed from heaven against all the godless-

32. Mavrodes, *Revelation in Religious Belief,* p. 96.

ness and wickedness of men who suppress the truth by their wickedness" (Rom. 1:18; for other instances of revelation and truth, see Deut. 13:1-2; 18:21-22; Dan. 10:1). This entailment is particularly clear in the case of propositions: a revealed proposition is a true proposition (but the opposite does not hold). So, granted that God has revealed X, it is true that X.

However, let us return to the the incompleteness of the human epistemic situation as it pertains to divine revelation and possible interpretative difficulties. From these it does not follow that divine revelation is less than worthy of trust. There may be various reasons for this situation, but it is at the same time likely that the most important things will be clear and plain. Yet our epistemic status must not be confused with the truth status of a purported divine revelation. According to Barth and others we cannot tell that some human statement contains the truth of some revelation, that it is a true statement of revelation. Even if we grant that, our epistemic situation does not exclude human statements from saying what the revelation is. From our inability to discern what are true statements, it does not follow that there are no true statements. Moreover, the truth value of a proposition (belief or statement) depends on whether what the proposition is about is as the proposition says that it is; and the truth properties that we grasp with our concepts may have traits that are not or cannot be conveyed by our concept of that property. Although for this reason our ordinary conception of truth may not reflect the traits that the property of truth actually has, the everyday conception is accurate as far as it goes.[33] This agrees well with what was set forth above in relation to the idea of revelation (e.g., appropriated discourse, the relation between proposition and presupposition, and context-relative standards of accuracy). God may well have truthfully revealed himself even though the human epistemic situation remains less than ideal.

What is perhaps of greater interest is the relation between true statements and what "really exists." According to the Kantian, revelation is what it is because of the conceptualizing activity of the human mind. Little or nothing can be said about the noumenon; what we are cognitively concerned with is constitutively dependent on human cognition. This is less than satisfactory for a realist account of revelation where the external reality is the truth maker. Yet, first, why suppose that human concepts formed

33. William P. Alston, *A Realist Conception of Truth* (Ithaca, N.Y. and London: Cornell University Press, 1996).

out of revelatory experiences cannot be true? Mental representationalism does not hold, and the alternative account given above seems coherent. Second, although there is "only the thinnest sort of significant connection between alethic realism and metaphysical realisms," realism about truth implies that what makes a particular assertion (belief) true or false is (almost always) constitutively independent of that assertion (belief) itself and its features, since its content concerns something other than the statement. What confers a truth value on a statement is independent of our thought and talk.[34] Even if the relation is weak between metaphysical and truth realism, the nonrealist position of revelation is unsatisfactory from the point of the Christian tradition where divine revelation is constitutively independent of human cognition.

In addition, Christians claim traditionally that God is the source of all other being and enjoys reality independently of us and our cognitive activity. We interact with this God in various ways both in this life and in that which is to come. He is actually present in upholding the world and redeeming humanity, so we can enter into personal relationships with this supreme personal being. Kantianism falls significantly short of the traditional Christian doctrine of God because it is committed to regard God as the cognitive system in which ultimate reality appears to us rather than as ultimate supreme reality.[35] Yet eternal life is to know (in a realist sense) the only true God and Jesus Christ, and this is overthrown by Kantianism.

Conclusion

In this essay I have argued that a view of revelation inspired by Kant's philosophy, according to which a purported divine revelation is inaccessible to humans since epistemic activities are about intuitions and concepts, is inconclusive. When it is claimed that revelation is not an external and independent thing but the product of our conceptual applications on some sensory data, one might well reject the Kantian assumption that the intuitional content of our mental life consists entirely of mental representations produced in us by reality. We do not have compelling arguments

34. Alston, *A Realist Conception,* pp. 83-84.

35. William P. Alston, "Realism and the Christian Faith," *International Journal for Philosophy of Religion* 38 (1995): 37-60.

against analyzing perception of an object as awareness of the object perceived, and mental representationalism raises serious difficulties. Moreover, if there are problems with characterizing the revelation as it really is, then similar difficulties obtain with inquiring into the conceptual scheme concerning that revelation. Concepts are rather the vehicles for grasping or the ways of gaining access to the things to which they apply. Humans may fail and characterization of the real is difficult, but that does not mean that it is impossible. Granted that humans interpret an alleged revelation conceptually, it does not follow that the object of that awareness is a mental state. Rather, humans manage to think and talk about the things as they really are because there are relations that tie the cognitive to the mind-independent and language-independent reality.

On the more positive side I have argued for the coherence of a realist conception of revelation. I examined the concept of revelation in everyday language and in the Christian canon and concentrated on two prominent models of divine revelation in the Christian tradition, that is, manifestation and communication. I asserted, moreover, that if we suppose a theistic Creator, it would seem plausible also to suppose that an agent of that sort would be able to produce some revelation to human beings by means of appearances and illocutionary acts. Indeed,

> there is no *a priori* reason why the God who is able to bring about revelatory events should not also be able to ensure that someone involved with the events draws reliably correct conclusions from them. It is not necessary, of course, that such conclusions exhaust the possibilities of interpretation, merely that they set forth reliably the essentials of what God intends to communicate.[36]

I do not find the realist view of mainstream Christianity incoherent, but believe that the Kantian view predominant among contemporary theologians is highly problematic. The exciting alternative of the traditional view is that humans can know that they enter into personal relationships with the living and true God on account of his trustworthy revelation.[37]

36. Fudge, "Can Doctrinal Statements Be Objective?" p. 123.

37. An earlier version of this paper was presented and discussed at Tyndale House, Cambridge, January 1999. I thank the participants at that forum for their questions and comments. Special thanks are due to Prof. Stephen Williams, Dr. Daniel von Wachter, and Mr. Mark Sluys, who made helpful suggestions on the draft of this paper.

RESPONSES

Trinity and Trustworthiness

Colin Gunton

There is some evidence, perhaps much evidence, that breakdown of trust is among the salient characteristics of our times. In the early 1960s it was rare for libraries, even the Bodleian, to have or need security devices; now — with good cause — readers are not trusted with the books, and that in an age of greater and increasing prosperity. It was recently commented that it would have beneath the dignity of domestic servants of an earlier era to reveal the details of the personal lives of their employers; now, it seems, few of the famous are safe, even given signed promises of confidentiality. These are two among many examples, the widespread breakdown of trust in sexual relations being another. Let me give one more that is perhaps contentious. It is a widespread complaint among educated but reluctant refugees from the bosom of the Church that the clergy and theologians have betrayed their trust in their abandonment of the gospel. One remark about the exhibition at the National Gallery, *Seeing Salvation,* was to the effect that its director, Neil McGregor, has done more to present the heart of the Christian claim to truth than the massed ranks of its official representatives. There is indeed evidence of a *trahison des clercs,* and in that regard, too, attention to the concept of trustworthiness, of God and more generally, is more than overdue. Stephen Williams is right: we may be at the stage of a choice between the void and a recovery of trust in the God of Jesus Christ.

Much of the attention of the papers in this collection is centered on the relationship between the trustworthiness of God and the trustworthiness of the Scriptures. That is one important need, especially in view of the fact that many of the Church's own members have thought it right to advocate a nontheological interpretation of the canonical writings. The Scriptures have indeed taken a battering, but times are beginning to change, with much attention being paid to the fact that Scripture cannot be interpreted in isolation from its theological content. How much impact all this will make on the now entrenched ranks of those who think they are paid to treat Scripture as nontheologically as possible remains to be seen, but at least it is there. That side of things, however, is the province of Francis Watson, and I shall assume that his response to the volume leaves me free to choose other directions. I shall begin with an observation of Craig Bartholomew to the effect that, according to Job 38–41, the doctrine of creation is the key to theodicy. It is also one of the keys to much else.

The problem is as follows, and it takes us to our modern dilemma again. We live in a culture where loyalties are divided between two incompatible conceptions of things, often held simultaneously, or so it seems, by the same people. The first is a kind of ideology of science, which depends, though it rarely admits it, on a doctrine of the world's essential trustworthiness that derives ultimately and fairly directly from biblical faith. The conviction has, however, in many places become paganized, so that we have not so much a trustworthy and contingent world but one whose structures are conceived essentially as fate. What else is the widespread proclamation of the gospel of the hegemony of the genes but a return to the view that impersonal fate directs our lives? If it is asserted that the Bible's God is "oppressive," who can doubt that this is more so? Many, it seems. We no longer have a fundamentally trustworthy world, trustworthy because of the creating love of its maker, but an impersonal determinism. We do indeed trust, and need to trust, impersonal entities, like the foundations of our houses and the brakes of our automobiles. *Etwas Festes muss der Mensch haben* (Matthias Claudius).[1] Yet the kind of trust on which our whole lives depend is something different.

That takes us to the second side of the polarity, or rather contradiction, at the heart of modern life. A large part of the response to the threat of determination by the impersonal, from the time of Immanuel Kant onward, and more recently with increasing desperation and irrationality, has been a kind of frenzied assertion of human freedom, most recently in the

1. A quotation I owe to my student Gunther Pratz.

extreme antifoundationalism of postmodernism, but also in absurd convictions that those who are determined by their genes will also be able to determine them, quite arbitrarily. (Surely it is that rampant and individualistic straining after the freedom of the void that underlies much of the breakdown of trust in the modern world.) The Pope's observation about the "culture of death" in the modern world is often quoted, and this is surely its origin. The world, it appears, simply kills us. In that respect, it is indeed trustworthy, and the modern world responds appropriately. Yet we cannot live in such a world, so that we at once systematically seek to avoid death's reality and to take the power of life and death into our own hands. That, as Paul would tell us, is simply another guise in which the rule of death imposes itself upon us.

Without a foundation for culture in a doctrine of creation that affirms both the trustworthiness of creation and its basis in the love of God who is faithful and reliable, there is no escape from the permanent threat of the void. Where shall we go from here? Inevitably, to the fact that the created world is not as it should be. As Carl Trueman perceptively observed, sin in the Genesis account begins with the serpent's attack on the trustworthiness of God. The result of the success of that temptation is that thereafter confidence in God's trustworthiness is hard-won. There is, it seems to me, a danger that in trying too hard to establish the trustworthiness from, in, and on the basis of Scripture, this aspect of things might be underplayed. Craig Bartholomew is right that the doctrine of creation is one key to theodicy, but he fails to develop the other side, that for Job trust is very hard-won indeed. Surely it does not follow from the brief early appearance of Satan that too much should not be made of the "test" aspect of Job's suffering. Is not the plot of the drama predicated on the test? Does not Job in that case enable us to realize that Scripture is full of tests imposed by God, from Abraham on Mt. Moriah to Jesus in the Garden of Gethsemane?

For that reason, we cannot found our attribute on the doctrine of creation alone but on the whole economy of creation and redemption. That takes us to Christology. The difficulty of belief in divine trustworthiness and the basis of that belief come together in the character and the outcome of God's testing of the one he had affirmed at both baptism and transfiguration as his beloved Son. Whatever we are to make of the meaning of Jesus' predictions of his resurrection, one thing is made abundantly clear by Gethsemane and the words from the cross, and that is that for this man, too, confidence in God's trustworthiness, as it affected him, was neither automatic nor merely theoretical. It is of no service here to claim that because Jesus was omniscient, he must have known everything that was coming. As a matter of fact, he denied that he was omniscient: "No one knows about that day or hour, not even the angels of heaven, nor the Son, but only the Father" (Mark 13:32). But that is not the important point. What is it that this man, the incarnate Lord, truly went into the realm of death — into the space whence God the Father had taken himself — in order "to learn obedience by what he suffered" (Heb. 5:8)? This is surely the point of his recapitulation of the path of Adam. As Adam is duped out of his belief in God's trustworthiness, so this man had to relearn it the hard way for the sake of those who would believe through him. Not that he faltered, but that he was tested to the uttermost: that seems to be a necessary stage through which any theology of God's trustworthiness must go.

That brings us to another matter of which somewhat more might have been made in this book: the resurrection of Jesus from the dead. Like the ram caught in the thicket, this is the historical confirmation of the fact that God is indeed to be trusted. Above all it vindicated Jesus' trust, as the ram vindicated Abraham's. For that reason, it is more surely a basis for our doctrine than creation, because as a result of the fall, the creation has been subjected to futility — surely there is an allusion in Romans 8:20 to Ecclesiastes? — and so does not unambiguously bespeak the reliability of its maker. The further point of the resurrection, however, is that it suggests also that we shall be in danger of too abstract a doctrine of God unless we pay attention to the context and implications of this definitive divine act. We shall come to the doctrine of God later, but before that, further remarks on the economy are necessary.

The context, as other writers in this volume have shown, is provided by the covenant promises of God. God makes promises that he appears not to fulfill, or at best appears to fulfill in unexpected ways. The monarchy proved to be corrupt, the land less than impregnable, the return from exile far from triumphant. It is not that God fails Israel, but that her failure to trust brings in its train a loss of confidence in his trustworthiness. In Jesus, therefore, there comes on to the stage of Israel's history one who embodies that history in concentrated form. Like Israel, he goes into the wilderness, and as an Israelite he engages in sometimes bitter, and ultimately deadly, disputes about his people's true calling. The outcome of disputes about Israel's faithfulness is a demonstration, in the death and resurrection of one man, of what it is at once to trust God and for God to be trustworthy. This one actually believes the promises, albeit only after a struggle replicating Israel's, and is vindicated.

The implications of this, however, proved deeply troubling, and this is why Romans 9–11 is so important, in ways beyond that discussed in Drake Williams's paper. It is not just, or even chiefly, that Paul demonstrates God's faithfulness by appeal to the Scriptures. It is rather that God's faithfulness to his own promises appears to have been placed in jeopardy by his own elect people's rejection of their messiah. Here another divine attribute must be brought into the discussion. God's trustworthiness is inseparable from his justice, and his justice consists in seeing to it that his purposes for his creation, partly summarized as they are in the story of the covenant with Abraham, are fulfilled. Yet how can they be fulfilled if Israel, rather than taking her place as the centerpiece of those promises, appears to be left out in the cold? Paul's solution to the problem is ultimately eschatological, which in his case means that he moves from the logic of the resurrection of Jesus to the logic of the end. Only by virtue of the resurrection of Jesus from the dead can we be certain that God is ultimately trustworthy. "Thou didst not leave his soul in hell. . . ."

God's trustworthiness is therefore demonstrated by the overall outcome of the history that takes place on the stage of creation. Two points would seem to follow. The first is that, as Paul Helm points out, this doctrine cannot be justified by a natural theology. Not only is the creation as it threatens us with death necessarily ambiguous theologically, but trust is placed in a cross that is also essentially ambiguous because it is the death of an executed criminal. Nor does the resurrection remove all doubt. The whole thing remains precarious, not from God's point of view but from that of the believer. Despite all the efforts of Wolfhart Pannenberg, the truth of the resurrection is simply not demonstrable by historical inquiry or rational exploration of its supposed necessity. It also means, as the First Epistle to the Corinthians argues, that for us everything hangs on the acceptance of the word of the gospel, that "Christ died for our sins. . . ." The doctrine of the trustworthiness of God is therefore and can only be the fruit of the faith that is the gift of the Holy Spirit.

That takes us to the second point, which is that we must alter the way in which we understand the relation between our attribute and a somewhat more celebrated, if recently much disputed, attribute, that of the immutability of God. Immutability is something that can at least in theory be demonstrated by reason alone. If it is of the nature of created things to be mutable, it is possible, and, as we know, has been argued by the way of negation, that God must necessarily be immutable. Recent debate has been much exercised over this doctrine for a number of reasons, biblical evidence of God's apparent mutability among them. That God can at first repent of creating man in the first place and then promise never again to inundate the earth shows at least a capacity for response to historical events that undermines an abstract belief in immutability. To this one can add the remark of Karl Barth that if by immutability we imply a sheer immobility, we must beware, for if the *immobile* is God, then death is God.[2] The dead and a certain conception of the immutable are not so far apart, and Barth can be said to have anticipated some of the concerns of this volume by more than half a century in advocating a preference for the term "constancy" in treatment of this topic.

At any rate, it might profit us to turn the thing on its head and interpret immutability in the light of trustworthiness rather than the other way around. It is because God is trustworthy in the economy of his creation, providence, reconciliation, and final redemption that we can argue also that the respects in which he is also immutable can be elaborated. God is immutable in the faithfulness and trustworthiness in which he maintains the steadfastness of his purpose that finally all creation should reveal the glory of its maker. Is that a full account of immutability? No, because immutability is more clearly an immanent attribute than trustworthiness, as is suggested by Paul Helm's contention that the latter is to be understood as a relative one. Let us see how far this claim can run, and whether, indeed, the distinction between relative and absolute or immanent attributes can in this context be maintained.

Certainly in its traditional construing, the doctrine of the immutability of God has been predicated on the eternal or inner being of God. It is, so to speak, a way of characterizing God's ontological stability and security. God is what he is eternally and reliably. In that sense, in the order of being, we must surely say that God's trustworthiness in the economy is a function of the ontological security of his being; without it, we would not be able to be confident that he would achieve his universal ends of creation and redemption. Thus, *ontologically* speaking, trustworthiness depends upon immutability. Yet, as we have seen, it is also necessary that this im-

2. Karl Barth, *Church Dogmatics*, trans. and ed. G. W. Bromiley and T. F. Torrance (Edinburgh: T. & T. Clark, 1957-75), vol. 2/1, p. 494.

mutability be the immutability of a living and responsive agent, if this is not to be the immutability of death. In that respect, in the order of knowing, the doctrine of immutability must be controlled by the economy of the way in which it is played out in time and space. The two ways of understanding the relation between the related attributes can only, it seems to me, be reconciled in a more securely trinitarian construction than is found in this book of both of their meanings.

What might it mean, in a trinitarian sense, to speak of the immutability of God? Primarily, I think, that the way in which the three persons mutually constitute each other's being is eternal and unchanging. The Father is unchangeably the Father of the Son through the Spirit, and so on. Not only is God unchangeably love, but he is love of a certain kind: love constituted by the mutual giving and receiving of distinct persons in relation. Thus God is eternally love: a *taxis* of personal giving and receiving, which is what he is eternally. It is this eternal being, immutably constituted by particular personal relations — *particular* by virtue of what Father, Son, and Spirit each are in the distinctness and particularity of their relations to one another — that provides the basis of God's movement into time in that complex of acts that we summarize as the economy of creation and redemption. It entails that all God's acts *ad extra* cannot but be the product of love, because a God immutably of this kind can perform only acts that flow from his being as love.[3] As John Calvin said in a rather different context, God cannot but do good, however much we may wish also to speak of him as doing what he does freely.[4]

For that reason, I would like to qualify Paul Helm's contention that trustworthiness is among God's relative attributes, one of those exercised only because there is a creation to relate to. Without wanting to suggest that Professor Helm in any way equates trustworthiness with wrath in its logical behavior, let us use the concept of God's wrath as the basis of a comparison of different attributes. Wrath exists only because there is sin and evil, so that there is a sense in which, as characterizing God's relations to any possible shape the world may take, trustworthiness is at the heart of

3. This is not to deny the necessity of showing, in the proper place, how apparently unloving acts, for example of wrath and judgment, are compatible with love. If the *particula veri* in the doctrine of the simplicity of God are not to be denied, it must be shown that all God's actions and attributes are consistent with one another: immutably the acts and attributes of the one triune God.

4. John Calvin, *Institutes* 2.3.5.

his *foundational* relations with the world; there would be trustworthiness, though not wrath, whatever happened, just as, it is sometimes though less securely argued, there would be an incarnation of the Son even were there to be no sin. Can one therefore speak of one attribute being nearer to the center of God's being than another? All this might appear very speculative, except for one important point concerned with the way all this bears upon our life on earth. One can conceive of love without wrath, at least in some hypothetical paradisal world, but not without trustworthiness, which seems in some way to be the very heart of what love means.

Does it follow that we should therefore make our attribute an immanent one, and speak of the trustworthiness of the Father to the Son, and so on? That seems to me to take us to the very heart of the kind of questions we ask of the divine attributes when we ask how their meaning is to be understood at the hinge of all history, the cross of Jesus Christ. What, in particular, is to be made of the cry of dereliction placed by some of the evangelists on the lips of Jesus on the verge of death, much used as it has been recently? With Jürgen Moltmann and his followers we must agree that the cry says something about the relations of the Father and his incarnate Son. In his dying, the Son's trust in his Father's trustworthiness is either broken or tested to the uttermost. It seems to me, however, that we must not suggest that it is broken if we are not to sunder the unity of God and breach his constancy. The Father is trustworthy even here, even before the resurrection demonstrates it beyond peradventure, or we do not have truly and securely the reality of God made man for the salvation of the world. Unless Jesus' act is in some way also the Father's, the basis of salvation is endangered. Must it not be said that we here need the doctrine of immutability if that of God's trustworthiness is to be maintained at the time of its greatest test? On the cross God proves trustworthy to his covenant promises even to the extent of his Son's descending into hell, for surely that is what the cry means (rather than some trip from the tomb on Holy Saturday).

Might we therefore not want to say that our attribute in some way characterizes the relation of the Father and the Son in the Spirit eternally? In that case, what happens here is an expression of what is the case in God's "inner" being, so that the love of Father, Son, and Holy Spirit can rightly be said to be a *faithful* love. Whatever we make of that, we have surely established that which modernity seems set to deny, the ineradicable link between love and trust. The trustworthiness of God is demonstrated even where it appears most in doubt, in the place where he made him to be sin who knew no sin. The eternal love of the Father for his Son is not denied but made actual in the complex of events from birth to resurrection. The incarnate Son's human faithfulness to his calling, realized through his dependence upon the Spirit, is the expression of the Father's relation both to him and to the world that was created and is upheld through him. Eternal love is made actual in time in expression of that covenant love that is accordingly to be understood as the eternal being of the triune God in act.

So, we return to the matter with which we began: the breakdown of trust in so many modern relationships. Whether and in what way divine actions and attributes are to be imitated by human agents is not a straightforward matter to decide. God being God, he is able to do the kinds of things that are forbidden to his creatures. For example, the exercise of judgment and the exaction of vengeance are, if not forbidden in the first case, certainly circumscribed, and forbidden in the second. The whole question of the image of God and its fate in Genesis 3 hangs upon a distinction between the ways in which it is and is not right to seek to be like God. Man, created male and female together, is created, according to Genesis 1, to be like God, while the serpent's temptation is for Adam and Eve to be godlike in ways other than that laid down for their condition as creatures. Their succumbing to temptation has the consequence that the succeeding episodes in Genesis and beyond take their relentless course downhill: murder and other offenses follow, and in Babel the pretension to divinity sums up the consequences, taking shape in a parody of the story of creation, so that the "let us make a name for ourselves" ironically echoes the divine "let us make" of Genesis 1. There are, then, respects in which imitation of God is expressly forbidden.

In our case, however, there is no doubt that the opposite is the case. Human trust, both in God and towards others, is part of what it means to be human. Human relations are to take a form similar to those intrinsic to God's triune being and action alike. Yet how do we bring all this to bear within the constraints of living in a world that appears to privilege other forms of human being and action? Intrinsic to the crisis of modernity is its rampant individualism, and its implication that the aim of life is the self-fulfillment of the individual, all other considerations being secondary to that. If, however, men and women are like the persons of the Trinity in being bound up in one another's being, then the matter is rather different. Mutuality and trust are of the essence of being made in the image of the trustworthy God. That brings me to another topic of which more might have been made in this volume, and it is that of the Church. Are not the congregations that make up that far-flung and diffuse body called the Church simply ways of being human in community? Are not those congregations primarily indeed dedicated to the worship of God, but also, and as a result of that, bound up together in a life of faith and love to which relations of trust are intrinsic? When trust is lost elsewhere, it is therefore of the essence of the Church's mission to be *godlike:* to demonstrate both the necessity and viability of trust in congregations formed by that Word and those sacraments that make present the utter reliability of the God whose Son's faithfulness took him even to the cross.

The point about the Church necessitates a final remark about the nature of Christian theology. Theology is not theology if it does not in some way shape the life of the Christian community and through that the life of the world. Without that, discussion of divine attributes and actions is in danger of becoming abstract. It is not that a theology is to be judged merely pragmatically. We are concerned with the truth of the way things are. If God is indeed trustworthy, that will include the truthfulness of our theology as one of the implications of the doctrine. That aspect is well set out in the various discussions of biblical themes in this volume. Yet that truthfulness is defined by and realized in Jesus Christ, who is the truth not abstractly but in effective action for human life in its setting in the created world as a whole. That is why we need to show something of how our doctrinal and biblical treatises bear upon redemption as it takes shape in the life of the Church in trust for the whole world.

An Evangelical Response

Francis Watson

What would an evangelical account of the trustworthiness of God look like? How closely would it resemble the position of the authors of this volume? Assuming that there is common ground between them, as well as the inevitable and necessary diversity, we must first attempt to summarize their view. Having assembled a composite picture, constructed out of elements drawn from the individual essays, we then return to the question of whether this is an adequately *evangelical* account of God's trustworthiness or faithfulness.

According to this book, divine trustworthiness is above all the trustworthiness of the divine *speaking*. Since the primary record and embodiment of this divine speaking is to be found in the Bible, which is quite literally "the word of God," we can speak of a trustworthy God only on the basis of a trustworthy Bible. If the human authorship of the biblical writings makes them in any serious sense untrustworthy, then divine trustworthiness is inaccessible to us, for trustworthy divine speech would then be so adulterated by untrustworthy human speech that discrimination between the true and the counterfeit would be impossible. How could we know whether the prophetic "Thus says the Lord" prefaced a genuinely divine speaking or an all-too-human speaking seeking to absolutize itself by claiming divine authority? If, however, the Bible is untrustworthy, then the trustworthy God would not have spoken clearly and unambiguously enough to elicit our trust. Yet divine trustworthiness must surely be manifested as such if we are to actualize the trust of which God is said to be worthy, and a trustworthy Bible is therefore a necessary condition for our ability to trust God — that is, to regard God as trustworthy.

A trustworthy God and a trustworthy Bible: the emphasis falls now on one and now on the other, for these are two sides of the same coin. Thus, the faithfulness or reliability of God as articulated by Deuteronomy has implications for the book itself: Deuteronomy cannot be seen as a seventh-century fiction, for that would make it unreliable and so undermine its account of the divine reliability. The reliability of the divine speech proclaimed by the prophet Jeremiah extends into the book that bears his name: its speech is God's speech. God's speech is always truthful, and that is why the Bible itself is to be regarded as truthful. (The apparent implication of one narrative [1 Kings 22], that divine speech was on at least one occasion *un*truthful, is therefore a serious problem that merits special treatment.) Old Testament statements of self-authentication are endorsed by the New Testament. Jesus himself solemnly attested that "scripture cannot be broken." He treated the early chapters of Genesis as straightforward fact, he assumed that David was the author of Psalm 110, and he took care to ensure that not a jot or tittle of the law was discarded. What Scripture says, God says: that was Jesus' view, and it is also Paul's. For Paul, possession of "the oracles of God" is the chief glory of the Jewish people. In Romans 9–11, Paul's extended meditation on the faithfulness of God entails a Scripture that faithfully articulates the divine speaking in the present (and without the need for allegorical interpretation). The same smooth transition between the pre-Christian, scriptural past and the Christian present is also attested in the letter to the Hebrews, where the revelation given in the prophetic Scriptures is regarded as no less authentic and trustworthy than that given in the Son.

This emphasis on the actuality, reliability, and accessibility of the divine speaking is further clarified at four main points. First, it is not denied that biblical interpretation is a complex and demanding activity. This was already clear to patristic theologians, and we have much to learn from their hermeneutics and their exegetical practice. Second, divine speech is not monotonous but "polyphonic"; its diversity of genres bears witness to the inexhaustible richness of the God of whom it speaks. Third, the fundamental mode of the trustworthy divine speaking is that of the unconditional *promise* (as John Calvin saw). The promising God and the trustworthy God are one and the same. Fourth, the divine trustworthiness is traced back to God's essential, nonrelational attributes of knowledge, power, and goodness. It is on this metaphysical foundation that the conformity between a trustworthy God and a trustworthy Scripture may be asserted. Anything that undermines the character of Scripture as trustworthy is ultimately destructive of Christian faith.[1]

If all this is a fair (though inevitably reductive) summary of the argument of this book, we may turn now to the question of its "evangelical" credentials. According to one contributor, "the key issue dividing confessing evangelicals from the rest of the academic world is still that of the *authority* of the text, and of the nature of the God who stands behind it." Assuming that "authority" and "trustworthiness" are closely related terms, some such position as that appears to underlie the book as a whole. The correlation of divine and scriptural trustworthiness is regarded as constitutive of evangelical identity. What Scripture says is what God says, and to be "evangelical" is to commit oneself to that equation.

This is a familiar enough position, and it has many merits. Yet is it the best we can do? In particular, can we offer an account of God's trustworthiness that is more attentive to the *specific form* of the divine self-disclosure that Scripture attests? Such an account might run as follows:

To be "evangelical" is to read Scripture in the light of the *euangelion* that lies at its heart. The gospel is the announcement that in Jesus' life, death, and resurrection God has acted definitively to reconcile the world to himself. In describing what God has *done* in Jesus, the gospel also tells us who God *is:* God is "the God and Father of our Lord Jesus Christ"; God is "the one who raised Jesus our Lord from the dead"; God is "the one who did not spare his only Son but gave him up for us all" (Rom. 15:6; 4:24; 8:32). What God has done (and who God is) does not end with the resurrection, for "God has sent the Spirit of his Son into our hearts, crying, 'Abba, Father'" (Gal. 4:6). According to the gospel, God is *triune;* that is to say, the word "God" is properly used only when supplemented by reference (explicit or implicit) to Jesus and to his Spirit. To be "evangelical" is therefore to see Scripture in its entirety as convergent upon *this* God — the God of the gospel. It is to see scriptural trustworthiness or authority as grounded

1. In this summary, I have not alluded to the contributions of Craig Bartholomew or Stephen Williams, which are less clearly focused than the others on the equation of divine and scriptural trustworthiness. I would also like to note that my response to this collection is generally in close agreement with that of my friend and former colleague, Colin Gunton.

in the single though complex *event* in which God definitively and unsurpassably announces who he is. This event has its antecedents and its consequences and is therefore attested in both an Old and a New Testament. To read the Bible in the light of this central point is not to reduce its polyphony to monotony, for the God of the gospel is inexhaustibly rich precisely *in* the concrete form in which he comes to us (and not in spite of it). This God is of course also the creator, the ground, and the origin of all reality, and he is the God of Israel; but it is only from the point at the center of the biblical testimony that the true scope of these claims becomes apparent.

"Evangelical" discussions of the trustworthiness of Scripture often seem to bypass the *euangelion.* Instead, they gravitate towards the prophetic "Thus says the Lord," and they find its endorsement in the New Testament: Jesus, Paul, and the author to the Hebrews all confirm that the statement "Thus says the Lord" means exactly what it says. The result is a doctrine of scriptural "trustworthiness" or "authority" in which Jesus himself is relatively marginal. The Johannine claim that "scripture cannot be broken" is treated in abstraction from the equally Johannine claim that "it is they [the scriptures] that bear witness to *me*" (John 10:35; 5:39). It is insofar as the Scriptures "bear witness to me" that they "cannot be broken": it does not occur to the fourth evangelist, or to any other New Testament writer, to endorse a doctrine of scriptural authority that overlooks the scriptural testimony to Jesus. The writings of both Testaments *converge* on the figure of Jesus and on the triune divine identity disclosed in Jesus, and this convergence is the basis of their authority and trustworthiness. Where this is not recognized, the result will be a doctrine of scriptural authority dependent on a sub-Christian, nontrinitarian, and unevangelical doctrine of God. The "key issue" for evangelicals in their debates with others is not "the authority of Scripture" as such and in abstraction but the authority and trustworthiness of Scripture in its manifold, variegated, infinitely rich testimony to Jesus, as the fellow human who, for Christians, is constitutive of God's own identity. If we could achieve clarity on *that* point and interpret Scripture accordingly, then the old, unevangelical, and therefore irrelevant anxieties about the historicity of Genesis or the date of Deuteronomy would disappear, and we might have a biblical scholarship focused on the gospel itself.

Scriptural reliability is indeed the correlate of the trustworthiness or faithfulness of God, but not apart from Jesus. Paul writes to the Corinthians:

> As God is faithful, our message to you was not "yes and no." For the Son of God, Jesus Christ, preached among you by us, was not "yes and no," but in him [the divine] "Yes!" has taken place. For all God's promises find their "Yes!" in him. . . . (2 Cor. 1:18-20a)

Here, the primary correlate of the divine faithfulness is the gospel message, speaking as it does of Jesus Christ as the Son of God (and therefore of God as the Father of Jesus [2 Cor. 1:3]). There is no divine faithfulness or trustworthiness other than that which is disclosed in Jesus. That is not to diminish the importance of scriptural trustworthiness; on the contrary, it is to establish it (cf. Rom. 3:31). The gospel is a scriptural gospel, inseparably bound up with the written texts that Christians call "Old Testament." In the light of Jesus these texts are to be read as "promises," pointing beyond themselves to that supreme divine endorsement and affirmation that takes place in him, above all in his death and resurrection.

God has shown himself faithful or trustworthy by uttering in Jesus the single word: Yes! In that one word the many words of the scriptural promises are summed up and fulfilled. Since the New Testament is the elaboration of the same gospel message, its trustworthiness too is to be found in its articulation in human speech of what God has said in Jesus. That is what would lie at the heart of an evangelical doctrine of the trustworthiness of God.